## Praise for "The One Thing"...

"Dave Drucker and 'D' Shannon have compiled outstanding information from some of the best industry coaches. Tiburon believes that defining your business goals and constructing systematic processes are crucial to building a great business, and the writers and contributors to this book have made this crystal clear. I would recommend *The One Thing* as a must-read for all advisors."

— **Chip Roame, Managing Principal, Tiburon Strategic Advisors**

"In *The One Thing*, Shannon's and Drucker's personal styles make you feel like you're sitting right next to them as they conduct in-depth interviews with 14 of the best known and most respected Coaches, Consultants and Visionaries in the profession. If you're not interested in developing your practice, increasing the quality of service to your clients and improving your bottom line, then you won't be interested in *The One Thing;* everyone else — order it now! You only need one idea from one chapter to make *The One Thing* a great investment."

— **Harold R. Evensky, Chairman, Evensky & Katz Wealth Management**

"In *The One Thing*, Drucker and Shannon give you the map you need to discover your personal brand of success, and a lineup of the best of the breed who can get you there. Now you can see what your future in the industry should look like and take action to make it happen."

— **Evan Simonoff, Editor-In-Chief, Financial Advisor Magazine**

"*The One Thing* is a must read for financial planners and anyone aspiring to be a planner. If you need to be reminded why you're in the business, or have the need to rekindle a passion for the business, or are simply trying to determine if you should be in the business, you'll find your answer in this book. Not only do Dave and "D" share sage advice, they remind us all why the role of planner is so important in the world today."

— **Virginia Stanley, CPA, PFS, CFP, CVA and Managing Principal, REDW Stanley Financial Advisors, LLC, a division of the REDW, New Mexico's largest privately-owned CPA firm.**

# THE
# ONE THING...

## You Need to Do

*as told by the*
*Financial Advisory Industry's*
*Top Coaches, Consultants*
*& Industry Insiders*

"D" Shannon and David Drucker

ISBN 0-9764974-0-9
Library of Congress Control Number 2005922511

First edition published 2005zzz

SAN 256-344

The Financial Advisor Literary Guild books are available at special quantity discounts to use as premiums and sales promotions, or for use in corporate training programs. For more information, please write to the Director of Special Sales, The Financial Advisor Literary Guild, 6288 Liberty Rd., Bealeton, VA 22712, or contact by phone at 1-888-567-4862.

**Publisher's Cataloging-in-Publication**
*(Provided by Quality Books, Inc.)*

Shannon, D.
   The one thing— you need to know from each of the
industry's most influential coaches, consultants and
visionaries / "D" Shannon and David Drucker.
      p. cm.
   Includes bibliographical references and index.
   ISBN 0-9764974-0-9

   1. Finance, Personal.  2. Financial planners.
3. Financial services industry.   I. Drucker, David J.,
1948-  II. Title.

HG179.S43 2005              332.024
                     QBI05-800231

## Featured Coaches, Consultants & Industry Insiders

Don Phillips
Leslie& Paul Strebel
Bob Veres
Deena Katz
Bill Cates
Mitch Anthony
Dan Sullivan
Bill Bachrach
Tom Gau& Ken Unger
David Grau
Mark Tibergien
Tracy Beckes
George Kinder
Jerry Reiter
Dave Drucker
"D" Shannon

*Dedicated to*
*1st Lt. Kenneth A Shannon,*
*KIA March 15th, 1964*
*in Vietnam*
—"D" Shannon

*Dedicated to*
*My beloved daughter,*
*Gracey,*
*and her search for*
*the truth within herself.*
—Dave Drucker

# THANK YOU'S

## Dave

I want to thank my Mom and Dad for my DNA, especially the part that makes me enjoy writing and editing (though not necessarily certain physical qualities, like prematurely grey hair);

I want to thank my wife, Susan, and daughter, Gracey, for their patience and love. (To them I'll always be a workaholic no matter how much or how little I work);

I want to thank "D" for his extreme wit and (almost) selfless participation in this project, Mary for her putting up with "D," and Beth (D's wife) for her hospitality;

I want to thank my dogs, the greatest source of humor and kisses in my life. (You don't know what a French kiss is until it's forced on you by a pit bull);

I want to thank all the editors I've ever worked with who helped me be a better writer and, particularly, Fran Hopkins for putting up with "D" (I already said that, didn't I?);

I want to thank all of our graphic support folks who did a terrific job. (Ric, my caricature is supposed to have brown, not grey, hair; I forgot to tell you);

And I want to thank all the others in my life who have seen fit to establish some degree of closeness with me; God knows we all need that, and it's helped me to be a better person.

## "D"

No serious book is written in a vacuum, although I'm quite sure that's where my dear wife, Beth, would like to place me!

To Beth: without you I would be a brilliant bum.

To David Drucker: you complete me. You had me at "hello"!

To Miemom: I wouldn't be here if it weren't for you! Thanks for hatching me!

To Fran, our awesome editor: I could tell the story; you made it readable. Thank you so very much!

To Dan Poynter: thank you! Your collective work made this project oh so much smoother.

To all of our coaches, consultants and industry insiders: my profound gratitude for joining Dave and me on this amazing journey. Your patience, willingness and collective belief in this book leave me feeling blessed. Thank you all!

To our production team: Michele, your designs rock! Galen, I'm quite sure I never want to know how you did it; I'm just glad you did! Thanks Kate, and if half of what you say about us is true, we're lucky! Ric, for the fabulous caricatures and even better friendship, I am eternally grateful. For all the folks at Berryville Graphics, thank you for letting me visit "Willy Wonka's!" Mary and Chris, especially, made life easy for this nascent author.

To my children Ainsley, Colin, McKeely and Ian: I knew I had to sell my business and write this when I told you I wanted to write a book and you all replied, "You mean I could see you on Amazon.com? My friends could see you on AMAZON? That is so cool!!!" I love you all more than you will ever know and I hope you find "your song" when you are big and sing it, flaws and all, just like I have.

Finally, to Tonka Dog: get some Beano!

# TABLE OF CONTENTS

"D"

Dave

# THE ONE THING INTRODUCTION

**"D":** Where to start? Why the beginning, of course!

It was drizzling outside the window of Strategic Coach that June day in 2004. I had just closed the sale of my financial advisory business three days earlier. With a good lunch under my belt, I sipped an iced tea and gazed out the window as I pondered my new future.

Turning, I almost bumped into some of my fellow Strategic Coach classmates in mid-conversation. "… I wish I knew more about their program. Hey "D," ever heard of this guy? He's supposed to help financial planners with…."

Colleen, Susan, Deborah and I chatted for a while. Just as I started to turn away, a thought popped into my head and I said, "Do ya'll think it would be valuable if someone compiled advice from all the great coaches and consultants into a book or website or something?"

These remarkable women quickly agreed that it would be a cool thing to do. We all returned to class for the start of our afternoon session with Dan Sullivan; my mind, however, was going 10,000 miles per hour on this idea.

That was the first birth pang of "The One Thing."

Later, on my flight home from Toronto, I kept noodling about this idea and started listing the folks whom I thought would be great to include. "Yep, he's good! Oh, this lady would be neat!" And so on.

As the list grew longer, a couple of points became clear:

- I knew a lot of, but not all of, the people on the list.

- This was a huge undertaking that would require skills that I, alone, didn't possess.

Then my sixth sense pinged me: "Hey! Didn't David Drucker just write an article similar to this idea for *Financial Advisor* magazine a month or two ago?"

The next day I logged onto Dave's website, pulled up his telephone number and called him. The rest, as the cliché goes, is history.

**Dave:** Yep, that was the beginning. "D" and I can say we've been friends for over 20 years, except we were out of touch for about 18 of them. Strange friendship but, I guess, once a friend, always a friend. So getting together on this project was both an exercise in bringing "D's" idea to fruition *and* renewing and building on goodwill established many years ago. Naturally, with two heads in the project, the original concept zigged and zagged, growing all the while into the book you now see before you.

## Why We Wrote This:

- It has never been done before.

- If it was going to be done, we were the ones to do it because we, together, knew all of the participants. Dave knew half and "D" knew half.

- We had been advisors and planners since the early '80s and had witnessed firsthand much of the tectonic plate-shifting within the business.

- We don't take ourselves all that seriously but we do take the subject material *very* seriously.

- We thought it would be fun, educational and profitable to do it!

## The Book Started Writing Itself

Over the summer we corresponded, talked and began crafting our ideas. Through phone calls and emails, we began conversations with those whom we wanted to invite to be in the book. As we floated the idea, we heard, in return, comments like, "Wow! What a great idea! I'd want to read that book even if you hadn't asked me to be in it!"

And yet that response wasn't universal. A vocal and irate minority had a strong reaction to the effect of, "There's no way I would lower myself to be included in such a book! If 'so-and-so' is in it, there's no way I would participate!"

Fascinating, huh? If you're thinking what we were thinking, it might be something like, "Hmmm, nine out of 10 of these coaches and consultants really like this idea, but the 10 percent who don't seem to almost foam at the mouth! I wonder what *that's* all about?"

As we expanded the list, the number of agreeable participants and disagreeable non-participants grew, and a pattern emerged. Those who were willing to become involved seemed to have a true appreciation for our industry and its evolution. They were grateful for all the opportunities it had provided them. They possessed a desire to give something back to it. Furthermore, they were naturally curious and wanted to learn what the other participants would have to say even though they, themselves, were already considered authorities in the field! Pretty cool, huh?

The negative 10 percent, we discovered, were noticeably ego-driven. Their motive seemed to be, "Enough about the reader. Let's talk about how brilliant I am!" They seemed to be threatened by the success of others who fished in the same pond they did — i.e., the financial advisory community. They reacted intensely, openly dismissed the other coaches, and extolled their own wisdom as the only true insight. One even had his secretary brush us off the very same week that Dave was speaking at the same conference on the same stage!

Don't get us wrong. Neither one of us has thin skin. (Hey, we've been advisors for nearly 40 combined years. Thick skin comes with the turf.) So we didn't take it personally. But we did *notice* the phenomenon and ultimately decided that, since this book's hoped-for result is to move the entire industry forward a few more (hopefully large) steps, then those who wanted to participate were self-selecting according to just the right criterion: the overriding desire to benefit the industry.

So the first lesson this book taught us is that some Coaches, Consultants and Industry Insiders (CCIs) come from a place of contribution; others, from a place of ego. You decide which you'd rather hire!

## Planes, Trains and Automobiles

We first met at Dave's Albuquerque, New Mexico home in early September 2004 after having contacted all the coaches whom we thought wanted "in." Still, we needed to put something together in writing and get a strong commitment from each of our CCIs. We sent out a bound, in-depth proposal enumerating our ideas on the book, our proposed writing schedule and, it seems, a novel idea: we wanted to actually visit and interview, in person, as many of the CCIs as possible.

In early October we began week-long sojourns to almost every corner of the United States. We ranged from Coral Gables, Florida to Boston, Massachusetts. We bounced from Seattle, Washington to San Diego, California. We visited the heartland in Rochester, Minnesota and we stopped in Chicago twice. We were gone for most of the month. Occasionally, when schedules conflicted, we arranged phone interviews, but never failed to ask each of our CCIs this question:

### *What is The One Thing you think an advisor should be doing today?*

## The Writing

By the middle of November we had concluded our interviews so we sat in front of our respective computers and began pecking away. We divvied up the chapters 50/50, with few preconceived notions about which of us would write about a particular individual. We put our heads together and reviewed our notes and the interview transcripts.

Sometimes we'd each blow through a chapter with near perfect recall. While some chapters took a day to write, others languished for a week or more for no apparent reason. As we wrote, we'd swap emails about a particular point or, punch-drunk, we'd send obscene comments to each other in a manner reminiscent of college friends studying for the same final exam.

Battling flu bugs, seeing relatives, negotiating the holiday schedule, and contending with the small bladders of our respective canine office mates, we forged on. Day after day the smoke arose from our clattering keyboards. Our copy editor, Fran Hopkins, guided us when we got off track. She'd settle disputes and merge our respective styles into one voice. Any remaining errors are ours alone. Most of the credit falls on Fran's graceful shoulders should this be a good read.

As the New Year approached, we began to slow down the writing and spent hour after hour reading, re-reading, marking and editing. That was when the chapters stopped appearing as stand-alone stories and began to merge their voices into one narrative. Which brings us to the point:

## Is There Only One Thing?

No.

And yes. No, there is no "One Thing" that is a universal truth for each and every advisor in the world. Yes, there are simple truths — each of which might be *your* "One Thing:"

1. It's relationships, *not* return on investment!

2. We need better conversations with our clients — open-ended ones that are all about their agendas, *not* ours.

3. You, the financial advisor, are the most valuable professional in the world.

4. Build a business, *not* a practice, using carefully-crafted systems.

5. Be passionate, purposeful and congruent about what you do.

These may not jump off the page at you as being revolutionary. Yet pause, rewind the tape to the last advisors' conference you attended, and recollect what the primary conversations were:

- It's all about the new product features and benefits, or

- It's all about the financial plan, or

- It's really all about compliance.

The new world that our CCIs painted for us exists today. It's a world where top advisors craft unique experiences for which clients are hungry. It's a world where, more and more, top advisors are unplugging from commoditized products and plans. It's a world where top advisors have built businesses that run on carefully crafted systems — businesses that have value and that will outlive the advisors.

Don Phillips tells us in his chapter that we need a "better investing experience." Deena Katz describes how we can catch lightning in a bottle by really "connecting" with our clients. Dan Sullivan demonstrates the importance of having a conversation that has the client visualize their future and emotionally buy in to it.

Time after time we heard from the likes of Mitch Anthony and Bill Cates that you — the advisors — are the only people who can have these amazing conversations so necessary for our world to grow. George Kinder, the father of the Life Planning movement, echoes that when he describes the three questions he asks prospective clients which engage them in their hearts. Kinder goes on to say that we, as advisors, are the only people hard-wired to create the personal transformations so many people crave.

Each participant in this book added another brick — a different take — to this collective story: Have a better conversation. Focus on the client's heart, not his wallet. Know you are valuable and can create a valuable business.

So after months of interviewing, reading and writing about this new paradigm, it's easy for us to lapse into a "This is obvious!" mindset. But each new financial magazine that lands on our doorsteps tells us that, still, these truths are *not* obvious. Each email offering us "Leads, Leads, Leads" reminds us that most of us are still trapped by our own scarcity mindset. Each new product offer claiming to "set you apart from the competition" and "take you to the next level" re-tells that same old saw.

Are products necessary? Sure they are. Are financial plans essential? Absolutely! Is compliance important for our world? Yes to that too! Yet — and we strongly emphasize this — they are not the *most* important things, much less "The One Thing."

Read this book with a highlighter in hand. Make notes in the margins. Challenge the assertions made. Most importantly, challenge yourself when reading this. Accept the challenge that you, in fact, are the most valuable professional in the lives of your clients and only through you can they live the lives of their dreams — *if* you jump into the deep end of this book and swim toward the new shore it offers.

And so we give you "The One Thing."

*Nothing is so firmly believed*

*as what we least know.*

—Michel Eyquem,
seigneur de Montaigne
1533–1592

## DON PHILLIPS

# Stewardship

*By "D" Shannon*

It was a windy early fall day as we sat in the Chicago Hilton. Over lunch I glanced anxiously at my watch. Our first interview for the book would be in two hours — wow! We'd spent months thinking about the concept, crafting the context, and talking with the possible participants about their participation.

One of the few people whom neither of us knew personally would be the subject of our first interview — Don Phillips. We'd each heard Don talk at conferences but, by happenstance, neither of us had met the man. I suggested to Dave that we walk to the interview so we could stretch our legs, shake off the comfort of a good lunch and have a chance to get our thoughts together. The concierge at the Hilton told us it was easily a 20-minute walk, which only emboldened us. Off we went out the revolving door onto Michigan Avenue.

Sunshine, breeze and lots of people filled the noon hour as we walked towards Morningstar's offices. Though not the first people on the planet to call ourselves financial planners, we felt our roots went back to the origins of the craft. As we walked, we each described to the other our experience of subscribing to Morningstar's *Mutual Fund Values*. What an amazing tool it was in it's time!

Before we realized it, we were staring at Morningstar's office building. With sheepish grins we plunged inside, signed our way through security (a dozing septuagenarian), and jumped the first elevator going up. We were received warmly and gazed at the modernistic office environs as we waited. Don's assistant came down and escorted us to a polished conference room, where we met one of the truly nicest people you'll ever meet.

## Good Guys Finish First

My Dad bought the Templeton Growth Fund for me when I was 13 years old. He sat down and he explained to me what a mutual fund was and how it worked. He showed me the prospectus and the annual report. He said you now own shares in all of these companies and it was terrific. A light went on. It was great because I became an owner of businesses, not just a consumer of products.

I was a pretty industrious kid. I always had paper routes; thus I had money and I invested it in individual stocks and other mutual funds. Because of that I got out of college without any debt. Part of it was due to the fact that college was much less expensive then. I studied both economics and English as an undergraduate and, in graduate school, I studied English literature. I wanted to become a professor, but I planned on being an active investor on the side.

I finished the Masters level at the University of Chicago and I had to make a decision: "Do I want to lock myself in a library for another five years working on a PhD, or do I want to be in business?" It was a tough call for me.

My wife and I got married after college. I guess I'm old-fashioned; it was really tough, having worked so much as a kid, to now be sitting in the library all the time while my wife was out making money and supporting us. I decided to switch things around and get a job writing about and researching investments, particularly mutual funds. I figured I would read the great books on the side.

Joe Mansueto, the founder of Morningstar, ran an ad in the *Chicago Tribune* that said, "Wanted — mutual fund writer" and I answered it. I didn't know Joe before that ad. I came in and we talked about John Templeton for an hour and the next day he called me up and offered me the job. That was 1986.

What was really neat for me was that I had a couple of job possibilities at the time. One was for a management consulting firm and the other was to work at Morningstar and become the company's first analyst. I had no idea that there was a career path called "mutual fund analyst" at the time. The management consulting opportunity paid literally twice as much as the Morningstar opportunity did. Because I'd gotten out of college without any debt, I could take a flyer. I could take a chance on my dream and do what I really wanted to do — something I held a real passion for — as opposed to just taking the highest paying job to pay off a lot of school loans.

That made me realize how taking control of your financial situation by saving more, earlier, could open more doors for you at some later point in your life that you don't even anticipate. It allowed me to pursue my passion.

## Morningstar

In the early 1980s, the mutual fund industry was experiencing dramatic growth. However, comprehensive information about fund performance was not readily available to individual investors. Most individuals — for whom mutual funds were created — lacked the tools they needed to track, analyze, and make intelligent decisions about mutual funds. Joe Mansueto, the founder, believed that fundamental information should be widely available and, in 1984, he created Morningstar to provide individual investors with much-needed mutual fund analysis and commentary. The name Morningstar came from Joe picking the last line of Henry David Thoreau's *Walden*: "The sun is but a morning star."

In 1984, Joe published *The Mutual Fund Sourcebook*™, a quarterly publication containing performance data, portfolio holdings, and other information on approximately 400 mutual funds. This large-scale collection of mutual fund data was priced affordably for individual investors. Morningstar started off as a company that was just sort of driven by our own interests as individual investors. Joe had been investing on his own in equities and doing equity research, whereas I had been investing since I was a teenager. I really believed in mutual funds. I really believed in the power of investing. To me it was transformative.

And Morningstar started as a company for investors and by investors. Certain financial planners, Harold Evensky being one of the early ones, started calling us and saying, "I saw this information you're putting out. This looks really interesting. Can you tell me more about what you're doing?"

Early on I was invited to speak at an Institute for Certified Financial Planners (ICFP) retreat in Rhode Island. I came out and met all these financial planners and they were just terrific people. They had the same passion for their job and passion for investing and passion for helping people that I felt at Morningstar. They were just a wonderful community. And it really was a community and I think it still is in many ways — a community of terrific people that have a purpose in what they do and a passion for what they do. It has been terrific to see this whole field grow and it has come so far in the 18 years or so that I've been involved with the financial planning community.

*The Mutual Fund Sourcebook* was a quarterly publication that just had data. I was hired to be the first analyst, to help create *Mutual Fund Values*; the idea was to add the text to that and to change the format around. We went to the one-page, one-fund format.

*I was as excited to get* Mutual Fund Values *as Don was to deliver it. Planners badly needed a tool like that in the days when it was first introduced.*

My first job was to pick the 777 firms we were going to cover and then to read 777 mutual fund prospectuses and write synopses of them. You quickly learn that reading 777 mutual fund prospectuses is not a fun task. And frankly, you realize that the prospectuses tell you almost nothing about what the fund actually does. So we picked out the funds and then it was my job to start calling up fund managers and asking them what they were doing in their portfolios, which was a little intimidating.

I began a program when I first started at Morningstar: to read one investment book per week. I lived way north of here, so I would get on the train, sit at the very back, and just read for an hour going into work and an hour coming back from work. I was reading everything I could get my hands on, trying to get a sense of what would be reasonable and intelligent questions to ask all of these managers.

At first, of course, they had never heard of Morningstar, so they didn't want to respond. And there were a number of prominent people in the fund industry who hung up on me the first time I called who would come up to me years later at a conference or something, and say, "Don, I always believed in what you were doing and wanted to help." I was always tempted to say, "I remember those early days when you wouldn't take my call!"

*Boy, can I relate!*

But the financial planning community was just the exact opposite of that. It welcomed Morningstar with open arms and, when I look back at some of the early work that we did, you can see that it's fairly basic.

The great thing is that the financial planning audience, in particular, saw our ambition and saw that we were making strides to make things better and better. And each issue that we put out was better than the one that it replaced. A lot of the ideas that Morningstar got known for came from just listening to and being a part of the conversation of the financial planning community.

## How We Got Style

The Style Box, for instance had its origins at that ICFP retreat in Rhode Island. A bunch of planners were sitting around talking about, "How do I explain to my clients why we own more than one domestic stock fund?" Their concern was that clients would respond, "We've already got domestic stock funds, why do we need two of those? Isn't that overlap?"

They realized that their clients were encouraging them to go out and do something really exotic. So once you've got a stock fund, you start doing sector funds. Advisors knew that that wasn't the logical next step, that there was more you could do to diversify the stock portfolio.

At that conference was a wonderful gentleman named Tom Ebright. He was Chuck Royce's partner. He made a presentation where he talked about a portfolio like it was a baseball team. He stated that you'd want some power hitters and some people who could steal a base and some good fielders; you wanted a collection of different skills.

He outlined a four-box style box, which was very clever of Tom because he ran small cap value funds. At the time, I would say that of 2,000 mutual funds, about 1,800 of them were large cap funds, which you could divide into large and growth. Immediately he had gotten rid of 1,800 of 2,000 competitors. And then, in the small cap universe, I'd say maybe 180 of them were small cap growth, meaning only 20 were locked into small cap value. So it was very smart that he reduced his competition from 2,000 funds to 20 funds. He was very genuine and was saying, "Here's a smart way of looking at things."

I tinkered with that and moved it from the four boxes to nine and when we introduced it a year later at the ICFP retreat in San Diego, Tom saw it and later sent me a note that said, "That's a better mousetrap." And that always meant a lot to me — a terrific guy and someone I cared very much about in this community.

I think planning is still in its infancy and it's changing the way people are making investment decisions all around the country and now even the world. So to be a part of the discussion of how this wonderful community continues to grow and evolve is a terrific opportunity and, frankly, it's an honor.

## The One Thing — A Better Experience

I see some advisors who are doing a great job of providing a better experience of investing today. Call it behavior-mod, call it life planning, whatever; they're getting across the importance of staying the course for investing and that positive results show up over the long run. It's not the highest return; it's thinking about engaging people and keeping them on board.

However, one of the sad realities is that, collectively, investors don't use funds nearly as wisely as they should. If you look at some of the really famous managers in this industry, if you go back and look at their careers, at first blush, they're very impressive. Their funds made a lot of money over time. But if you go back and asset-weight the performances, you realize that a lot of very talented people collectively aren't making any money for investors. That's because so many people buy at the top and sell near the bottom.

To me the issue is, "Well, let's roll up our sleeves and see what we can do to create a better investor experience, finding ways to keep people on board so that they get the full benefit of a full cycle of a great manager." I think that financial advisors are a huge part of the solution here.

You asked me, "What is The One Thing?" Creating a better investment experience for the client is the one thing I think advisors should focus on today.

You enrich that to make it more of a life experience — which makes a lot of sense because investing is a means to an end. It is the engine that drives the ability of people to do other things with their lives. It goes back to my story of being an investor early and being fairly disciplined about it, and the doors that later opened up for me.

How do you do this? I think you need to know the value of the advice you bring. When you are convinced, as I am, of the power of investing and the positive effects it can have on people's lives, it creates a level of emotion that engages the client and keeps him or her on board.

I'd also recommend seeking short-term wins. For example, many advisors I know advised their clients to refinance their mortgages to lower interest rates over the past few years when it was difficult to see a win in the markets.

Another example is that some of the fund companies will tell you *not* to put money in a particular fund at this point. The intellectual honesty they have is akin to the movie *Miracle on 34th Street*, where Santa Claus told people they could get a better deal at Gimble's. It comes back to the fact that putting the client's interest first is good business! That, to me, is the lesson in the fund industry and the advisory industry of the last decade.

Sometimes I think advisors worry that they're not doing enough, that it's too simple, that the client is going to think you're a fraud because you don't have some complexity to this whole process or you don't use hedge funds. But it's the complexity that's the enemy. That is what you want burned out; it's the simplicity and the ability to have that elegant, simple solution that really is the value you have. It's sometimes just that simple. It's the basics.

*I see this all too often — advisors not realizing how much value they bring to their clients' world! Keep it Simple!*

## The Future Challenges

The challenges ahead of us are so much more complex than the challenges behind us. I think of the demographics from the baby boom generation and it seems to me that the accumulation phase of financial planning is the easy stuff. You know, that's just much ado about 60/40.

The tough stuff is when you start thinking about transition into the retirement years. Most advisors have been focused on accumulation because the baby boom generation delayed saving and investing until later in life and a lot of them had the twin challenges of retirement and college payments for their kids at the same time. So they became fanatical as savers and accumulators.

But a lot of baby boomers have been focusing on transitioning to retirement and trying to put together a stream of income. Now they're asking much more complex questions, and ones that I think make a lot of individuals realize, "I really, really need an advisor's help in answering these."

When I started at Morningstar, the challenge was, "How do you get a hold of some good information on which to make a decision?" Today the challenge is, "How do you make sense of this overload of information?"

The way I think about it today is that we've saddled the individual investor with all the disadvantages that traditionally only the pros have had. The public's just being completely inundated with information. CNBC's a part of it, the Internet's a part of it. All of this data is overwhelming. The key is to rise above the noise and get that picture on the longer view and that's where financial advisors create so much value.

## KISS

I was at a conference in Europe when the mutual fund scandal story was going full tilt. In the states, the U.S. managers of a particular fund were claiming the SEC had it all wrong and they were right, blah, blah, blah. At this European conference, however, I heard the managing principal of the firm speak.

He said, "When I got into this business, I was told, rule number one, do not lose money for the client. And we forgot that over the last 20 years."

As soon as I heard those words come out of his mouth, they reminded me of the old boss in the Jerry Maguire movie that kept harping to Jerry about taking care of the client. I thought to myself, "There's no way that these guys are going to continue that stance in the U.S. if their boss is saying this in Europe!" And they ended up settling very quickly after that.

 *In my opinion, too many advisors overemphasize the investment component of planning. As Don said earlier, engaging clients and keeping them on board should be the objective. Obviously, within that framework, clients' return needs must be met, but attempting to create an exotic investment experience at the expense of other planning goals serves neither the client nor the advisor very well.*

He continued to say in his speech, "Somewhere along the line, we lost the sense of stewardship and we got more focused on salesmanship."

I'm not suggesting that the core community of financial advisors has ever forgotten that sense of stewardship. But I do worry that in some cases we're over-engineering the investment process to give it more sex appeal. Keep it simple, silly — KISS!

I'm worried that many advisors are branching into the esoteric nowadays. Instead of buying good companies at good prices and holding them for long periods of time like a Graham & Dodd approach, I see hedge funds with exorbitant fees and very elaborate strategies. I see portfolios that have a core index fund with satellite offerings and I frankly find it worrisome.

I think there are really two viable ways to invest in mutual funds. One is low-cost asset strategies and the other is great managers at moderate cost. And there are lots of choices in both of those camps.

I don't think it makes any sense to argue which of the two is better. I think any combination — 100 percent in one, 100 percent in the other, 50/50, 75/25 either way — can be a winning investment decision. What I worry about is when more money, for whatever reason, starts going out into things that are untested, that are higher cost, that are more sizzle than steak.

Finally, I often see independent advisors who try hard to recreate what Goldman Sachs and other large firms offer their white-glove clientele and I think that is a mistake. It saddens me a little bit when I hear that happening, because the financial planning community left all those shops because they *didn't* want to be a part of that and now they're turning back, suddenly feeling jealous of them or wanting to be like that. What makes you special is the fact that you don't have that!

**In summary,** create a better investing experience for your clients by:

- Keeping your clients engaged and on board so that they receive the benefits of great managers.

- Keeping it simple.

- Knowing the value you bring.

- Not trying to be like the big guys — that's what makes you special!

As I watch the advisory world, it's a great thing that the good guys are winning and continue to win. To me, that's a wonderful and heartwarming thing to see!

**Don Phillips** has been a managing director of Morningstar, Inc. since 2000. He is responsible for corporate strategy, research, and corporate communications. He has served on the company's board of directors since 1988.

Phillips joined Morningstar in 1986 as the company's first mutual fund analyst and soon became editor of its flagship publication, *Morningstar Mutual Funds*™, establishing the editorial voice for which the company is best known. Phillips helped to develop the Morningstar® Style Box™, the Morningstar® Rating™, and other distinctive proprietary Morningstar innovations that have become industry standards.

Journalists regularly turn to Phillips for his insight on industry trends. *Investment Advisor* magazine has named him to its list of the most influential people in the financial planning industry. *Financial Planning* magazine has named Phillips one of the planning industry's "Movers and Shakers." *Registered Rep.* has named him one of the investment industry's 10 key players.

Phillips holds a bachelor's degree from the University of Texas and a master's degree from the University of Chicago.

For more information please go to ***www.morningstaradvisor.com***

**Leslie**

**Paul**

## PAUL AND LESLIE STREBEL

# Willingness

*By Dave Drucker*

Neither "D" nor I had heard of Paul and Leslie Strebel until Bob Veres wrote about them in *Inside Information* and suggested we include them in our book. The Strebels are both certified as *"E-Myth Consultants"* and, having known some of these in the past, I was a little dubious. Efforts I'd seen by those preaching E-Myth principles to reform their clients' businesses were often heavy on theory and light on procedures.

However, the Strebels are different, and that's why they're in this book. They proved to me that they knew their stuff and that they have a unique message vis-à-vis our other "subjects" when they told us about their own transformation and that of their business. They based much of that transformation on getting a handle on the management of their employees. As one who subscribes passionately to the virtual-office notion that building a well-oiled team of employees is about as easy as building a pyramid out of marbles, I was instantly impressed.

---

* The key point of the *E-Myth Revisited* by Michael Gerber is that you must be more than a good technician to be successful at running a business; you must also be an entrepreneur and a manager. Your business will run better when you systematize all parts of your business and when you hire other people to operate and improve those systems for you. Ultimately, the goal is to have your business run effortlessly without you.

So "D" and I decided we had to meet Paul and Leslie in person, and all agreed on a spot convenient to both D.C. and Ithaca, NY (from whence the Strebels hail): a folksy little diner in Syracuse, NY. Not an auspicious setting, but one with decent breakfast fare and relative quiet — at least until a family of eight sat down next to us. With Sony recorder rolling, we changed venues several times until we got what we needed: the story of a husband and wife, working together, knowing that they needed a better quality of life and figuring out not only how to get it, but how to teach others to get it too.

### Getting Religion

We've been planners for 20 years and Paul has been a CPA for 14 years as well. We have always worked with small business owners and intentionally designed our business to meet their needs on several levels, from accounting and tax prep to personal financial planning and employee benefits. It was not unusual, though, for clients to express gratitude and delight with the work we had done for them and yet cringe when we asked how things were really going. Their entire demeanor changed as they described to us the disenchantment they felt with their businesses. When they got started, they visualized a life of independence, measured both by the time they spent at work and their degree of financial success. Their reality, though, was very different. They were working tons of hours and were responsible for every aspect of the business. They felt that nobody cared as much about the business as they did so they couldn't leave it for any length of time.

And because they worked so many hours, they were missing their kids growing up. Their health and their marriages were suffering and they saw no way out. Well, we could certainly empathize. We were helpless to help them, because we were unable to help ourselves out of the exact same predicament! We'd relocated and set up shop in Ithaca and the response was tremendous. It did not take long for our business to consume our lives. Finding the tool to help clients (and ourselves) out of this situation was the missing link in offering comprehensive support services to business owners.

So we were quite open to a mailing from (what was) the E-Myth Academy, now E-Myth Worldwide. It was directed toward CPAs who wanted to help business owner clients take their businesses to another level. Paul signed up immediately and returned from training in California with new hope and excitement for what these tools represented. Training continued remotely for three years, although after one year,

Leslie started her training because she saw the difference it was making in the businesses and lives of those Paul was coaching.

Five years later, the Strebel Planning Group is a much different business than the one that was consuming us earlier. It's been rebuilt in an intentional manner, with a dedication to strategic work and company-wide systemization as its foundation. We had to relearn much to get here… things like how to manage employees (one of the biggest challenges for us and for many of the business owners with whom we speak) and how to provide clients with top-notch service.

It surprised us to learn how much we did not know about tracking the financial health of the business, a skill that we have imparted to many other businesses as an enhancement to our accounting and tax prep services. The biggest innovation, though, was creating a track to run on — once we'd defined our destination, of course. The progress was slow, yet steady and intentional. It didn't take long for us to feel better, though, for we finally saw that the tools were available to us to make this happen.

### The Old Belief System

The old belief system is that of the technician vs. the entrepreneur. The technician says, "How can I possibly take the time to do the strategic work you are telling me about when I have all these piles of work to do?" So instead of creating a system that will enable someone else to handle pervasive problems, and handle them in a consistently high-quality manner every time, the owner goes from one fire-fighting activity to another. Nothing ever gets permanently fixed!

We need to give ourselves permission to work strategically on our businesses and not treat strategic planning as a luxury we can't afford. It's an absolute necessity. Many business owners we meet are unhappy and frustrated; yet when it comes right down to it, they are not *really* willing to delegate anything. In order for things to change, we must be willing to give up control of every single aspect of our businesses. We must, instead, create systems to run the business and hire competent people to run the systems.

 *"We must be willing to give up control of many aspects of our businesses"… particularly, those things we don't enjoy doing.*

This is not abdication. Leadership means holding people accountable for their areas of production and for running (and improving upon)

the systems that were provided them. If you are not willing or able to let go, then you have two choices: either stay very small and have nothing of value to sell in the end (because the business cannot run without you), or get out. If you refuse to get out of your own way, then attaining true freedom is, sadly, not in your future.

 *Boy is this true! It does not mean you have to be gargantuan — rather it means you need to operate like a business, not a practice. Even if you want to be small in scope, systems — to me — are the only way to go. In fact, systems are almost more important for the small shop than the large!*

## Scarcity vs. Abundance

By concentrating on what we don't have, on what we feel we don't do well and on what others have, we sabotage our ability to get what we really want. There really is something to a positive mental attitude, to feeling grateful for what we do have. Most of us have minor problems — inconveniences really — but get so caught up with what is going wrong that we cease to see all that is right.

Our health and the health of our families is of paramount importance. Can we put a price tag on this? Of course we can't. Do you have enough to eat, heat in the winter and adequate shelter? If you do, then you are far better off than many on this planet. Yet we still pine for bigger and better, and even feel like failures if we are not earning more than everyone else we know. Is this really the yardstick by which we want to be measured? What does it really cost us to see the world this way?

## Our Primary Aims

A Primary Aim describes the essence of who you are. Maybe your Primary Aim is to be healthy, complete and peaceful, with great capacity to love and share. Or maybe it's to keep the child inside you alive and well — to play like a kid and have fun. Many people think in terms of what they want from their business, family or community as their Primary Aim, yet it is even more fundamental than that. A Primary Aim tells the story of what gets you out of bed in the morning and should be attainable even if you no longer have a business, if your family status changes dramatically, or if you move halfway around the world.

We start business development work by identifying our Primary Aim so we can then build a business that enables us to live it — every single day. The Primary Aim becomes an acid test for every decision that we are faced with making. If something contributes to the attainment of our Primary Aim, we should go for it. If not, we should avoid it, if at all possible.

Creating a Primary Aim requires introspection. What do I want out of my life and what is stopping me from getting it? How would I like to be remembered after I am gone? What is it that energizes me, and what is it that sucks the life from me? Can the business I'm currently a part of ever help me live my Primary Aim?

Sometimes the greatest thing about a Primary Aim is figuring out what else you may want to do with your life. There is nothing wrong with finding out you are in the wrong place; in fact, it is very useful information. Things just may be inconvenient for a while! But you must be willing to be introspective.

## The Right Stuff

Not everyone is willing to be introspective. On one level, a lot of people truly want their lives and careers to be different, but when it comes down to "the rubber meeting the road," they're not adept at the introspection necessary to make real changes. Or they're not willing to delegate. Or they have a difficult time with change. It's sad when we have a situation like that. It's frustrating for us. But introspection is just not something everyone's willing and able to do. For some of those folks, they're going to get what they've always gotten. There may be some minor improvements, but not the type of impact that we know they can achieve.

We get paid month to month for the coaching we do. We want clients who are getting value from the process and relationship... unlike one of our current clients. He is an advisor who works alone and we don't particularly look forward to or enjoy our calls with him. We're considering firing him because he's not engaged. Instead, he continues to focus on minute details as we try to drag him towards seeing the bigger picture. Each time we speak, he has completely reversed his thinking and strategy from the prior meeting. There is definitely a mental shift that people need to make. Some clients haven't attained the ability to think strategically about the bigger picture.

To have a successful coaching experience, there must be an openness to making changes, a recognition that change can be your advocate rather than your enemy.

How do we sometimes find ourselves working with clients who don't have the right stuff? They hire us saying the right words: "I'm ready to delegate to somebody" or "I'm ready to make changes." But what they *really* want is a magic wand. They want to wake up the next day and find everything done for them.

We can tell pretty early on, though, if someone has the right stuff. To begin with, their Primary Aim is very telling. The next part of the process is defining their strategic objective and goals. These things can be very telling too. We observe whether they have an unrealistic expectation about the timeframe for the results they hope to achieve. Many want instant results. But good clients understand that it's a long-term process.

## Goal-Setting

Having goals is absolutely essential to your existence and to achievement of your Primary Aim. We move toward and become like that which we think about. So if you don't deliberately anticipate the way you want your life to be, the way you want your family to be, the way you want your career to be next week, next month, next year, then your sub-conscious will duplicate your presently dominant picture.

Successful goal-setting requires adherence to these 10 principles:

1.  Your most important goals must be yours;

2.  Your goals must be meaningful;

3.  Your goals must be specific and measurable;

4.  Your goals must be flexible;

5.  Your goals must be challenging and exciting;

6.  Your goals must be in alignment with your values;

7.  Your goals must be well balanced;

8.  Your goals must be realistic;

9.  Your goals must include contribution;

10. Your goals need to be supported.

## Getting the Right People on the Bus

Hiring the right employees and developing them properly was one of the hardest things for us to do and is a common problem among our business clients. Hence, we subscribe to Jim Collins' notions about employees from his book *Good to Great*. First, you must get the right people on the bus (and the *wrong* people *off* the bus); second, you have to figure out where to drive the bus; and third, you must build a superi-or team. We believe the right people, once assembled, will figure out how to take the bus in the right direction.

To make this happen, hiring must be systematic. The business owner must be rigorous in her hiring practices. If she interviews a prospective employee and has any doubts, she must not hire that person but, rather, keep looking. There's no reason to settle for mediocrity. And when an employee isn't working out — that is, you know you should make a people change — then act!

 *Can I get an Amen? AMEN! This is so salient! Having the right team is one of the most important attributes to get right, in my book. I value it so much that I am in the process of creating* The Experienced Assistant System™, *an audio-based system to help financial advisors hire, train and manage the right team members and fire the wrong ones!*

One of the greatest lessons we've learned is, if somebody's not pulling his weight as a team member — and we're not necessarily talking about productivity, but how he interacts with other team members, which is equally critical in our eyes — he's done. The mistake we made over and over again is we would try to work with an employee on his personal development. We were always telling ourselves this employee was too important production-wise to let go. But that's a "Catch-22" because that employee would be poisoning our other staff with his cynicism or back-biting behavior.

So we've come to the decision that it's the attitude of a person who works for us that determines whether he stays on board. When a prospective employee applies and interviews for a job, we're looking for the right attitude, a record of cooperation, and his or her personality and style to determine whether we believe there's a good match.

Technical skills are very important, of course, but without the right attitude, all of the applicant's degrees and technical capability won't help us build the organization we want to build.

## Getting Off the Bus

As we've realized this, we've had to let people go who'd been here a long time and even worked hard for us but had become a drag — a cancer. So we've learned to look for attitude first and aptitude second. We can provide employees, through our systematic approach, the training to do the things we need them to do. We don't need them fully-equipped with every skill in the book when they start working here. We're looking for people who are creative and outspoken. We encourage varied points of view and opinions. We respect our employees' outlook as to where we're going and what we're doing right or wrong. Someone who just sits in a back office doing nothing but paperwork isn't going to be a valued member of our team.

Resisting our team culture is now a reason for a quick dismissal. It wasn't always this way. We had one employee who was extremely productive. She could really crank out tax returns and would work very late to get her job done during tax season. However, her attitude was a big problem. We tried for years to change her, always hoping things would someday be different.

One of her problems was that she was disrespectful of other employees. We had a dedicated employee who drove 35 to 40 minutes each way to commute to her job with us (that's considered a long commute in the Ithaca area). Rather than saying to this person, "Wow, you must really like working here," our problem employee would say, "You must not value your life to drive that far to come here."

Our business development process was threatening to this person. She was uncomfortable having open and frank discussions since her modus operandi was trying to position herself to the best political advantage within the firm. She might say something very positive to Paul and then walk upstairs and say something derogatory about him or our strategy to another employee. There were many other examples of this individual's unwillingness to participate in our brand of team building. Needless to say, despite her high productivity, she is no longer working for us.

## Introducing the Team Culture

Once employers adopt a true business development mentality and employees understand that it's not just a "strategy-du-jour" the employer read about somewhere, it becomes clear that there's going to be a change in the entire culture of the organization from the top down. Teamwork and attitude and client service really matter and will be scrutinized on an ongoing basis.

When this happens, some employees start to worry about being found out. They become threatened and it's not unusual that some people have to go because they don't want to be held accountable and they don't want the visibility they've been able to avoid in the past. Some will "act out" to try to preserve their position in the staff hierarchy.

After a high-producing but problematic employee had gone and not been replaced one year, it was getting close to tax season. Paul was thinking about a CPA he knew in town and mentioned him to Leslie. Next thing we know, Leslie runs into him in a store, so he calls up Paul and they go to lunch. He starts telling Paul about the local CPA firm where he works and how dysfunctional it is. Paul tells him about our accounting firm, our teamwork, and the CPA is saying, "Wow, you do that, you have these meetings, employees have input into this and that?"

He came back to the office with Paul and met our employees and saw how high the morale was and it blew him away.

He was working for us within two to three weeks after giving notice at a job he'd been at for 15 years. He's been with us six or seven weeks now and it's been awesome. He's brought clients with him; he's a total team player. We believe with all our hearts that it was eliminating the negative influence of his predecessor that enabled us to attract someone who better fits our culture.

## Building the Team Culture

In the beginning, maybe four-and-a-half years ago, when we realized we had problems with employee attitudes and team building, we only had five employees. It doesn't take that many to have problems, or that many to introduce new processes. We now have 12 employees on our team.

We're looking for people who are willing to look inside themselves, to improve themselves. Our new CPA, the fellow we recently hired, is a Buddhist teacher. We follow some of those principles. Some of the firm members also meditate. They're used to looking inward where the change really occurs. So we ask new hires how open they are to change, to looking inward, to being critical and being willing to explore.

It's helpful to team-building to promote from within when possible. A great support network develops when someone comes into a position an employee used to occupy. The new employee has systems to rely upon and his or her supervisor is responsible for training, but there's also another person there to shed some light on the job.

With all of our precautions, until a new employee is in your company and interacting with others, you never know for sure if that person is a team player. We had someone who worked out just fine through our 90-day probationary period and literally unraveled on Day 91. She apparently had "forced" her attitude for 90 days and then the real one came through. She became uncooperative and the things she'd been doing correctly, she suddenly lost her drive to do right.

Once you begin valuing the right attitude in your employees, the same thinking extends to clients as well. That is part of building the culture. Rather than kowtowing to certain clients, we have ceased to tolerate abusive behavior from our clients. We've even fired clients over their treatment of our employees.

A few weeks ago, we heard from an employee that one of our business owner clients had been abrupt with her on many occasions. We made a call to the client and had a talk with him about that. It means a tremendous amount to your employees when you go out on a limb like that — maybe even fire a client — rather than subject your employees to the client's abuse.

What's the number one impediment to growing an organization? Business owners themselves are the number one impediment. Employee problems are merely a symptom. It all comes back to the business owner allowing those problems or not knowing how to correct them. It's not necessarily a character flaw. It's a combination of fear and a lack of skills.

## Keeping Teams Working Together

One way we keep employees working on the same team is to conduct what we call "Employee Development Meetings." These are regularly-scheduled meetings between employees and their managers that become a forum for problem-solving, conflict resolution and planning. It is just as important to hold such meetings to discuss these critical business matters as it is to let employees know that they are being listened to and that they are empowered to take action.

In addition to Employee Development Meetings, the firm as a whole schedules four-part "Business Development Meetings." Employees come together in management teams and each week we address one of the four parts so that, in the next month, we start the rotation all over again. They debate vigorously in search of the best answers to the problems they are having. And yet they unify behind their decisions, in spite of their own interests.

The first week of these Business Development Meetings, we hold what we refer to as our "Systems Meetings." Employees answer and discuss questions such as "What was the best thing that happened to you either at home or at work this month?" "What issues have you brought to your manager's attention that remain unresolved?" and "What do you think is the biggest issue facing the company at this time?" Every employee is expected to bring at least one new documented system to this meeting.

The second week we spend doing "Strategic Training" on such issues as lifetime learning, mastery of E-Myth principles, and training for personal and professional development. The third week is to go over performance: how are we doing overall? We pore over statistics as well as intangible indicators of where the company has been and is going.

The meeting every fourth week of the month is about the direction our company is taking and our strategy for getting there as quickly, easily and profitably as possible. In this meeting, we embrace another *Good to Great* principle: the Hedgehog Concept. As Collins states in his book, truly great companies have a simple core concept that drives everything and it's embodied in these three questions that become the focal point of this week's meeting: 1) What can we, The Strebel Planning Group, be the best at in the world? 2) What drives our economic engine and what could accelerate the engine? and 3) What are we deeply passionate about? Collins says you need all three to be great and we agree.

The Hedgehog Concept is based on the notion that hedgehogs reduce all complexities into one unifying thought that guides all of their efforts. The three key questions are designed to achieve the singular, hedgehog focus.

Part of team maintenance is making sure that the individual employee is getting frequent feedback. Instead of doing annual performance reviews, we conduct them every month. We employ a process whereby the employee answers 10 questions and grades himself on each one. The manager grades the employee too and then they compare answers to work out differences. The 10 performance questions include such areas as the employee's attitude, teamwork, client service, ability to meet deadlines, and so on. Employees always know where they stand.

We also have a goal-setting process. At the beginning of each year, employees set goals for themselves for the next 12 months.

Of course, there are fun things that draw us together as a group too. One of our employees came up with the idea of noontime exercise sessions. We had a small office not being used, another employee had a spare VCR and TV, so we fixed up the room so everyone could do yoga or Tai Bo. It ended up being a low-resource, high-team-building activity. We'd be in there too, just sweating away, having a good time. We all support each other's physical/mental/emotional well-being with ideas like these.

Every month we go out to lunch to thank our employees for bringing documented systems to our systems meetings. No one forgets to bring a documented system now because they don't want to jeopardize this lunch we all look forward to.

Of course, no discussion of people management and E-Myth would be complete without touching on delegation. It's only through delegation that management can:

• provide visionary leadership;

• achieve strategic and operational objectives;

• increase participation in company decision-making with more confidence and less top-down control;

• create a learning organization for continuous improvement, and

• coach personal growth.

We find that managers make quantum leaps in "getting the job done" when they discover how to decide what work can be delegated, match the right task with the right position, and follow up with feedback — all toward the end of accomplishing quality work, within budget, and on time.

## Why Planners Seek Our Services

Business coaches specialize in working with people who wish to bring their businesses to another level. There are two categories of business owners who seek us out. The first group includes those who are hurting and have come to the realization that their situation won't improve, or won't improve fast enough, without help. They are often working too many hours or not making enough money.

Some experience high turnover of staff and/or clientele. Others feel as if they can never get out, that their clientele are completely dependent on them and would go into a state of shock if the planner retired, sold the business or just closed up shop to do something different. Their health and their relationships are suffering. In short, they are headed to burnout. This group is rewarding to work with because the impact is so great when they turn the corner, reclaim the passion they once had for their business, and see that they can build the business of their dreams.

The second category includes those who have built a good business, sometimes even a great business (by most of their peers' standards), and want to bring it to another level. They have often been through other coaching programs. They attend conferences and read professional journals. I call them students of the art of building a business.

People in this group are great fun to work with because they are generally enjoying their lives and their businesses. Their businesses are more stable, giving them the opportunity to have greater control over what they do at work and with whom they work. Money is generally not a problem, so they can hire staff to whom they can delegate the things they don't want to do anymore.

All realize that, with the help of a coach, they can do it faster, easier, and have a track to run on — many know what to do, but not in what order — and can benefit from what many before them have done in similar situations. Most important, both of these groups realize that with accountability to their coach, they are much more likely to get the work done.

## What's In It For the Advisor?

By making a conscious effort toward business development, our advisor-client stands to create the business of his or her dreams. She gets to choose with whom she works, what she does while at work, and how many hours she does it for each week or month or year. Building that business enables the client to live out her Primary Aim.

The business becomes a servant to the client, rather than the client being enslaved by her business. When she wants out, she has an asset that is quite marketable because it has been built on processes that will endure and on the knowledge and talents of the business owner. The business' fortunes, however, are no longer dependent on the continued presence of the business owner.

### What's In It For the Advisor's Clients?

Clients also get what they want out of their relationship with the advisor. What do they want? In general, they want to feel cared for and attended to. They want to feel that the advisor has the ability to help them achieve their goals and not subject them to undue risk. They want to know that they can get accurate answers to their questions and action on their requests without the advisor necessarily being there to do it.

They also want to feel secure in the continuity of the business should the advisor be unable to continue running the business or decide to leave or retire. Clients want to work with an advisor who enjoys hearing from them, seeing them, keeping up with their lives; who never makes them feel like a burden. More than anything else, they want to establish a relationship with an advisory firm and feel that it is permanent.

### Why Should You Run Your Practice Like a Business?

Because it *is* one! We are not only creating an income stream for ourselves during our working lives, but we're also building an asset that can be turned into an income stream for our retirement and/or provide a professional path for our employees or kids. A business allows the owner to experience the things she went into business for: independence, flexibility with her time, higher income, and the intrinsic reward of having built something significant.

If we have not done the strategic work necessary to create this type of business, then we have merely created a job for ourselves… the kind of job that keeps us engaged 24/7 and is constantly frustrating to us, our clients, and our employees, with no prospect of a pot of gold at the end. In most cases, it is the person with strong technical capabilities who concludes he can do it better than the firm he's currently working for. He tells himself that he can realize the independence, unlimited income potential and freedom he wants.

What he fails to realize is that being good at the technical aspect of a business has little to do with effectively running a business that does that technical work! Rather than being a great financial planner, he now finds himself the personnel manager, bookkeeper, operations manager, client services manager and marketer. All of a sudden, his initial vision has turned into shackles.

*I have learned first-hand that, by running even a small practice like a business, one can eventually sell and realize value for that practice. Technical expertise isn't what does it; it's creating repeatable systems and annuitizing cash flow — whether or not one has a large staff.*

## The One Thing — Willingness

Willingness, alluded to earlier, is our One Thing. To guide the creation of their Primary Aim and the development of a business model that will satisfy it, advisors must be willing to engage in introspection. Introspection doesn't have to be a negative experience. Planners simply need to be introspective about their personal lives in order to articulate and visualize how they want things to be. Only then can they determine what kind of business they must build in order to live that life. We have to be open to hearing what type of impact we have on other people; to ask this of our employees, our clients, our vendors, and our peers.

Once we know where we stand, we need to determine our willingness to do something about it. Some may conclude the job seems too big and make a conscious decision to just live with it or get out entirely. Those who can visualize the end result, who really want that end result, find themselves open to doing what it takes.

Willingness is an important principle. It's about finding the help you need to get there faster and easier. It's about studying what others in similar situations have done and determining how those strategies can help you, too. It's also important to be willing to try new things, to quantify the results and refine the strategy when it's not working. In other words, it's a willingness to make mistakes, but more importantly, to observe these and learn from them.

Some might expect E-Myth consultants to say systems are the One Thing. After all, systems are what the E-Myth is all about. In our firm, we reward people for contributing new systems or systematizing internal processes that haven't yet been documented. The systems reward the employees, too. They come to see them as a way of avoiding the need to remember everything as they free up that brain space for creative solutions, new service offerings, and system enhancements.

Yet, as important as systems are, they always come back to Primary Aim and willingness. It's the Primary Aim that must guide all systems because, if your systems don't contribute to your Primary Aim, then — no matter how good they are — they're not the right systems.

Demonstrate a willingness to develop and run your practice like a business by:

- Identifying your Primary Aim.

- Setting goals for yourself and your business.

- Getting the right people for your team.

- Delegation — it is the key.

The strategic purpose of The Strebel Planning Group is to contribute significantly to the personal well-being of our employees, clients, and others who come into contact with us.

We do this by exemplifying the caring we have for all of our constituents by our commitment to offering services and products that truly help people to realize their dreams and by offering a workplace environment that supports attainment of the employee's dreams.

We want to be perceived as the only place to go to access the full scope of planning services, all offered with the highest degree of professionalism, knowledge and concern for others' well-being.

### The Strebel Planning Group

The Strebel Planning Group
400 Warren Rd.
Ithaca, NY 14850
(607) 257-0858
(607) 257-0859 — fax
(800) 597-1181 — toll free
***results@strebelcpa.com***

## BOB VERES

# Advisors Achieving Their Potential

*By Dave Drucker*

Ever since Bob Veres, publisher of *Inside Information* newsletter, moved from Atlanta to a place called Mars Hill, NC, I've wondered just what Mars Hill looks like. I was picturing, perhaps, a hollow somewhere in the North Carolina woods reminiscent of the Appalachian battlegrounds of the Hatfields and McCoys. Well, I still don't know what Mars Hill looks like, but I've learned it's not too far from Asheville, which is where we found Bob waiting for us at the appointed street corner.

Starting out in a vegetarian restaurant and finishing up in an outdoor café (where we learned, first, that a digital recorder must be programmed to eliminate background noise, and second, that a Centrino computer may find lots of wireless networks in a trendy area of town, but that doesn't mean it will actually connect to any of them), we queried Bob about his current views on the industry.

I've learned over the years that Bob's thinking changes rapidly, not in the sense of contradicting itself, but much like a never-ending movie continuously offering up new subplots for the audience's consideration. Therefore, a talk with Bob is a snapshot of his thinking at one point in time; a similar talk a year or even one month later may reveal a new subplot that has caught Veres' attention.

Here's what Bob had to say.

❖❖❖

## The Profession: Its Strengths and Its Potential Downfall

Ten thousand years ago, we humans embarked on a new experiment. People were living a hunter-gatherer lifestyle roaming the earth at the top of the food chain and, as nearly as the anthropologists can tell, working at most five hours a day. It was a pretty good life.

Then, a bunch of them suddenly said, "Let's go down there in the Tigris-Euphrates Valley and start digging ditches and doing back-breaking labor for 12 or 14 hours a day and build permanent settlements." I'm not sure these things were actually said in a conscious way, but humans changed their lifestyle in a way that basically introduced workaholism into the human sphere of activity.

You have to ask yourself, "What were they thinking?" There is actually credible evidence in the book of Genesis that the hunter-gatherers up in the hills looking down at these people were given to wonder what these people *did* to deserve this? What sin did they commit that they had to live this way, and I think pretty much everybody knows the answer now. The answer is that we are embarking on this journey because we are hoping that, sooner or later, someday, we humans would become the first species on the planet to escape from a life of drudgery — a subsistence lifestyle.

I'm pretty sure that the people who were digging those ditches were thinking, hey, all we have to do is dig just one more ditch and we will be there, you know?

And the great news, the news that I think everybody should hear is, we have now for the first time in the last 10,000 years reached the point where people are capable of achieving that dream. Now here's the punch line: Nobody knows how to walk through that door. We are conditioned by ten thousand generations of genetic and cultural heredity to be subsistence creatures. As soon as things get easy, we put our nose to the nearest grindstone just by instinct, because that is the kind of creature we've evolved into.

So, in this land of opportunity, in this world where it is possible for people to live — and there are people who, with a great deal of effort, *are* living — happy, fulfilled lives, most people are living lives of quiet desperation. They just don't have the skills needed to change things.

You see this every day, so often that the stories are lost in the background murmur of daily white noise. People win the lottery, they blow the money in two or three years, their equilibrium is lost forever and they are worse off than they were before. People with inherited wealth are powerless and disenfranchised. People work every day of their lives and never work on the things that are theirs — things they want to achieve. It seems like whenever you read about someone who seems to be in danger of living that kind of life, they blow it somehow, and you see these stories over and over again.

There are two obstacles that have to be overcome. One is their genetic heritage — if you will — their training. And the other is that we live in the most complicated society ever imagined by the human mind.

So what do we do?

I think financial planning is destined to become the solution to both of these problems. It is, number one, a profession that has the skill set to handle all the complicated procedural challenges of addressing life issues, which requires training and an understanding of how the economy works, how investments work, how to navigate through the jungle to get from one place to the other. (How many people have this kind of training in this world?)

And number two, financial planners are developing the skill set to make that service relevant to what people really want, which is to lead a fulfilling life. They are learning to help people ask the right questions about their lives.

 *"Ask the right questions." Seems so simple yet so profound! Over and over I keep hearing this refrain in these chapters. I believe the quality of your life depends on the quality of the questions you ask yourself!*

Why is this second issue important? Because you have to know where you want to get to before you can get there, before the financial planner can help people get there. And this is an area where there are enormous benefits to be gained simply by working with somebody who asks the right questions.

If you look around closely, you will discover that most people have gotten sidetracked from their goals, so far that they have forgotten that they once *had* goals. They're living what I call "lives of expediency," making the best of what comes up. Typically, they are working a job that they just kind of fell into, a job that they don't really enjoy, and they would really like to do something else. Other people doing a different job are not enjoying *that* job and would rather be doing something else — and sometimes this is the job that person number one fantasizes about.

So you have this tremendous systemic underutilization of God-given talent, skills and inclination all across the global economy, because people — and this is the most important thing to know about human beings, I think — come to believe, over the course of their experience, that they can't have what they most want and, therefore, they won't pursue it, because they believe it would be just too wonderful for them to have. They unconsciously adopt a belief that some mystical force will stop them from getting it.

I have talked to people who told me about a wonderful opportunity that came up in their lives, and then they would say, but of course I didn't follow up on it.

"Why?"

"Because it would just be too wonderful."

"Is that a *bad* thing?"

"I just can't imagine me doing it."

After having this same conversation a few times, I started asking people to start out by envisioning the most wonderful thing that could happen to them, something that would be too wonderful for them to deserve. And they start fantasizing and I would tell them: *This* is what you have to pursue. And chances are, the person who is doing whatever it is *you* want to do hates that job.

 *Bob's description of what a financial planner could or should be sounds a lot like a coach, except planners work the numbers in addition to nagging the client — not that the numbers are necessarily any more valuable than the nagging.*

So we've got a mission ahead of the planning profession, which is allowing people to believe in their goals and giving them their goals back. Nobody is selfish enough to pursue their own agenda. We go through our lives surrounded by a million competing agendas, all on our desks from the outside world — from our bosses, from our friends and neighbors, from our families, from advertising agencies — everybody has an agenda for us and we are not selfish enough to screen all those out and focus on our own agendas.

So one of the services of the future in the financial planning profession is something I call "creative nagging," which is really a tremendously profound service. Advisors will learn their clients' goals and objectives, their life missions, the things their clients most want to achieve, and then they will keep it in trust and give it back to their clients, with more force than all the other agendas. Suddenly, the client's life agenda is coming back from the outside world with more force than all the advertising messages and the work screaming for attention on the desk and everything else, and the funny thing about *that* is that people will do things for other people that they won't do for themselves. If somebody else is holding them accountable, they'll do the work necessary to achieve their life goals.

Financial planners are becoming the people who help their clients recognize what it is they want. If they do that and nothing else, their clients will be in the upper one percent of the human population. Number two, they take that agenda and they hold it and they give it back to their clients on a regular basis. Number three, they navigate a course from here to there, wherever here is and there is. And number four, they handle the paperwork of life in between, which is probably the most complicated aspect of all.

*Bob is so right! I mean, let's get serious — who else can do this? No one else is nearly as skilled at good conversations as advisors. We only need to upgrade the conversations to ones that are more meaningful!*

You ask who else should be doing this. The laugh line I give during presentations is when you're thinking about fulfilling your dreams and living an actualized life, the first advisor that comes to mind to help you with this is *lawyers*, right? Of course not! Dentists? Doctors? Accountants? There isn't another profession with the skill set or the inclination to address these issues.

And, of course, those other professions are locked into addressing different needs. Financial planning is young enough that it can adapt its service package to address the single biggest need in human society right now.

What I see in the future is a new society that will be different from this society — as different from civilization as civilization was from the hunter-gatherer. I think the financial planner is the catalyst that will bring about the "Age of Aquarius" — a world where we start meeting our inner needs with things that actually *address* our needs, and follow our true talents in a straightforward way, with some expectation of success. Society becomes a superconductor of human potential.

## Dry Rot?

Another thing I've been wrestling with lately is the dry rot at the center of the profession right now. Most financial planning professionals you talk to are established, they've got their client base, they're not growing, they're comfortable, and we have a word for not growing and evolving: stagnant.

Now "stagnant" is a harsh term. But I think there is nothing more dangerous to a service firm than complacency, because the world and the profession are evolving at a rapid pace, and there is a real danger of becoming obsolete, even if you feel successful today.

There are several aspects to this. Advisors who have reached a certain stage don't believe they can be competed with effectively (about which they're probably right) and they don't believe it's necessary to do what every normal business takes for granted, which is to develop new capabilities and expand their service menu. They've looked that assumption in the eye and rejected it. But rejecting that assumption has really weird consequences for the profession. It means that there is no growth opportunity for new people coming into the business — no career path. It means that the established founders of the profession are not creating a legacy business that will survive them.

This is one of the reasons FP Transitions [*www.business transitions.com*] exists, because now people want to have their lifestyle met by their business and eventually leave [the profession] *without* any business. They leave and their influence and their way of doing business dies. The torch flickers out, because it hasn't been passed to anybody.

 *Bob's identified one of the great debates of the future: what constitutes a legacy? Will it be necessary for a firm to grow and sell to an insider in order for its legacy to be perpetuated?*

I would like to see some rethinking about what it means to create a financial planning firm, and to look at it from the client's perspective, and also from the perspective of the future. What is best for the client? What is best for the future of the profession? It's for the successful advisors to create a business that will outlast them — an idea that should not be incompatible with lifestyle issues.

What I'm worried about is that the visionaries are all going to retire and die before their visions get transferred. It's true that the concepts are laid down so that other people can pick them up from writers, speakers, and those in the profession who teach. But [reading about] how to do it and inheriting a firm that does it are two hugely different things. Ten generations down the road, a pioneering advisor's original vision is not going to be read in a manifesto anywhere. But it *will* live on in the firm if the torch is passed, if the advisor passes on to the successor team at the company a certain way of treating clients, of doing business, of providing service in an ethical and idealistic way.

## The New Journalism

A couple of years ago, I moderated a panel discussion for SABEW — the Society of American Business Editors and Writers — and the panel included some of the smartest people in financial journalism: Herb

Greenberg from the *San Francisco Chronicle*, Alan Sloan from *Newsweek*, and Floyd Norris who, at the time, was writing for the *New York Times*. Yet my feeling was that most of what was said by my fellow panelists was old-paradigm thinking. I think their — our — profession is changing right underneath us in ways that will make the world fundamentally better and more democratic.

My contribution to the panel was the suggestion that journalism is being changed, as it always is, by the medium that we work through. In the history of my profession, journalists have worked first with newspapers, then magazines, then radio, and then TV. And each time a new medium was introduced, people were clueless about what it meant until finally, by trial and error, people *stumbled* onto what it was good for. Radio was oral print journalism for a while. TV was radio with pictures for years. Radio finally stumbled onto music and discovered that that's what it was supposed to be for, and TV stumbled onto the sitcom.

Now we have a new medium that I think most journalists would agree is the new forum for us — the Internet. And you have to ask yourself, if you're looking for the end game here, what is different about the Internet than about any of the other media? Stop me if I say anything even remotely profound here, but it's *interactive*. You and your audience talk to each other on the Internet.

So my thesis was that journalists of the future will be interactive with their audiences. Instead of throwing informational thunderbolts down from on high, as they do now, they and their audience will talk to each other. It will be a far more democratic, interactive process. Journalists will harvest the wisdom of their audience and give it back to them. I told the SABEW audience that their readers know more than they do, always collectively and sometimes individually. You've got to be able to ask the audience for advice and you've got to be able to deal with it when they come back and say, "Bob, you're full of shit, and here's why." And it turns out that *those* are the great messages. Ninety percent of the messages that disagree with what I said are the messages that I learn something from. Today, because they've been functioning as information gods for their careers, most journalists can't deal with that. The transition is too hard for them.

The other interesting thing about the Internet is how it changes the dynamics of advertising. In general, it seems to me, the people who need to advertise are, generally speaking, the people you don't want to deal with it. Vanguard doesn't advertise. Dimensional Fund Advisors doesn't advertise. You could argue that advertising has been the great equalizer of the people of less quality.

But if the Internet makes it harder for large organizations to create artificial demand for their services, to bully their way, by the sheer expenditure of money, to front-of-mind awareness, then what happens? Personal recommendations become much more important. Having a big media budget becomes less important. It will be really interesting how society is going to change as a result of that one simple thing. I'm envisioning a world without Coca-Cola. The soft drink industry won't be able to create an artificial demand for a product that's really not healthy and costs a great deal more than fruit juice or water.

## The Early Days

Where did I start out? I was a freelance writer in Atlanta and I sort of had the reputation, "If nobody else will write it, call Veres because he'll think about some way to do it." So, you know, I was not a great writer. I was a great researcher. I was able to get to the bottom of stories. I found that most writers on that level are not really too deeply involved in research issues. They want to get the information quickly and then write glibly about it, and I was sort of the opposite. I made a decent living, not a great living. No freelance writer ever makes a great living.

So one day I was asked to write an article about Republic Airlines' air freight operations, which were based in Atlanta. I interviewed the management team and they told me how they ran their cargo terminal and what the logistics were of getting freight into and out of Atlanta versus other airports in the area. And they told me funny stories like the time a large snake that was being shipped to a zoo got out of the cargo area and somehow was loose in the terminal. I finished the article, and it turned out that that was going to be published in the very last issue of *Air Cargo*, which was a Dunn & Bradstreet publication that had been losing money since about 1946. Of course, as a writer, I was more concerned about getting paid than whether this was the first or last issue in the history of the publication. I just made a mental note not to worry about receiving a check from them in the future and that was that.

So not long after that I got a call from a local organization called Communication Channels in Atlanta which had bought *Air Cargo*. The conversation was interesting. They said, "Bob, we'd like you to be editor of what we're going to call *Air Cargo World* magazine." And I said I wasn't qualified to edit and that I'd only written one article for the magazine and they said, essentially, "Well, we've asked everybody else associated with the magazine and nobody wanted to be editor and move here to Atlanta and so if you want to interview for the job, we would certainly like to talk to you."

As a writer, I'd never been on the editor's side of the table before, and the negotiating position was not so terrible, so I decided to try being an editor. The only problem was that I didn't have any experience in the air freight industry, or any real knowledge about it, which meant that I had to learn in a hurry and meanwhile rely on contacts in the industry to help me understand the things that everybody else knew and took for granted. It was a steep learning curve.

The magazine did not have a great stable of writers for me to inherit. One of the feature writers for the previous editor told me early on in our relationship that he wanted to be put on the masthead as the "Associate Editor" because, he told me, it was good for getting girls. Apparently, he would go to bars and show [eligible ladies] the magazine with him listed as Associate Editor, and this would impress them somehow. I phased him out of the lineup as quickly as I could.

That was when I honed my essential interviewing technique, which I use to this day. Whenever I sat down with an industry executive or source of information or interview subject, I would start off by saying, "Now, please remember that you're talking to a dumb journalist, so speak slowly, use small words, and you're going to have to repeat yourself a lot." It was a very good formula for making sure I was grounded in the information that I was writing about.

Before long the magazine was profitable, and I was hearing from readers who were telling me how much they liked the new writing and format — and I realized that despite my obvious knowledge shortcomings, I was not the worst editor in the world. It helped that this was the dawning of the small package overnight delivery era — with new companies like Federal Express and Airborne and UPS getting into overnight shipping. So I adapted the magazine's coverage to include couriers and overnight delivery business and mixed those stories into the typical profiles of an airline's cargo operation or a local freight forwarder. The articles were fun to read, which had not been the norm for the industry.

After I'd been on the job for six months, I attended the World's Fair of air freight in Amsterdam — my first, and still my only, trip to Europe. I flew in on KLM Airlines, and KLM had a young PR guy who was assigned to me to show me around and keep me out of trouble and show me the sights and also take me on a tour of the company's headquarters. And at KLM headquarters he said to me, "You know, I have always wanted to be a magazine editor and writer in this field." In Europe they had several air freight magazines, but he was looking at years of getting in the door, and he would have to start off way at the bottom. So he asked me, "How did you ever become editor of America's leading freight journal?"

I told him my story and he winced over and over and over again, and finally looked off in the distance and said, "Only in America."

At the time, I was also writing a fiction series for *Atlanta Magazine*. I was halfway through a five-part series and the editor of *Atlanta Magazine* left to become communications director for the International Association for Financial Planning. He called me up and suggested that I talk to him about becoming editor of *The Financial Planner*, which was the IAFP's association publication. The plan was to rename it *Financial Planning* magazine.

I said, "Well, you know, I don't know anything about financial planning. I've never even balanced my own checkbook." And he said, "Well, I've asked a lot of other people and nobody else wants to do it."

By now, this had become a familiar story, and the execution was very similar. I developed a whole new crowd of writers and I would re-report everything and I would call people and I'd say, "Talk slowly, you're talking to a dumb journalist, use small words and be prepared to repeat everything because you're liable to lose me." In that first year, *Financial Planning* magazine took off and became the number one member benefit at the association and immensely profitable.

Trouble was, I was never really an editor. I was a journalist. I could never stop writing. What really drove everybody crazy at the IAFP was the fact that I insisted on writing four or five cover stories a year and maybe a practice profile every once in a while, when I was supposed to spend my time on executive activities.

## Life Planning

Life planning is the endless pursuit of what you can do better in your life. So what do people need to do? The first thing I think everybody needs to do, as a member of the human race, is to hire somebody else to help them uncover what it is they want to do and what it is they can do most effectively. What is their highest and best use? What does a fulfilling life mean to them? How can they contribute uniquely, and what do they want in return for contributing? How do they want their lives to look? And a lot of financial advisors have that answer in their business lives. They're working in one of the most fulfilling, psychically rewarding businesses ever. Now it's time for them to spread the wealth.

The first thing they do is help their clients identify their ideal life, and what they're good at, and create a map to pursue that. And they need to be consumers of their own service. That's an enormous challenge for some of these guys for two reasons. One is finding somebody who knows how to offer life planning services, because at the moment very few advisors do this. And number two, they start looking at their own service and say, "I don't do this either, even though this is what I would want if I went to somebody." *That* is the key insight; one of the key benefits of getting life planning/financial planning help is you can look at your own services from the perspective of the client.

It astounds me that financial planners are reluctant to get help, because they live on the idea that delegation is beneficial. If they can't delegate their own service to another advisor, how can they expect their clients to delegate so many important things to them?

 *Your authors have taken this advice to heart. "D" and I have both worked with coaches, and I no longer manage my own investment assets. As for those earth-shaking questions about life, my wife guides me in that arena.*

If advisors start out by going through this process themselves, then they need to make progress toward becoming citizens in the next society where they live a life of fulfillment. And that requires actual courage. You have to be willing to leave behind a lot of default assumptions about life. If I'm busy, I must be important. I can't make a lot of money unless I work really hard. I can't add value unless I'm diligent about this or that. Taking off three months a year is obscene. There are all sorts of assumptions in our society you've got to let go of. And only when you've walked through that door can you pull other people through that door and really offer the service that's in demand right now in the world at large.

Success in the future will not be defined by wealth or the purchase of status objects. It will be defined by having the most fulfilling life.

## The One Thing

When I look at financial planners as a group, I see a lot of minor dysfunctions — and one big one: The way people charge for their services. In the history of the profession, the amount people paid for a planner's services has always been set by somebody else. You've got commissions, which are set by the product company and the broker-dealer. You have the assets under management fee structure, which is really a variation of the same type of compensation, with the money coming directly out of the portfolio.

Sooner or later, we need to get to the point where advisors are actually setting their compensation themselves — a compensation that is visible to the consumer.

That's the setup to The One Thing. The first thing they have to do from a practice management standpoint is to assess how much each client is costing them compared to how much each client is bringing in. I give this as a homework assignment to my audiences. Create a spreadsheet. Write down how many hours a year you're spending on each client. For most clients, it will be some standard number of hours, because you have a relatively systemized process. If you have a few pain-in-the-ass clients that require more time and energy, you should appropriately document that. And then multiply that time you're spending by, say, $300 an hour... more if you feel comfortable with that, but no less. Then do the same thing with significant staff people, the case writers or the senior planners, if they're serving the clients. Bill them at $200 an hour or $150. And then multiply *that* out. Then allocate your overhead on a per-client basis, and put that figure on the spreadsheet, and total them up, so that you have a column which shows what each and every one of your clients is costing you.

Then, in the next column, type in how much revenue you're getting per year, subtract the money they're costing you from the amount they're paying you, and rank them according to the highest positive down to the lowest negative.

What you discover is that 10 or 15 percent of your clients are generating 115 percent of your profits in a given year. Once you know that, then you can start charging appropriately.

*Planners no longer have to feel guilty about jettisoning smaller clients whom they can't serve profitably. In most communities nowadays, there is at least one middle-market planner who would be grateful to receive and serve these clients, as well as future middle-market prospects who don't fit fellow planners' business models.*

There's a wonderful line by Larry Carroll, who practices in Charlotte. He said he has to charge a great deal more for things he's incompetent at and knows nothing about because he has to do a lot of research. The things he's really good at, he charges less for because he can do them instantly. This is the best argument I've ever seen for not charging on an hourly basis. I think you have to charge by the value you offer, which means retainer fees, or some combination of retainers and asset management fees.

But if you are going to charge retainer fees, and make the fees more visible to the client, you will also need to make your services more personal. If there is one thing we've learned these past 20 years, it is that people are reluctant to pay for the generic financial planning service that's traditionally been offered: I manage your assets, I organize your paperwork, I make sure you get a will, I make sure your assets are properly diversified, I give you a quarterly statement. These are incredibly valuable services, but consumers don't really see what's in it for them. The value has to be made real, tangible, and personal. That's one reason why I'm so excited about life planning.

1. Financial planners have two enormous advantages over everybody else in delivering that personal service:

2. They hang around successful people on a regular basis, and so they see what success is like and have some confidence that they know how to get there.

They have mastered the ability to take complicated goals and break them down into individual manageable pieces. That's what retirement planning is. You have to save this much per month and you'll have "x" million dollars in retirement money at some point. Mission impossible achieved. It's the same thing with life planning goals.

In presentations, I talk about a life planning scene in *Bonanza*, still one of my favorite TV shows of all time. Ben Cartwright, the family patriarch, is turning the Ponderosa over to his son Hoss. And Hoss, never the sharpest tool in the shed, is nervous about taking over the Ponderosa — which is a spread that takes up half the state of Nevada. And so the father takes his son outside and he picks up a bundle of sticks and he hands them to Hoss, and he says, "Here, son. I want you to break these sticks." And Hoss, who was not a small man, starts grunting and straining and pulling on the sticks, and he finally drops them at his father's feet and says, "Pa, I can't do it."

And his father, unfazed, says, "Okay, son. Now this time I want you to pick up the sticks and break them one at a time."

That's what financial planners do very well in the financial services world, and what they need to do procedurally with their clients. They need to show them that the sticks that represent the obstacles to reaching their goals don't all have to be broken at once, and then show them how to break them one at a time.

And that's a service nobody else provides. What financial planners are uniquely capable of doing is creating a path that'll get their clients to what the clients perceive to be their most unreachable goals. Doing that for your clients is The One Thing.

**In summary:**

• Lead by example by being a participant in the Life Planning process.

• Ask the right questions of your clients.

- Give your client's agenda back to them on a regular basis.

- Leave a legacy of your business and its practices by passing the torch — that certain way of treating clients, of doing business, of providing service in an ethical and idealistic way.

- Create a path that will get your clients to what they perceive to be their most unreachable goals.

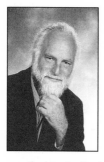

**Bob Veres'** *Inside Information* service has evolved into a community of the top professionals in the planning profession, who share their most successful ideas and best practice management and marketing solutions with the membership as a whole. His Media Reviews service addresses one of the biggest new practice management issues in the profession — staying on top of the published materials — by summarizing the contents of the four leading trade publications and many articles in the consumer press, allowing advisors to get the important information that is published each months in minutes instead of hours per week. Mr. Veres is author of *The Cutting Edge in Financial Services*. For more information on the *Inside Information/Media Reviews* service, visit ***www.bobveres.com***.

*Everything is complicated;*

*if that were not so,*

*life and poetry*

*and everything else*

*would be a bore.*

—Wallace Stevens, Esq.
1879–1955
Former VP of Hartford Insurance Co.
and renowned poet

## DEENA KATZ

# Lightning in a Bottle

*By "D" Shannon*

We woke up at the Marriott Residence Inn at Washington's Reagon Airport at "Oh-dark-thirty" in the morning. I felt near death after fighting the East Indian food that Bob Veres had "treated" us to the day before. In an effort to survive, I'd spent most of the night gulping down Pepto-Bismol.

The flight down to Florida seemed uneventful for the first hour when all of a sudden, a commotion arose from behind us. We turned around to discover a man having a heart attack. This is not your normal, everyday flying, I thought. Luckily, the man sitting in front of us was a doctor from Walter Reed Hospital who quickly got the situation in hand with the help of the flight crew; the automated defibrillator most planes carry proved unnecessary that day. The man seemed to have had only a minor event and we didn't have to detour or stop. Still, it was more excitement than we needed as we proceeded to land in Fort Lauderdale.

What a wonderful day it was in Lauderdale compared to our previous day in windy, cool Asheville, North Carolina. Lauderdale was everything you dream of that time of year: sunny, white puffy clouds, about 85 degrees. I piled into the cab after Dave, gave the driver directions, and we roared off towards our appointment with Deena. The cabbie headed for Coral Gables as if he'd been there all his life, which we suspected he had. As we got close to the address, we weren't sure what the actual building looked like and had to U-turn and proceed back down to the Omni Hotel.

Deena's offices were in the penthouse of the Omni, a building with retail shopping and more offices on the lower level. We quickly rose in the penthouse elevator and, as the doors opened, were immediately greeted with a wonderful reception that embodied the concierge level of service Deena and her husband and partner, Harold Evensky, provide their clients. Graciously ushered to a comfortable living room, all three of us took our seats on plush sofas and overstuffed chairs for a comfortable afternoon chat.

## Figure Out Who You Are

Most people pigeonhole me as a practice management person. And practice management is really important to me because I think it is the place where people need the most help. I'm not in a position at this time in my life to help people with their life questions or with their ability to communicate. These are not jobs I think I'm equipped for and I don't think I can do it in a book. So that is a piece they have to get someplace else.

The practice management stuff that I do is pretty simplistic in terms of Harvard Business School teachings but, somewhere along the line, I put other ideas out there that may lead them in the right direction or that may support them as a whole person. It's important for advisors to think about being whole persons themselves before they try to figure out how to support somebody else. I give out what I know and, if it helps somebody, that's pretty cool. Even if it doesn't help them, it does crystallize things for me.

What do I get out of it? I think fairly well on my feet. Sometimes I may have an idea that has not gelled very well in my thinking process and the ability to verbalize it for my audience is an immediate "aha." Telling other people about the things they might think about doing comes back to me in ways I can sometimes refine for myself and my practice.

Many times when I'm with advisors in a consulting environment I do a *Harvard Business Review* case on Shouldice Hospital. It is one of the most fun presentations I do and takes a couple of hours. I give them the case beforehand so they can read it and get their ideas together.

Harvard Business School takes on a different business every year. They work all the issues into a case study and then they tell you at the conclusion what the business should be doing. So one year, 1984 I think, it was Shouldice Hospital.

Shouldice Hospital is a hernia hospital in Canada that was having growth problems. It was trying to figure out how it should grow. It wanted to know whether it should build a new facility, add on to the old one, or perhaps add procedures. It was seeing some competition from hospitals in the United States that were copying its unique operating style; yet it believed it had enough business and didn't think it was necessary to meet this competition head-on.

So I lead financial advisors through this whole process, talking about hernia procedures, doctors, and how the doctors treat their staff and patients. It's really amazing stuff. And at the end I say, "Does any of this sound familiar to you?" Everybody nods their heads as they recognize how similar our issues are. Then we talk about our own practices and our growth decisions.

I gave this case study to one group and it was the best thing I ever did with them. We had such a good time with it, lots of interaction, and it stirred up a lot of issues for all of us about our own business challenges.

Then one time I did it with some high producers at a large brokerage house. One guy sits down and in the first five minutes says, "Hold on, before you get started on this, I need to let you know something. I didn't read the case. I don't *want* to read the case. I'm *not* reading about hernias. If you think this is so important, cut to the chase. From reading this, what should I be doing or not doing in my business?"

I was devastated. He didn't want to explore changes; he just wanted to know what would help him make more money. Somehow or another I made it through the whole case study but I hated the thing.

 *The day when wirehouses figure out how to motivate their financial consultants without the need to leave their humanity at the door can't come soon enough for me.*

What I realized then was the difference between people who want to improve what they do for themselves and the people they help, and others who simply want to improve how they sell. This particular man wanted, "Give me stuff to make me a better salesperson so I can make more money," not "Give me something so that I can think through what I'm doing to have a better relationship with the people I work with."

These are two very different views of the world. If I can be better for you, my client — if I have my vision intact — then I can help you. But, if I'm floundering, what good is it for me to talk to you? What could I possibly offer you?

Then there are a lot of people in the world who think that the most valuable thing they can give to others, especially their clients, is to show them how they can buy more or, in the case of the advisors, sell more. And that is actually a great thing to know. I took a class that gave me 112 ways to close a client. In one instance you say, "Do you want this, on the one hand, or this, on the other hand?" But one day I woke up and said, "Why do I want to close everyone?"

Let me give you an example of my own consulting that I think is illustrative. I used to do this with individual advisors. I would send them a consulting case study beforehand, a self-assessment thing, and then spend an hour with each one of their staff members. I would go through some of the things with them and, when I was finished, I would come up with a strategy: where things were weak, what changes might need to be made. I did an assessment of where people were. Maybe they were not placed in the right spot. As I went along I gave hints: "Well, what if this happened and what if that happened? What would that be like?"

Doing these interviews was really interesting because, while a lot of the questions I got were fascinating, one was more so than most. I had interviewed this one gentleman who was a salesperson who wasn't doing that well. He was complaining that he didn't have any tools to help him do a better job. His company had some software but he wasn't encouraged to learn it. Somebody would input the data for him and he wanted to know more about it. So I was talking to his sales manager later in the day. I said, "What kind of tools do you have available for your people?" And he said, "Oh, we've got lots of stuff. They can do whatever they want. They really don't need anything more."

And I responded, "I'd like to offer an observation. This particular man is *not* a natural salesman. He needs a different framework."

He said, "You know, it's funny you say that because I know he has an issue in closing sales and I haven't quite figured out what it is. He won't give people opinions, I think, and that's what's keeping him from closing. He won't tell them what he thinks they should do."

So I responded, "He doesn't tell them because he doesn't have anything to support it. He doesn't have any analysis. Many of the people that you have working with you," I said to him, "are yellow-pad guys. They can sit down with a yellow legal pad and say you need to do this and you need to do that. Let me take care of this and we can do that."

But in this particular situation, this young man needed to have more support and more detail to feel confident in presenting what he believed needed to be done. He needed more analysis. So, in this particular consulting arrangement, there wasn't one thing that worked for everybody. However, there was one thing that worked for each of them and it was different for each. This man needed to learn how to use the software and understand it. I'm happy to report from what I hear that his sales have gone up and he's more successful now because he actually got a solution that was uniquely specific to him, as compared to other people who were perfectly happy just drawing out their ideas on a yellow legal pad… which brings me to what I think The One Thing is.

## The One Thing — It's the Connection

When I am connecting with people, an audience, a client, whatever, there is an energy that seems to pass between us that you can almost see. I really enjoy a picture I saw once that somebody sent around the Internet. It showed an older couple holding a jar and, if you look inside the jar, there is lightning in there. Literally lightning in a jar.

And you look at the man and he has really been picking this lightning out of the sky and capturing it. That is what connecting is — to be able to reach out and touch the energy that we feel in each other, to be able to open yourself up to somebody else and to be able to connect with them.

It's beyond having an institution or something that dictates what we are; it is pure energy. It's speaking without words, it's knowing without knowledge, it's connecting. It's harder than anything we might be able to do because it requires us to be less self-conscious about ourselves, not to be conscious about how we appear and how others are thinking about us. You have to stop the stuff where you are trying to impress someone. It's more about, "How can I look into that person's soul and see something that I can connect with?"

When we were young, as advisors, a lot of our processes were motivated by things like money and cars and status or image, and that's good and probably appropriate. But as we grow, we can only grow by connecting with people and getting focused on what's important to them. Some of this is taught in the Certified Financial Planner (CFP) program in an oblique way. They do pay some lip service to listening skills. Most of what is taught, though, is pretty technical stuff.

What it tells me is that, if somebody is a newly-minted CFP, they are really good at the technical stuff and the product knowledge. But to me the best way to form a relationship with your client is to sit there and talk like we're talking now. And nobody ever really tells you how to do that. The operative term is "collaborative interactive." It's a soft word. We do not put things on paper. We simply let the client talk.

 *I'd go so far as to say that, when you've got the kind of client relationship Deena describes, you can walk into a meeting with no more than a one-page agenda and maybe a few pages of backup material.*

When I first got started, I wrote my first financial plan. It was 103 pages. My client looked at it and said, "Oh, my God, you're published!"

In those days that's what we thought we had to do. Today it's about understanding: "What do you, the client, need to do and how can I synthesize the technology, analysis, the world picture, the experiences that made me who I am today, and help guide you in a meaningful direction?" That's my job.

What I do is help you get where you want to go and if I can't connect with you, if I can't communicate with you, then I can't help you. Filling in all the forms in the world and sending them to some idiot to put into a machine and then send back a bunch of boilerplate documents is garbage that is not going to help you.

So what I would say before you ever take on a client is: you better know what you have to offer. Paramount to that is knowing the value of what you have to give. Often our view of what is valuable is entirely different from what our clients think is valuable, and that is the disconnect.

I don't mean to go off on a metaphysical tangent. I am pretty grounded. But a quantum physicist would describe it as this: we are taking people and their money (kinetic energy) to a higher valence. It's almost spiritual.

*Deena foreshadows so much you'll read later in this book, e.g., know your value to the client!*

My primary purpose and what pushes my buttons is to create a connection between one person and another, between myself and others, between their energy and mine. Sometimes I can do it and together we become an extraordinary force; and sometimes I can't. The hitch is to know when you can't do it and to move on to the next thing.

The ability to really listen to people and what they're saying and what they're not saying is so important. My Mom used to describe what I do as 95 percent shrink and five percent number crunching. She said, "You know, there are a whole bunch of idiots out there who could number crunch for you, a bunch of idiot savants who could do a whole bunch of calculating, but can't seem to function in the world." So Mom asked me, "So what do you want to be? Do you want to be a great communicator and have the ability to get at things with people and join in with them, or do you just want to hand them numbers?"

## Practice Management

I know you might have expected me to talk more about practice management. But what I write about is not necessarily who I am. Practice management is really important to me, as I said earlier, but I think the essence of The One Thing is to really connect with people, to reach out and make that bond, to catch that lightning in a jar.

We manage the quality of our clients' lives, not just their dollars. In the opening part of my first book, *Practice Management*, I told a story about how I met with one of the top money managers today and described to him my brother-in-law who had invested in his fund. You may remember that if you read it. If you don't or didn't, I'll summarize it by saying that he jumped up from the table and, in horror, screamed, "Now you've done it! Now you've put a face on the money!"

Well, I think that's what our jobs are and that's what separates money managers from successful advisors and planners. We put a face to the money. We are concerned with our clients' holistic interim and long-term goals. We don't have to maximize returns because we're more concerned about our clients' achieving those goals.

We're not just managing clients' assets independently of their goals and objectives. If we are, then really all we have to offer is performance. If we tout performance as our value as planners, then we're attempting to deliver something over which we ultimately have no control. The cure for this is to know what we do for a living and how to express it to the world.

### Family Values

This brings up another good point I'd like to talk about, and that's what I would call family values; not like what we've heard about in recent political elections, but family values with regard to our planning industry. What I'm specifically referring to is the values that we impart to young advisors and planners today, the ones coming out of school, many of them with baccalaureate degrees in planning.

They need to have role models provided to them to help them understand how important the connection with clients is. They need to have people who give them the strong guidance and example of connecting with clients, where it's about the relationship and not about the performance. And it concerns me. I think what David Grau at Business Transitions has done is really cool. But a concern on my part is… what happens when firms are sold as part of an exit strategy? Who's going to provide the continuity and legacy that the next generation will need to pick up from us? And so I've been thinking more and more about that lately.

### What It Is Not

I'll tell you what The One Thing is not; it's not that tired old saw of the compensation argument. I've been in this industry for about 27 years and we're still having the same old argument about compensation that we've been having forever. Here is my view of that.

*Amen!*

Let's say that we're some large lion on the plain of Africa and we're looking at a herd of zebras. And we go over and get one of those zebras, not worrying about the rest of the herd. The truth is, there's so much of it that all of us lions can eat and do comfortably well. Instead of fighting over which one of us is going to get this part or another of the zebra, we should remember that we have the rest of the herd out there

And it has to be the same way in our industry. Because when we start talking about middle markets and lower markets, perhaps the only reasonable way these markets can afford to pay for our services is through the implementation, i.e. commissions, and it's not wrong or dishonest. It does not mean that everybody who implements plans through commissioned products is unethical.

Anyway, I'm tired of having this conversation. I know I'm comfortable working fee-only. That's just my background and education, and it doesn't have anything to do with my ethics. As far as conflict of interest, we all have conflicts of interest; they're just packaged differently.

Many people know that we had an issue for a long time with the National Association of Personal Financial Advisors (NAPFA), but recently we encouraged two of our advisors to join NAPFA. I think that's because they have moderated somewhat and I think it's because it's an important thing to do. And I've moderated somewhat too. But for a while I thought that the way the fee-only planners presented themselves really disenfranchised the rest of the world and I don't think that's appropriate or right. But remember, I've always been a fee-only planner. That's the way I do business. It's not necessarily the best way for someone else.

I just don't think we need to have these roaring battles over compensation. I'll have roaring battles over disclosure any day of the week, though. The issue is not how we get paid, but that we disclose our compensation to our clients.

There are some things we're not going to be able to get done without a commission. I've been going through this fee-only insurance route six ways from Sunday and have come to the conclusion that we're going to have to start providing insurance, so a lot of my guys are going out and getting licensed. It's just not going to change in the foreseeable future. What really rubs me raw is that I've given my clients to other people for insurance and they've been chewed up and spit back three times and are very unhappy with me. So I've had to make some changes to my model that accommodates what my clients want me to offer them. Bottom line:

- Clients are not averse to paying you.

- They just want to know *how* you get paid.

## Professionalism

I'm excited to see us all move toward professionalism. We still need to get our act together, though, because we're still haggling over that same old zebra as opposed to presenting a united front to our consumers. Still, I get pretty excited about our progress, even though sometimes it seems like a huge struggle. Watching financial planning grow globally is really thrilling for me.

As a metaphor, let me describe my experience of watching this growth. I used to be in Rotary in Chicago and our project was The Rehabilitation Institute. I used to go and dress up as a clown every year for their Christmas party. The only way I could go and face those children was to do that. You would see the same faces year to year but, instead of being in a wheelchair, they would be in a walker. It was good to see the progress.

And that's what I view as happening in the financial planning industry globally. Each time I visit a place I've been to before, I see huge inroads, huge changes as these people embrace a discipline that I love. That is a very exciting, heady thing. Still, it's a pretty slow process sometimes and we need to be patient. I like to feel that in some way I may have had a small part in that process. It's very gratifying when somebody walks up to me and says, "Thank you very much for writing the book you wrote. I got this out of it and I've applied it to my practice, and I'm doing so much better." That's probably one of the best things that can happen to you, you know? That's feeling like you've made a difference!

I think we have legitimately moved from product, to process, to advice. We're now seeing the process emphasis in all the broker-dealers and the 800-pound gorillas out there. Whether or not they are getting it is another thing; but just progressing to the advice model tells me that we're moving very much in the right direction.

And I think the biggest change we've made is that it's not about the product anymore. Let me give you another metaphor.

Recently I spoke in China. I noticed that everyone in that country has a mobile phone. Everyone! When we developed the telephone, we needed to put up telephone poles all over the place to facilitate calls. Today, we still have that structure, even though we started offering cell phones about 20 years ago. What's amazing for me is to see a country that went from almost no phone service to leaping immediately to wireless cell phone technology, skipping the entire part of needing telephone poles and telephone wires.

And that's what I see when I travel around and speak to people — that they're able to make this huge leap of progress from where they were years ago and catch up very quickly to where we may be here in North America regarding financial planning.

### Does My Success Surprise Me?

That is a great question. You know, I don't take it real seriously. Sometimes I'm fascinated with it from time to time, and at times people will come up to me and ask me, "I have your book. I just wanted to meet you. I've followed your career. Etcetera, etcetera." There's almost a knee-jerk response I have of, "Do you have a life?"

Truly, I'm moved by their attention and feel grateful that I've been given this chance to help so many people, but I'm not an icon. I just don't put myself up on that pedestal.

I'm just doing my thing. I've got a big mouth. And I have a lot of opinions on stuff. In fact, I have a lot of opinions on everything! And I don't take any of this celebrity seriously. Those planners out there in the trenches... those are the people I admire. I do think I've been very fortunate, though. I've been given an opportunity to have a forum somewhere and I hope I don't screw it up.

What's funny is I actually didn't even start out to write a book. I wrote my first book because Mary Rowland and I were doing a talk together and, in front of the whole audience, she announced that I was going to write a book for Bloomberg. She didn't even ask me beforehand. She said, "Deena is writing a book for Bloomberg."

I almost fell off my chair! After that speech Mary called and she said, "I gave your name to the acquisitions editor. You need to write a practice management book." And I responded, "I've written little things, but I don't know that I can do that. I don't know what I have to say."

She responded, "Trust me, you can write. It'll just flow out of you," and she was right.

I sat down and it was almost like I was channeling. I think that's because I'm really passionate about what I do. I know that when I'm speaking it's like live theater where there can be this tremendous connection and energy. You can feel it coming back to you. And that describes exactly the kind of connection that is The One Thing that we as advisors need to have with our clients.

### Postscript by "D"

After we turned off the tape recorder and walked out the door to lunch, Dave and Deena started talking about how important it is to reveal yourself to your clients for who you are. Your authenticity is part of that connecting, Deena remarked.

Dave mentioned that he'd given a presentation to advisors about connecting with clients through authenticity and had described his passion for pit bulls, Harley Davidsons, and body art. He quickly pulled up his right shirtsleeve and showed Deena his tattoo of his pit bull "Angel."

With characteristic aplomb, Deena said, "Well, to celebrate life after the passing of my sister last year, I decided to get a tattoo of my nickname. You may or may not know that my nickname is 'Pepper.' So I went out and got a tattoo." And quickly scooping her blouse down, she showed us a hot chili pepper emblazoned on the upper portion of her left breast!

Falling over with laughter, the two of us staggered out the door with Deena and proceeded to have an amazing lunch and a wonderful conversation with somebody who truly is an icon to us. We're eternally grateful to her, both for her hospitality and for letting us into her life a little bit.

### In summary:

- Figure out who you are before you try to support someone else.

- Know the value of what you have to offer.

- Really listen to your clients goals.

- Put a "face on the money" — manage your client's lives and dollars.

- Connect with your clients and create something extraordinary.

**Deena Katz** is President of Evensky, Brown & Katz. Prior to joining EBK, Katz owned an independent financial planning firm in Chicago.

Katz is an internationally recognized financial advisor and is the author of various books on financial planning. Her book, *Deena Katz on Practice Management*, along with her newest best-selling book, *Deena Katz's Tools & Templates for Your Practice*, have become the leading texts on management of a financial services business. Another book, *Long Term Care*, has been reprinted six times and more than 125,000 copies have been distributed to clients by major insurance firms. Katz was Editor-in-Chief of the *Journal of Retirement Planning* and has been a contributing writer for *Investment Advisor, Financial Planning* magazine and *National Underwriter*.

Katz was named *Financial Planning Magazine's* "Most Influential Person" (one of five) for 2001 as well as one of *Accounting Today's* "Top Ten Names to Know in Financial Planning" in 2001 and 2002. She has been included on *Worth Magazine's* list of top financial advisors numerous times, including the most recent year. Katz has held many positions in the financial services industry, including member of the CFP® Board Examination Audit Committee, the International Association for Financial Planning (IAFP) Strategic Task Force, and board member of chapters of the IAFP and the Institute of Certified Financial Planners™ (ICFP).

Katz is often called upon to speak at national and international financial forums and has spoken in Australia, Canada, Japan, England, Ireland, Singapore, New Zealand, Malaysia and South Africa, as well as throughout the United States. She is also frequently quoted by major national news media and has made various television appearances on local and national network programs for CBS, ABC and PBS.

Katz was the first woman member of Rotary/One, Chicago, as well as the first woman to serve as a Director of a United States Rotary Club. She received her Bachelor's degree from Adrian College and was the 1993 recipient of the College's Young Alumni Achievement Award. Katz is a trustee of Adrian College and received a Doctorate of Humane Letters from the College in 2001.

Look for Deena's Books on our website ***www.onethingforadvisors.com***

*Courage is a mean
with regard to
fear and confidence.*

—Aristotle

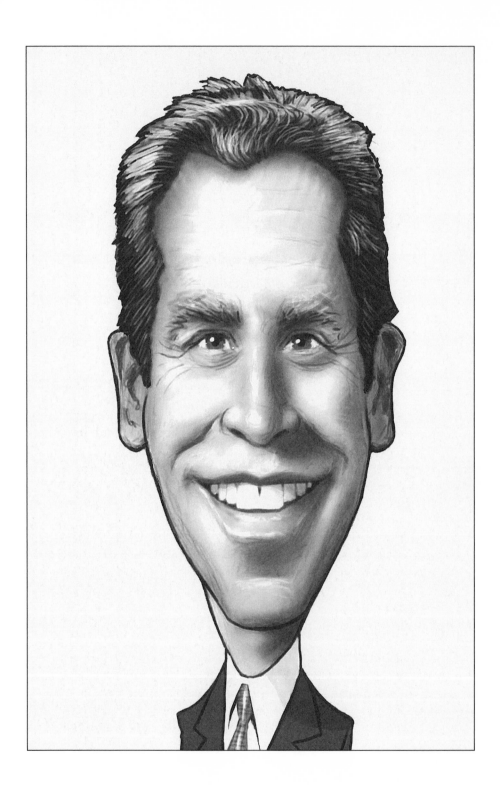

# Don't Keep Me a Secret

*By "D" Shannon*

We were near Dave's old stomping grounds in Columbia, Maryland. Dave reminisced about growing up in Silver Spring and how the area had changed so much since he moved away almost seven years ago. Bill Cates was an hour-and-a-half from "D's" farm near Warrenton, Virginia on a drive that took us past the Pentagon, the Capitol Building and RFK Stadium. Occasionally Dave pointed out a landmark and related a story about his roots there.

Seventies music blared from "D's" F-250's speakers as we sang out of tune, "Anywayyyyy, whatcha gonna dooooooo?" We looked out opposite sides of the truck to keep from cracking up at each other's inability to carry the tune. Our musical inspiration seemed fitting because not only is Bill Cates known as "The Referral Coach" but, at one point in his life, he made his dough as a rock 'n roll drummer. (Needless to say, Dave and I didn't make the band.)

I explained to Dave how I had met Bill years ago and had reconnected this past February through the National Speakers Association as I was beginning to explore the sale of my advisory business. All three of us share a common affliction of middle-aged men: teenage daughters. So as we pulled into Bill's parking lot, courtesy of his very able assistant Karen guiding us in like an air traffic controller, we lamented how each of our 14-year-old girls owned us. We remembered that Bill was being besieged by his daughter to get a dog. As the proud owners of seven dogs between us, we decided that Bill might not be as inclined to talk "dog" as we were under the circumstances.

After signing in through security at Bill's new office building, we were again met by Karen in the lobby and escorted back to Bill's brand-new space. Bill greeted us at the door, obviously in mid-conversation on his cordless headset as he wrapped up a call. With a warm "hello" we took the quick tour before settling down in his conference room.

## The Referral Process

In my new book, *Get More Referrals Now,*[1] I outline five major steps that advisors can take to help them create an unlimited flow of quality prospects. Not only will these skills help them eliminate cold-calling forever, but they'll be meeting high-level prospects in exactly the way those prospects want to be met: through a referral from someone else they already trust.

These steps are as follows:

### 1. Adopt a Referral Mindset

I believe you must embrace referrals as the best way to build your business. Referrals are not just something nice that happens every now and then. They are the primary part of your overall marketing and growth plan.

### 2. Enhance Your "Referability"

You must be good at what you do; you must be good at your relationships with your clients. To be referable, you must create a "Wow!" experience.

### 3. Prospect for Referrals

I believe you must be proactive in making referrals happen to obtain the clients you want. You do this by "planting seeds" and knowing how to ask for referrals in an effective way. You must also create a profile of your ideal client so *you* know who fits your business and who doesn't.

### 4. Network Strategically

Not all of your referrals will come from clients. However, "networking" is an overused term and often does not lead to the results people want because, in my opinion, it is not approached strategically. Networking in a strategic manner is more effective because you are targeted in your approach. Every advisor should have 10 to 20 high-level referral alliances who send them a steady flow of great prospects.

---

[1] *Get More Referrals Now* (McGraw-Hill, 2004)

It was my publishing business that taught me the value of a niche. When you target a niche, you bring more value to your clients and you're more referable. It's the fastest way to building a referral-based business. My niche was cookbooks sold to gourmet, kitchen, and gift stores. I didn't sell to bookstores much. I sold over 40,000 books a year just to pick-your-own fruit and vegetable farms. I learned about these niches that were out there and produced these books that these guys would sell by the truckloads.

Years later I reached a point with the publishing business where I knew I had had enough. So I made the decision to sell it. And as I was selling it a friend of mine said, "You should be a professional speaker." And I said, "Great, what's that?"

I had never seen professional speakers before. So I checked it out, attended some seminars, and joined the National Speakers Association. My first "gig" (musician's term) was doing sales training for a Virginia-based firm. When the guy who owned it moved his business, I found my way on my own. For a few years, I was a generic sales speaker and had some very happy clients. But I didn't have a thought-out process to teach salespeople.

One morning, while driving to Philadelphia, I listened to some tapes from a guy named Scott Kramnick who was in the insurance industry. I really liked the topic of referrals as an area of expertise for me. So that was when I made the decision. I had been looking for something to really go deep with. By the end of listening to his tapes I knew this was it. I was going to teach referrals. I was going to write my next book on referrals. From there, things took off. When I started writing, the book ideas just flowed from me, from a place I didn't even know I had.

The book was written generically — not specifically for financial services. However, the financial services industry really latched onto my message and the rest, as they say, is history.

## Producer-Centered Referrals

One thing I learned in teaching referrals is that many people see the referral process as something being *pushed* onto someone, something they *do* to someone. It's almost like the old way of selling as opposed to working collaboratively.

The old way is, "Let me tell you how I get paid. I get paid in two ways. First, I get paid through the products I sell and second, I get paid through the referrals you give me." It becomes an obligation for someone whom you haven't really served yet. A lot of clients or prospects will be offended when you come out heavy with the "here's how I get paid" spiel. They are far less likely to appreciate that old way of doing referrals.

It is very centered on your needs as a "producer." While a producer-centered methodology can work, it's not the most effective way.

I was working with a manager who was trying to build a referral culture in his organization of 300 to 400 advisors. So I went to their meetings. They met weekly, sometimes by videoconference. Everything was focused on numbers: numbers of clients, numbers of plans sold, numbers of assets brought in. Nowhere was there a discussion about how the clients were being served. Not a word was said about bringing value to the clients. It was entirely producer-centered. *Every* business is based on bringing value to clients/customers. If you don't bring value, you don't make money.

*"If you don't bring value, you don't make money." This should be tattooed on the insides of our eyelids!*

In the beginning of the very first meeting, they advertised the fact that they were going to ask for referrals at the end of the meeting. I said "Don't do that!" I went on to say that it can't be producer-centered. It has to be about the value — the value clients receive and the value that can be provided to others. Sure, I stated, with a producer-centered methodology, you may walk away with 15 names and phone numbers. But with the Do-Not-Call regulations, you might not be able to call them! Even if you could reach them, your closing ratio will not be as strong.

When clients feel obligated to give you referrals — because it's how you get paid — you usually don't get their closer relationships. You get a list of people with whom they have less influence.

## Client-Centered Referrals

Talking to clients about referrals from a client-centered perspective — where it's all about the value you bring — comes from a place of success. It comes from a place of your knowing that you do important work for people and that your clients know people like themselves who need to know you.

*"With" versus "to" is an important distinction. Advisors who don't sell products often fall into the trap of thinking that any type of selling — including asking for referrals when they have real value to provide — is somehow "unclean."*

You must perceive this work as something you do *with* people as compared to something you do *to* people. It is fairly simple when this is your position: all I've got to do is identify the people who are willing to collaborate on referrals! There are enough of them out there. I'm not pushing them to do something they don't want to do. So it becomes a very natural, easy, collaborative process; not with all clients, but with enough of them.

I often use the term "missionary zeal" as it conveys a sense of true passion for the work you do. It conveys a sense of purpose and the deeply-held belief that people will be much better off because of the work you do. It is easy, when you have this missionary zeal, to feel comfortable asking your existing clients to collaborate with you on bringing such good work and tremendous value to others they know.

### Know Your Value

I think that part of your missionary zeal comes from understanding how much value you actually create for your clients. When you internalize exactly how much better off people are because of the work you do with them, then the referral process becomes easy and effective and you enjoy your work more. Few people in your clients' lives come close to making such a profound impact as you do (maybe a doctor or a teacher). It is a truly an awesome responsibility that you carry and an amazing gift you offer to the world through the work you do — if you're good and if you maintain a high level of integrity.

Larry, my financial advisor, is the guy in his company who teaches all the other people how to charge for financial planning. He gets $8,000 for a financial plan. Other advisors charge only $200 to $2,000. He can do this because he is very clear that his work is so valuable that $8,000 is a bargain relative to the value he brings to his clients. Other advisors' confidence on this matter is so low that they almost give it away.

So it is about knowing the value you bring. But, on another level, you almost don't need to know how much value you bring to your clients because all you've got to do is ask them. Ask your clients and they'll tell you how valuable you are.

 *In studying the subject, I've been amazed to find that only a tiny percentage of advisors actually survey their clients to find out what the clients value about their services.*

That's why I say to new advisors that, if you don't know the value of what you offer, if you haven't internalized what other people are telling you yet, then just start asking your clients and pay attention to their answers. Internalize what they say to you.

## Have a Process That Creates Value

I like working with advisors who are real financial advisors or planners in the sense that they actually do a financial plan for someone. They really have a bona fide process through which they put their clients. I believe that they, as far as the referral process goes, become more referable more quickly.

When I did my financial plan, my advisor talked with me for two hours in our first meeting — and we barely talked about money! We talked about other things, things that were a lot more important to me than just money, but things that money might influence at some point.

In terms of bringing value to your clients, first, you've got to be good at what you do. Your prospects and clients should see the value in meeting with you and the value of your process. To borrow a term from *Star Trek*, your "prime directive" on every appointment is to bring value. If you bring value, you'll likely make the sale *and* become referable in the process.

Second, you have to build business friendships. Remember what they had to drink when they were in your office the last time, send hand-written notes after every meeting, host client-appreciation events. These things seem small but they play a large part in making it a pleasure to do business with you.

One of the advisors who uses our referral system in Florida has an office on the first floor because he works with seniors. At 9 a.m. he places a sign out in the parking lot: "This space reserved for Mr. and Mrs. Smith." At 11 a.m. the sign reads: "This space reserved for Mr. and Mrs. Gold." You get the idea. His clients walk into his office with smiles on their faces because he treats them like kings and queens.

So being referable is about being really good at the work you do and being really good at building business friendships with as many of your clients as possible.

> **Never forget that your business grows at the speed of relationships.**

## How Well Am I Doing?

The barometer of how well you are doing is your receipt of unsolicited referrals. I believe that everyone should always be getting referrals without asking. Any business, financial advisor, dry cleaner, anybody, should receive unsolicited referrals because there are plenty of people who like to give referrals. Most people like to make the connections under the right circumstances.

Haven't you raved to friends about a new restaurant you found or insisted they go see a certain movie? It's the same thing. I would just tell you, as an advisor, that if you are not getting referrals without asking for them, then there is something missing. Something is missing in your relationships or in your value creation process. That is the ultimate barometer of the question "Are you referable?" — receiving, or not, unsolicited referrals.

## The One Thing

What is The One Thing from my perspective? It is what I said before: know the value you bring to your clients. If you are absolutely convinced of the value you provide people, you will possess a missionary zeal and not see the referral process as something selfish — as being all about you. Rather, you will feel an obligation to help more people and will work cooperatively with your clients to help more people through their referrals.

Your client wins because she feels good when she plays a part in helping someone through the work you do. Her friend, family member or colleague is better off because of the work you do. And yes, you are better off because you get to help another client, you make more money and, most important, you have had it affirmed that what you do is important and necessary in the world.

**In summary:**

- Have a process that creates value.

- Adopt a referral mindset.

- Enhance your referability by being good at what you do.

- Proactively prospect for referrals.

- Know the value that you bring to your clients.

**Bill Cates** has revolutionized the way financial professionals use referrals and other powerful marketing strategies to attract more clients and increase sales. Top producers call on Bill to help them leverage their book of loyal clients. Rookies get the right strategies from the very start of their careers.

His popular books, *Get More Referrals Now* and *Unlimited Referrals,* have established him as America's foremost expert in attracting high-quality clients through referrals. Bill's Unlimited Referrals® Marketing System has been featured in *Success* magazine, *Entrepreneur* magazine, and *Selling Power* magazine. His own business success has been featured in *Money* magazine. Bill has spoken twice for the Million Dollar Round Table. He has earned the professional designation of CSP — Certified Speaking Professional, held by fewer than 400 speakers worldwide. Bill's speeches and seminars are high-energy, entertaining, and filled with strategies and tactics that can be put to use immediately.

Bill Cates is the president of Referral Coach International. RCI specializes in working with financial professionals who want to perfect their referral-based business and with companies that want to build stronger referral cultures.

For more information about Bill Cates and his company, Referral Coach International, please contact him at ***www.referralcoach.com*** or 800-488-5464.

*They say the seeds*
*of what we will do*
*are in all of us,*
*but it always seemed to me*
*that in those*
*who make jokes in life*
*the seeds are covered*
*with better soil and*
*with a higher grade of manure.*

—Ernest Hemingway

# MITCH ANTHONY

# Getting the Client's Story

*By Dave Drucker*

We got into Minneapolis at 10:37 p.m. on a cold, rainy Monday night. With only two minutes to spare before Enterprise Rental Car closed, we were rewarded with an upgrade from a compact car to a Chevy Suburban. Fortunately, "D" had rented a Suburban the previous summer so there was a minimum of confusion about the location of the headlight switch and windshield wipers. We departed Minneapolis-St. Paul Airport for our suite at the local Residence Inn.

The next morning we woke in the shadow of the Mall of America to another overcast, drizzly day. After a hearty breakfast, we headed for Rochester in our Suburban, our MapQuest directions as our guide. Within 20 minutes we'd left the confines of the city and were rolling up and down the gentle slopes of the upper Midwest Prairie. We commented more than once about the rich darkness of the prairie topsoil compared to our scruffy local earth.

When we finally arrived at Mitch Anthony's house in Rochester, Mitch and his lovely wife, Deb, invited us into their home for a sit-down around the kitchen table. "D" and I proceeded to pick Mitch's brain until he was virtually speechless. We learned that Anthony is a man of many ideas and many accomplishments who has much to teach the advisory industry. (And he's got a truly classic 'Vette for sale, if anyone's interested).

❖❖❖

## Context

I don't want to be seen as someone who helps advisors increase their production — and that strikes at the heart and soul of what's wrong with this business and this industry. What I've been saying to people in leadership at these companies is, you need to pay attention to the language you use because the language you use shapes the culture you live in and it shapes people's expectations.

Here's an analogy I began to use with management at companies that stress production. "You're telling your people to take clients on a long walk into the horizon. And you're encouraging them to build that sort of long-walk relationship. But, at the very end, you tell them, 'Oh, by the way, we'll have a stopwatch on this walk.' Make up your mind. Either this is a stopwatch race or it's a long walk. You can't have it both ways." And that's where they're at right now. They know that to succeed, it has to be a long walk. But they're still running stopwatches every 30 days.

The best phrase I've heard in 15 months is the one that says context is worth 50 IQ points. And what I've been trying to do is get people to think about the context they're creating in their conversations. Because if you paint the right context, everything just falls into place. And this is where I think firms are failing at the retail level — they're not painting a context that gets to the heart of what matters to clients.

What I'm warning the leadership about is, you've got to pay attention to your language, to every word you use. For example, what is the archetypal metaphor that runs this industry? That's not an easy question to answer, but I'm talking in a very large-scale context. It's "track record."

If you watch the language people use, a discussion by investment managers about returns almost sounds like a gambler going to a track and studying the numbers to find out who did really well in the last race so he can bet on him for the next race. And for those who don't really believe that that's the archetype, we now have this very sophisticated planning tool called Monte Carlo simulation that'll go out and project all the possible returns. I think the problem with that is that it sends a message, at the emotional level of the client, that this is really a gamble. And what I'm trying to get the industry to do is say, "We need to shake off that metaphor. We don't want to be associated with gambling."

A better metaphor is "wealth care." We're very close to the Mayo Clinic here in Rochester. Around the turn of the century when the Mayo Clinic was established, William and Charles Mayo made a statement that became the foundation for their entire organization: "The only interest that matters is what's best for the patient." So, whenever the Mayo Clinic has a dilemma and it doesn't know what to do or what direction to take, that statement settles the argument. And every doctor, every nurse, every receptionist, every finance officer, every person who works in that organization demonstrates a patient-centric attitude in the form of confidence, caring and integrity.

Everybody knows those three words, and "caring" is the spinal column of the whole thing. Doctors aren't afraid to let you know they care how you're doing. What a difference that makes. And no wonder the Mayo Clinic, year after year, is rated the top clinic in the world. I've had five family members go through the Mayo Clinic for surgeries and every single time I've been blown away with the empathy they've been shown.

So if an advisor calls me and says, "I want to start having that bigger context conversation... I want to start addressing the big picture," I say, "Describe the conversations you're having now." And if they're product-driven conversations, I simply say to the individual, "You need to go through a brainwashing course."

There's a local advisor here. Great guy, nicest guy in the world. But he never calls me unless he's got a stock idea. If he called me in and sat me down and all of a sudden wanted to have a big-picture conversation, I would be looking at him cross-eyed, because he's never had that kind of context with me.

 *I wholeheartedly agree! I have often made the analogy that we need better bedside manners — look up from the clipboard and the numbers and pay attention to the patient/client!*

Looking at the industry's opportunity to introduce a new context, I think it's the insurance companies' game to lose because, if you've ever had to deliver a benefit check to a widow, you've learned to have a real-life conversation. I don't see many people in the wirehouses delivering checks to widows. I think that makes a phenomenal difference in your ability to have a real conversation with someone.

The other day, a very highly qualified Certified Financial Planner said to me, "I am so tired of this return-on-investment conversation." Now, I probably had too much Starbucks in me at the moment, but I asked, "Who do you suppose started that conversation?" I said, "You chose to create that context. You chose to offer that value proposition. Now you're stuck." And I think what we've got to begin to do in the beginning of the relationship is to paint a different context.

You explain it this way: most studies show that most Americans' lives revolve around trying to get ahead financially. They make decisions, they do what they do, they go where they go because they're trying to get ahead financially. At the end of the day, sooner or later, every one of us comes to the epiphany that that model doesn't work. It leaves empty places in our lives.

What the client really wants, and what the advisor needs to learn to do, is to shift this context, turn it inside out. The advisor has to say, "I'm here to discover what your life's about, where you've been, what's going on right now, where you want to go and the principles that guide you. And then let's do everything we can with your financial situation to make that life work." Money is the servant, not the guide. But most people — just by virtue of getting in debt early and not realizing that they have choices in all these things — end up in that subservient position. So that's the first way I offer to describe the new context for the relationship. In the first five minutes with a client, you can completely shift the context.

## Advisors Need Life Planning Too

I've actually got a major national firm that I'm working with right now to create a program called "Advisor Life Planning." You can't offer what you don't know. Most advisors' lives are out of control. They don't enjoy what they're doing. They're not passionate about what they're doing.

 *This theme of advisors getting their own lives under control and doing their own Life Planning is one that was voiced over and over again among those we interviewed.*

I'll sit down with an advisor and say I want to have a meeting with you and I'd like you to bring me eight envelopes each containing a check for $250. I'm going to make a trade with you that I think you're going to like. I have eight envelopes too, and we're going to trade envelopes. You're going to open your eight envelopes and find that for every check for $250 you gave to me, I gave you a 20-dollar bill. You'll say you've gotten ripped off, and I'll say well, that's the way you deal with yourself every day. You trade $250 worth of value and skill in the marketplace for a job you can hire someone else to do for under 20 bucks. And you wonder why you're not happy with your career. Until you get paid for the value that you bring, or that you *could* bring, you're not going to be happy.

I happen to believe that the best gift you can give to a client is a snapshot of a life that's working really well. And we all know advisors who are doing this — people like Ross Levin in Minneapolis, whose life is working really well, and he's helping his clients have lives that work really well. I like people like that, because they've got a balance in their life. They're prospering. They bring value and they charge what they ought to get for that value.

I believe you set a boundary for the life you want to have. An opportunity doesn't get past that boundary if it's going to shake the core of that life and mess it up. Along with this — a really, really big issue — is we've got to help people get better at painting a larger context for their lives.

## The Process of Discovery

How do you go about it in a very disciplined and predictable manner that gives you a repeatable experience with clients, a discovery path? What does that discovery path look like? I spent quite a bit of time working on that riddle and came up with this model: picture a heart and its four chambers. Actually, put the heart in the middle of a circle that represents the six-step planning process: assets, risk tolerance, estate, debt, cash flow and tax. In the middle of that circle place the heart and label it "My Life."

Now we're going to go ahead and do a little discovery — some surgery. We're going to divide that heart into four chambers we call My History, My Transitions, My Principles and My Goals. Now, I'm from Iowa originally, so I have this penchant for reducing things to the simplest terms, which means I describe these as "where you've been," "where you're at," "how you got here," and "where you're going."

A great many of you in financial services work around the financial planning process with just numbers and treat all clients as the same person. The process is, "Just give me the numbers, let me work the numbers." Many of you think you can work in an isolated, quantitative vacuum without getting to the larger context of what it's all about.

But here's the interesting thing. In the financial services industry, when you start talking about the quality of discussions, it's pretty much from the hip. Everybody comes up with their own serendipitous route or path of getting to know people. The process, however, isn't always repeatable; there's no discipline to it. So I set about designing a disciplined process for discovery or, as one person put it, "You've almost left-brained the right brain." You need a predictable format for getting at what's in that right brain, what's in the heart and soul of the client.

Here's what I've noticed with financial services companies. Out of History, Transitions, Principles and Goals, what area are they telling people to go have a conversation about? Goals! That's the last place you should have your initial discussion. I ask these companies, "Which one is the most important for your financial advisor to understand?" They need to know where the client has been — the client's history.

*Goals are the focus of the CFP program too, which is largely ignorant of the fact that a larger context, or conversation, is possible.*

I pay a lot of attention to the discovery, or data-gathering, forms people use in the industry. Look at how little information we get on our client's history. Instead, we spend our time as advisors collecting information on their numbers. We can get somebody else to do that for us.

## Why Personal History Is Important

My financial advisor happens to be in Iowa and he's been with me for 24 years. And the reason he's been with me so long is because he knows my story. He knows how I got started. In 1983, exactly 365 farmers hung themselves after getting foreclosure notices. I did not grow up on a farm but my mother's family did. For me, however, this was deeply personal. I ended up running all over the state finding out, "Where's the help for these people?" There was nothing.

So I decided to set up a Suicide Prevention Hotline for farmers. I wound up in the lieutenant governor's office and they wanted to make a political thing out of it. I said, "Phooey!" I went on a road tour for nine months, raised money in churches and service clubs, and trained a volunteer staff to answer the phone. We put up billboards and did television and radio ads all over the state saying, "Suicide's not the answer." We plugged in the phone line in March of 1984 and the first day, nine farmers called.

Have you ever had a conversation that starts this way? "I've got a loaded gun in my hand and if you don't give me a reason to live, I'm pulling the trigger — and I might do it on the phone." Here's what I discovered: these people's lives were ruined; not only their lives, but their legacies. Whole families, the generations to come, were ruined by bad financial choices. This was at a time of 20 percent interest rates and inflated land valuations. As we answered the phone we would learn so much about the experiences that had shaped these farmers' lives — their values, their fears, their hopes — while trying to help them.

So I ask, "How much about these things, these personal histories and stories, do advisors know about their clients? And what methodology are they using to get this information?"

Returning to the example of the Mayo Clinic: Mayo will get two types of patient history. They'll get some personal history, but they also want to know if you're allergic to anything. I ask, "Where is the allergy question in the financial services questionnaire?" Analogously, I ask, "Where do we ask the client about what experiences, good or bad, he's had with other financial services professionals?" Tell me the best experiences and the worst experiences you've had with your money. These are allergy questions.

We have designed this path, literally a path, with the History questions you have to ask, and then we ask the Transition questions. Then we move to Principles and finally we move to Goals.

## Take Your Conversations to the Next Level

I define my audience as advisors who want their businesses to emanate from their heart. I don't advertise myself with phrases like, "Take your business to the next level." I have utter distain for those terms. Who's that about?

You should, I believe, describe your business with phrases like, "Take your client conversations to the next level." "Take your life to a better place." My audience is those people who work from the heart, have a philosophical bent, and who really, truly, have come to this epiphany that the numbers side of this business is actually rather mundane.

My audience says, "I'm going to get bored if all I do is put together plans." They express, "I want to be invested in my clients in a way where I actually help shape some destinies. And I happen to believe that money is a profound thing."

Is this Life Planning? You know, I think the language, the term "Life Planning," and even the term, "Financial Life Planning," which is a term I created, marginalizes the conversation. Really all we're talking about is emotionally intelligent advice. This is advice that takes the emotional issues and the rational issues and pulls them together. And we all know that the issues of the heart, the emotional issues, are the context for all this. But we never really had a disciplined process for getting at that. And that's where I'm coming from.

 *It's truly refreshing for someone to have the integrity to back up the bus and call a foul on his previously-held idea. Mitch does that exact thing here by challenging himself on the term "Financial Life Planning."*

George Kinder gives you three questions that open up a larger context. Bill Bachrach gives you a question that you keep repeating in an effort to open up the larger context. We've got to have a continuing conversation with the client and that's why I've created the Life Transitions methodology.

Let's go back to the Mayo Clinic analogy. Let's say your doctor has that initial context-opening conversation. He gets some history and learns what your concerns are. Does that end the relationship? Does he say, "All right, let's put together a health plan and you just stick to that"?

You know the term "financial planning" is really an oxymoron. All you need to do to be a good planner is to have a crystal ball. All you have to do is to know what's going to happen. Then you can be a planner. And we're not really talking about planning here. We're talking about preparation.

## Life Transitions Conversation

I got an article from a guy who created a metaphor called "financial scanning." I thought that was quite clever because what we're really doing is watching a pattern in people's lives and just keeping an eye on what's changing. Planning is a static term; scanning is a dynamic term. Using the Mayo Clinic analogy, what the doctors do any time something flares up is have a conversation. Any time something changes, they're going to want to have a conversation. So I took that model to heart.

I think the most powerful framework you bring to a conversation is your experience. I personally believe that we have entered an age that I characterize as the Experience Age. The Information Age ended the day Google appeared on our computers because you can punch in a name and get so much information that it's overwhelming. That ended the Information Age. Information now has become pretty much useless. It's actually disabling.

What's powerful now, what has importance in the market and what will pay, is your ability to *sift through* information; your ability to say, "I've got 20 years in this business." Gray hair is now an indication of gray matter. It's not an indication that you're on your way out; it's an indication that you know what you're doing. That's why I'm on this new "Retirementality" thing — because the world's changing. And the attraction is going to be the gray hair, not thin waistlines. So I tell advisors, "Here's how you start this conversation."

## How to Start

You say, "In my 20 years in this business, one of the greatest lessons I've learned is that we do our best to create a financial plan, but life doesn't necessarily comply. Life has a way of taking its own twists and turns. And what we've learned is that we need to keep in touch with the twists and turns in your life and make sure that your plan is keeping pace with that, because if one thing happens in your life that we don't know about and don't address in your financial plan, it can literally undermine the whole thing. So to do that, what we would like you to do is just go through this 'Checklist of Life Transitions' in advance and tell us what's going on right now or what you see on the very near horizon. And only check the ones that apply to you."

Now, I've got four years of research in this Checklist, and I'll tell you how it started. A guy walked up to me after a speech and said, "You know, that's all great what you're saying. But I don't need to talk to my clients about their lives. I'm good with numbers, I'm good with investments, I know what I'm doing and that's why they buy my services." What ticked me off was not what he said, but the fact that he represented a very large contingency of this industry that actually believes you can carry on this conversation without getting to the heart of the matter. So this guy says to me, "I don't need to talk about life." And what disturbed me was that he had been successful in the marketplace without ever actually getting into the real context: the client.

I don't think that model can last. Why? Because the relationship has got to resonate with the client over the long term or he or she is going to go elsewhere. We need this conversation that some people would call "the soft side." And at the end of this conversation, we'd better have something financial to talk about.

## The Financial Implications of Life Transitions

Now let's go back to this transition conversation. I said to myself, "All right, I need to come up with a powerful thesis to rebut what this guy just said to me." So the method I chose was to list all of the transitions one can go through in a lifetime — from the cradle to the grave. What could possibly happen in life? And we came up with about 60 different transitions and events that could or might or will happen to you. They fell into the categories of personal family events and transitions, work and career, financial, community and charitable or legacy-type events.

I then went out and started doing research on every one of these events and studied the following issues:

- What do you need to know to get through the transition? What are the considerations here? What questions do you need to be asked or to ask yourself?

- Are there financial institutions connected with these events? Do these events impact your wealth-building or wealth-protecting process? And finally,

- Where do you go to learn more?

All of that information is a part of our online tool now (*www. flpinc.com*).

Here's what we learned in our research. We found that every one of our 60 transition issues has financial implications. You want to just deal with the financial implications without knowing the issue? Where's the life in that? So what we're saying is, instead of starting with the financial implications of people's transitions, find the context for the transition in their life.

At our Financial Life Planning website, the planner can kick out a customized Life Transitions Summary Report for the client. Let's say his client checks off five issues. With that information, the advisor can then construct financial solutions for each of those transition issues.

Here's a personal example for you. My father worked for 25 years as a television broadcaster. The company he worked for changed hands five times. What that meant to my father is that he now receives a pension check for $53.22 a month. My brother and I are baby boomers, and I think baby boomers have had an impressive capital opportunity. I mean, we don't work harder than our parents, but we get better financial rewards. So my brother and I got together and decided we needed to do something to give our father a margin of comfort.

Our father isn't retired in the traditional sense; he works odd jobs to supplement his pension. I found a study that showed an extra $200 to $400 a month can give a person in that age group some breathing room… the ability to go to a movie and not worry about it. So my brother and I sat down with our father, right here in Rochester at the Grubers Bagel Shop, when he turned 65. This is not an easy conversation to have with your father. How do you tell your father that you're going to do this for him? And my brother and I, we didn't know how to start the conversation even though we're both fairly articulate people.

So my brother finally just started talking and we described what had happened to his pension and how that bothered us, and what a great father he was. And how we decided to create something called a "parental pension," and that he didn't have any choice about this. And that he'd begin receiving this check for a few hundred dollars a month till the day he died. Our father broke down and bawled like a baby. And now what do we do? Our dad is weeping in Grubers. He says through his tears, "No one has ever taken care of me." My father's father left when he was two, his mother didn't want him, he was in five foster homes by the time he was seven years old. "No one has ever taken care of me."

That is easily one of the top five events in my life: that moment. And that moment got repeated with my mother, who's separated from my father. This time, we were wise enough not to do it in Grubers.

## Solutions That Work — the Ongoing Conversation

So what I'd like to tell the planning community is this: if you're the kind of advisor who isn't afraid to talk to me about my life, who isn't afraid to ask me to fill out a Life Transition Profile, then you could make that moment possible in my life because, by the end of that conversation, we would have a financial solution that worked.

And we go down the list. I have a child preparing for college. Well, you know the financial preparation involved there. I'm starting a new business. You know they keep changing the laws on business structure, so you always keep an eye on what kind of structure your client needs to have.

I have a charity called One Life, and we put the majority of the income we get from our business into that cause. I have a book on suicide prevention that I wrote in 1991 and it's been translated into numerous languages. We just finished a Slavic translation because Hungary has had the highest suicide rate in the world for 20 years. We pay for the translation, we pay for the printing and we pay for distribution. Last month alone we gave out 3,000 copies around the world. And we also pay the expenses of people who are out doing this stuff.

My advisor knows that. Now he's something other than somebody who just does financial stuff. He's in it full circle. He knows me. And he knows what Mitch and Debbie and my family are all about. He sends a check to my mother and father every month. We're talking about a personal engagement here.

And he's going to be the executor of my estate. He just sat my wife and me down and had a very difficult estate planning conversation with us. He said, "Mitch, you're putting all this money into charity, you're doing this and that. What about Debbie and the kids? I mean, is this thing set up properly?" You know, he broached that difficult conversation with us.

But this is the ongoing physical, or "fiscal" conversation, if you will, that the advisor is going to have with the client every year, because it only takes one change to turn things upside down. A parent falls down and breaks his or her hip and all of the sudden a whole new world opens up. So this is how these planners are using this tool. They just have the client fill it out each year and they keep the conversation moving along.

The first thing we give the advisor on this issue is the Discovery Guide because they don't know what to ask. They can't possibly be a student of all 60 areas of life. So we went out and did the homework. And I'm now creating — and I think this is going to be the Holy Grail — I am creating a way to turn every annual review into a joyride. I'm moving the context away from "Return on Investment" and changing it to "Return on Life." And I'm creating a template that will allow you to sit down and show the client the qualitative progress you've made together.

Here's the analogy I'm using right now with the advisor community. I say, "I want to make a proposition to you. I want you to pay me and here's the service I'm going to provide. I'm going to be your weather advisor. You bring your calendar to me. Show me the dates that you want to have outings, picnics, ball games, whatever. I'm going to tell you if it's going to rain or be sunny. Now, raise your pinky if you think I'm a little off here, if you think I'm just a tad insane." Of course they all raise their pinkies. I go on, "Now you tell me the difference between what I'm doing and what you're doing when you tell your clients you will get them a better return than an index. There's no difference. You have based your entire life and career and business on something that you have no control over."

## Making the Conversation Better — PROFIT

This speaks to why advisors have stress in their lives. Their lives and careers are something they have no control over. And they build a conversation that's no fun.

Now I don't want this next point to slip by. Let's say you guys are my advisor, we just spent 40 minutes talking about my parents and what we might do for them. When that conversation's over, I guess my time's up. So you say to me, "Mitch, the next time we meet, which one of these issues would you like to talk about?" And I say, "Actually, I think I'd like to work on the starting-a-new-business issue." What happened is we've completely redefined the context of our relationship. This relationship is now about the client's life and associated financial issues and, from now on, we're having conversations about his life, even though we never actually said that.

What I've done is I've created a new report that advisors can customize for their client and it's called the PROFIT statement. PROFIT is an acronym that stands for Progress Report On Financial InTentions — not financial returns, but financial intentions. And here's what it's going to look like. It's going to say "Your Concerns" up here, and then down here it's going to say "Your Goals." And up here's my aging parents. And down here's my college tuition and the names of my children. And over here it's going to show how we made progress this year. For the parents, we've got the income stream going. We took out an LTC policy and we made an adjustment in the will.

This is what the conversation should have been about all along. The return on investment is a peripheral conversation to this. We address the core first and then say, "The 529 college funds earned 12 percent this year." The market might have been up or you might have made some additional contributions. Either way, we're that much closer to your goal. They're going to ask the kind of questions we taught them to ask when we started the relationship. What's going to happen, eventually, is that people are just going to stop saying, "How did we do against this index?" You created that stupid conversation.

The reason I worked on this PROFIT statement was to solve the riddle that's bothered me, which is: how do we make the conversation better? And I finally came to the conclusion that you have to change the topic and get to the heart of what the topic's about. By the way — and this was a shock to me — but when we went out and did our survey of clients who are using this tool, we got our top 10 concerns. Do you know that "re-evaluating my investment philosophy" was number five? There are people who don't know what to think any more. The whole world's going to turn upside down philosophically as to what works and what doesn't work.

Take the question, "Are there any investments you would avoid as a matter of principle?" I've done a lot of surveys on that with my advisors. Fewer than five percent of advisors ask that question. When I go to clients and ask them if they would like to be asked that question, over 95 percent say they would.

## Boomers: Learning What's Important

I had a call yesterday from a lady who is an expert on Gen-X and she said she'd read my book *The New Retirementality* which, ironically, I wrote for baby boomers, and she said it resonated with her. She said, "We had a party the other night. We're all about 30, 31, and every one of us agreed there isn't a single advisor we ever met that had a conversation we were interested in. And advisors aren't even interested in talking to us because they don't think we have any money."

So I ran my conversation by her and she got all excited and said, "Oh my God, what a great conversation." I said, "The reason the value of this came to you is because you know about the boomers; but they're just now learning about themselves. You knew it growing up. These people are chasing stuff. They're chasing status. They're chasing bigger, higher, better, and you knew that wasn't it. The boomers are just now figuring out about themselves."

Gen-Xers tend to want a life with purpose. Boomers are just now realizing this. I was offered a consulting job in 1995. This guy heard my radio show and he called me and said, "I want to sponsor your show," and he showed me his products and I proceeded to stick my foot in my mouth and told him that that was probably the worst-looking display I'd ever seen in my life.

So the net effect of the conversation was that he asked me to be his marketing director and he offered me 160,000 shares in the company plus a full-time salary for showing up two days a week. You can imagine how long that conversation lasted between my wife and me. He's taken three companies public. He just offered me 160,000 shares. We're already doing the math. So I said "yes" and I proceeded to trade my life for this financial promise.

One of the things that happens when people are worth $100 million is that they begin to believe they know everything about everything, even though they don't. And he was impossible to work with. I'd come up with a great idea and it would disappear into a black hole. Then he started taking more of my time and, pretty soon, I'm on the road a lot, which wasn't part of the deal. Now, all of a sudden, he wants me to show up three days instead of two days a week and I've got to drive 90 miles one way just to get there. By the time I'd get home, I was about one-tenth the father and husband I used to be.

So I was driving home one day and I was about halfway there when I looked down and saw I was literally choking the life out of the steering wheel. And I'd been doing that for 45 miles and didn't even know it. I was looking at my white knuckles and they spoke to me. I realized that the night before I couldn't sleep because I was so angry at this guy. I was putting on weight and my asthma and allergies had flared up to the point where I couldn't even breathe on the phone. You'd talk to me and I'd be wheezing on the phone

And I let go of that — I just put a light touch on the steering wheel, and then the real impact hit me. I had the thought, "The writer inside Mitch Anthony is going to die if I don't get out of there." And that's when I realized that I didn't have a choice — I had to get out. I came home and I told my wife, "I'm leaving and we're going to put together a financial plan to be out of this thing as soon as possible." It took six months to get out and I've written seven books since then. I extricated myself in 1998. That experience gave me a lot of empathy for the snare that America is just getting hauled into.

### *The New Retirementality* and Life Conversations

My book *The New Retirementality* is about choosing from a core of passion. You know, everybody in this business says retirement planning is the business they're in, and most of them don't know the basic history of retirement. They don't know it was invented in 1875 and that it was an effort to move old fogies out of the German government. They don't know that the retirement age was set at 65 back then. They don't know that the average worker died at 46. Retirement was never designed to be a 30-year subsidized journey. It was designed to be a one-year bridge from the loading dock to the loading dock. One year, okay? In 1937, if you retired at age 62, you were dead at 63.

Retirement is an artificial finish line. If you remove the finish line, what changes? You're 45 years old and we just removed your finish line. It forces you to think in a much more fluid way about "How do I get money, how do I spend my time, what do I like, what don't I like?" — all those things that are suddenly on the table. You see, I believe retirement is a failed social manipulation. It's damaging to the spirit and, for those who are of a religious persuasion, retirement is something you won't find in the Bible. There are only two negative references to it in the Bible: one is in *Leviticus* — priests who had served too long and had fallen into cronyism were "retired." And two — it was Moses' form of punishment for killing an Egyptian. Those are the only two references you will find in the Judeo-Christian ethic. So it's unnatural.

And I like the term fluid because life is a fluid event. It's not a static event and retirement imposes this artificial finish line that people shoot for, thinking something's going to happen when they get there and it doesn't. For a lot of people, it ruins their life. And then they also realize that they have no life. So when you remove that artificial finish line, it brings you back to this question: "What am I passionate about?"

Or to quote — I think it was Jonas Salk — who said, "Figure out what it is you're passionate about and see if there's any way on God's green earth to get paid for doing it." Now you start having that kind of conversation. And isn't it great when we can develop skill sets and intentions for a life that age really doesn't impact?

I just created a new conversation called "Retiring on Purpose" — double meaning intended. It's all about having a retirement that a) connects you with others — because that's one of the indicators of successful aging, b) challenges your capacity, and c) has a charitable pulse to it. You're helping, you're bringing transcendent value, to somebody.

I got this book by Viktor Frankl called *The Doctor and the Soul*. He was a big believer in logotherapy, which is about finding meaning in your life. You've got to have a meaning that's beyond you. He parted with Freud and others because he said they missed the mark. It was about meaning. People are driven by finding meaning. He said people talk about freedom. And that caught my eye because I've asked thousands of people, what does retirement really mean? And they always say freedom.

But Frankl said what they don't understand is that they're talking about freedom *from*, not freedom *to*. They're only thinking of what they're going to get free from. He said it's our responsibility to determine what we are free to do. What are you going to do with that freedom that will have transcending value?

So this is a conversation we're having through *The New Retirementality*. I just ask people, "How do you want to do your business? Do you want to do it from your heart? Do you want to do this business in a way that it's joyous, that when the day's over you're fulfilled, you've gotten properly recompensed for the value you brought to the conversation, and you can't wait for tomorrow?" The only way that kind of life is possible is to have life conversations.

## Find Out What's Important to Each Client

So we set these conversations up with this: "You can't measure a person's wealth by a checkbook alone or by an account balance alone. If you could, there'd be no such thing as a happy poor man or an unhappy rich man. So, what we like to do is have every client define for us what they mean by true wealth. How do you define success in your family life, your working life? How do you define balance?" And that opens up a conversation at the end of which the advisor says, "I want to work with you on making that picture happen."

You have to eventually get into the conversation of what's enough money; how much money is it going to take to make all this happen? Then we get into the conversation about financial history: lessons, memories, biggest threats, best and worst decisions, experiences with advisors, and main sources of information. Then we have our principles dialogue, and then the one about transitions. And then we get into their goals, making sure they include the category of "leisure and recreation."

When we ask people to give us a goal, there's a 50 percent chance they're going to hand us a seed and a 50 percent chance it will be a weed. But do you really want to get engaged at that level? I mean, do you want to help somebody grow a weed? So I think that the goals conversation has to get way more open-ended, and I use this natural metaphor of weeds and seeds.

I've actually got a discussion guide called "The Garden of Goals." We talk to people about tending a garden by breaking it into the family plot, the work plot, the community plot, and the personal improvement plot. When you're tending a garden, it's not just about sticking seeds in the ground and watering them; it's also about pulling the weeds. What's your goal? What do you want to take out of your life? Those are good questions.

What do you want to take out of your family life? What do you want to take out of your personal life?

Then you ask the client, "What do you want to do in your retirement?" and now they get a reality check. They say, "Oh, my God. I don't have a plan for my life." So I think we need a new conversation. You can't just talk to people about their dreams; you've got to talk about survival. You've got to touch survival first, so what I've done is I've created this whole conversation where we lay survival over a financial conversation by asking, "What are your survival expenses? What is it going to cost for you to survive? How are you going to pay for survival?"

Okay, we've got that; now let's talk about safety. You do it in that order. And next we talk about insurance issues where you get into safety — protecting what you have. Then we get to where we talk about freedom. What do you want to do with your time? How are we going to pay for that? We literally itemize all the things you've got to pay for to achieve those emotional ends.

We're entering into an age now where the boomers are going into retirement, so this is a conversation that people have to master.

### The Conversation Has Value

I'm very passionate about *The New Retirementality* because the core of that message is life. It's the conversation we've been having all along. This new online tool (*www.flponline.net*) has 100 customers. I'll probably have 500 by the time 2005 is over the way things are going because, this month alone, I think we had 20 people sign up. It hasn't been an easy business to build, but I think we've finally figured out that what advisors really want is some coaching. They also want some encouragement and they want fellowship with other people who are operating this way and doing it successfully.

So we have a forum online, but we also hold what we call the FLP Fellowship Meeting in the Chicago area, which is advisors sharing their success stories. Once every quarter we have a phone call where I spend 20 to 30 minutes teaching and we spend another 40 minutes interacting with each other — asking questions and sharing ideas. And that seems to be the connectivity the advisors want. They don't know each other, but they all want to do it right. They have in common that they're talkative, they're caring and they're motivated. They want to make a good life.

And I'm pretty clear, when I talk to these people, that I'm not about having a great conversation and starving to death. I mean, when you bring value to the table, you better get paid for it. If you don't get money for it, you rob yourself; but I think, more importantly, you rob the client and we rob the future of this industry. It won't be here. We'll be back to stupid numbers and other stuff.

We've got to keep this conversation moving forward and let it continue to evolve, so that if you want to do this business the way it should be done, you can make a good living at it. Talk to Deena Katz, talk to Roy Diliberto, talk to Ross Levin and talk to other people who are doing business right. They're making good money and people around the block can't compete with them.

### The Curious Biographer

So what we're doing is introducing a new skill set here that I would define as "biography." The people who are going to be the best at this business in the future are going to be those who are the best biographers. How skilled are you, how willing are you, to sit and listen? How skilled are you at asking questions and how curious — and this is the topic of my next book — are you? Because if you're not curious, then we don't have a foundation for this conversation.

Everybody has an interesting story. The earliest piece of parchment known to man is in a museum in Turkey and it has two things written on it. One is about unruly children and two — and bear in mind that they had just discovered a way to record a story — is that everybody thinks he's a writer.

Clients want to tell their story, especially retired people, but nobody wants to hear it. That's what they have left to share with the world. That's their legacy — their story — and you should be sitting there saying, "Tell me your story." When you cross that bridge and you take the time to hear their story and you have the natural curiosity to really want to know that story, something amazing happens at that level.

And natural curiosity is such a pure thing. Curiosity is the driver of all great success in the world. So if the financial advisor marketplace is sincere about having long-term relationships, then they need to invest themselves in the process of being better biographers.

### The Discovery Dialogue

A client of mine hired a firm to do a study on this thesis I'm developing now about how curiosity leads to empathy, leads to trust, leads to more assets under management and a more trusting relationship. We studied how many cents on the dollar the average client entrusts to the average advisor. The average across the United States is around 30 to 35 cents.

Then we started looking at people who would give an advisor 100 cents. Wow, a carte blanche relationship! What we studied was the method of discovery used. The discovery method that led to the 30 cents on the dollar relationship was, "What do you have and where is it?" The discovery *dialogue* leading to 100 cents on the dollar was, "Who are you, why are you here, and how can I help you?" *Then* the client was asked what do you have and where is it? But in that order.

In this statistical study, we also took eight life categories and asked clients whether their advisors understood them in each of those areas. If their answer was that the advisor understood them in eight out of eight categories, then the advisor had 100 percent of their assets. If, in their perception, the advisor knew them in five out of the eight categories, the advisor was managing about 70 percent of the client's money. If the advisor understood two of the eight categories, he was managing around 50 percent of the money, and so on. What we established is that there is a true link between biographical knowledge and assets under management — which is a signal of trust.

So it's a pretty simple message, isn't it? Know your client. But it's like one guy said to me, "You're talking about taking a handshake conversation to a hug." Not literally a hug, but a hug conversation. That means I want to get my arms around your story. I've probably got an obnoxiously big vision about all of this. And the vision is that I want to have a conversation with everybody. Everybody, in my opinion, deserves a conversation.

Let's talk about what it means to the financial services industry. It means that we finally figured out that you can't have trust without understanding. You can't build a bridge of artificial trust. You know, it's like something an old friend of mine told me about golf. I was nervous about playing a certain person, and my friend said, "Don't play his reputation; play who he is today."

 *I am glad Mitch has an obnoxiously big vision of this — nothing great ever came from having a timid small vision!*

Your reputation's important, but you've got to build it right now; and you can't build trust without understanding who this person is you're talking to. Once people are doing this, then we'll have a dynamic, vibrant industry. And I think people get hooked on this sort of relationship. Once you have this sort of relationship with your client, you get hooked. It's a beautiful thing.

## The One Thing

Here's a little story on the welfare of the client and the welfare of the industry. In May 1953, two men became the first to climb to the top of

Mount Everest: Edmund Hillary of New Zealand and this guy from Nepal, Tenzing. On the way down, Hillary slipped and began to fall to a certain death had it not been for the quick thinking of Tenzing, who slammed his ice stick into the ice and created a temporary brace for the rope, just long enough for Hillary to re-establish his hold.

Upon reaching the bottom, they were surrounded by international press. When they heard about the amazing rescue by Tenzing, they were quick to call him a hero. Being somewhat of a modest man, Tenzing's only response was, "Mountain climbers always help each other. After all, we are tied together." I think that story is almost a perfect explanation for why we have to completely consume ourselves with the client's story. It's their money, not ours.

That's The One Thing. It's their story. And the one thing you're looking for in their story is their purpose. That's why you want their story. You want to know their purpose. You want to be a part of that. Financial planning and implementation help them move toward their purpose; they help them live out the life they've dreamed of.

So how do people really transcend the habits they've learned throughout a career of working for big firms? How do they begin to transcend the sales process? What do they do on a regular and consistent basis to move over to focusing on the client's story, to aligning their purpose with their client's, and to working with these tools?

Well, everybody comes to a level of learning at a different point. You know, you're either cut from a cloth where you know immediately that a decision is gratifying, or you beat your head against the wall year after year until you suddenly hear of a better way to do it which you decide to try.

I think that futility drives change. People do things they hate until they realize how badly they hate them.

**In summary:**

- Conduct yourself with confidence, caring, and integrity.

- Advisors need Life Planning.

- Know your clients' personal history.

- Have an ongoing conversation with clients and provide them with progress reports on their financial intentions.

- Paint a context that goes to the heart of what really matters to the client.

- It's their story—it's their purpose.

❖❖❖

**Mitch Anthony** is the founder of the *Financial Life Planning Institute* and is the founder and President of *Advisor Insights, Inc.*, a firm specializing in training financial service professionals in relationship building skills. Mitch is the author of several books for financial advisors, including *StorySelling for Financial Advisors, The New Retirementality, Your Clients for Life, Selling With Emotional Intelligence* and most recently, *Making the Client Connection*. Mitch's work has been featured on *ABC Evening News with Peter Jennings, CNN, Bloomberg, CBS Marketwatch, Kiplingers Magazine*, and many other media outlets. His radio program, *The Daily Dose*, is heard daily on 170 radio stations nationwide.

and then advisors will learn how to custom design it for themselves. So The D.O.S. Conversation consists of two parts. The first part is called The R-Factor Question™, and R stands for relationship.

What the question immediately does is determine whether the other person actually wants to have a relationship with you because, if they don't, they'll never answer the question. It's a very confronting question if you don't want to have a relationship with someone. We find that people usually size each other up in about ten seconds and decide as to whether they want to pursue the relationship.

And there is a basic buy-in or a cancellation that happens in the first ten seconds. So you're going right after the first sale, and the first sale is the relationship, because if you don't buy the relationship, then everything else is meaningless. The other thing is that it's a question not about the present, and most people go in and they ask a question about the present, "How do you feel about what's going on right now?"

Well, most people are all over the map right now but when you move them into the future — for example, three years out — in their mind they have to do a lot of distilling and they have to make all sorts of choices, and the human brain is really, really fast. So when someone says we're having this conversation three years down the road, first of all they've bought into the premise that they're going to be having a relationship with you three years down the road, but then you're asking them to actually describe what their measurements are. You're asking them for a template. Essentially you're getting the person's template or their yardstick out on the table. This is how I'm going to measure my progress over the next three years such that I will be happy with it. It's useful to know because there's only one person on the planet who knows that. And they are the expert. What you're doing is you're getting the person to actually define how they measure their life. You've told the person right off the bat what this is going to be about, and it's not going to be about you; it's going to be about them.

And for most people, in any kind of transaction, it's actually one of the questions that we really want to know the answer to. If I get to deal with you, who's this really going to be about. Is this going to be about me forcing something on to you, or is this going to be about me finding out about you and seeing where I can be useful? And that is very powerful.

Now, in that illustration did I tell him anything about my program? Most people say "No." And I say, "Actually I did." I told him who the program was going to be about, which was him.

That's all he really wanted to know — who is the program going to be about. So as a financial advisor, the biggest thing that the client or prospect really wants to know is:

## Who's This Going To Be About?

If you're selling a product or you're selling a service, immediately the person on the other side of the desk knows that it's really about you, it's about your sales projections, it's about your commission income for this year, it's about going to president's club and everything else, so the very way in which the financial services industry teaches its advisors and salespeople how to sell immediately tells prospects and clients that the game isn't about them.

I'm saying that, as a salesperson, if you lead with your information you immediately commoditize yourself because you're just like everybody else. This question is a particularly open-ended question. The client can go anywhere he or she wants. This is very, very scary to a lot of advisors. Because in the past they've been told, if the prospect does *this*, you do *that*. They have learned sales karate. Now they have an open-ended conversation and that's scary.

*I can tell you from first hand experience it's a great world where you don't have to "overcome" objections!*

And so we do channel the question with the second part of The D.O.S. Conversation which we call The D.O.S. Worksheet™, and The D.O.S. Worksheet is actually either a worksheet that you have out for taking notes or it's a template that you have in your brain. There are three things that we want them to give us the answer to. And we call it D.O.S., which stands for Dangers, Opportunities and Strengths.

In response to their vision for three years down the road we want to know, first of all, what dangers are in the way of getting what they want over the next three years. Danger relates to fear: fear of losing things. Everybody, on a daily basis, in some area of their life, big or small, is confronted with losing something. And what could they lose? They could lose opportunity, they could lose reputation, they could lose money, or they could lose capabilities. I always say that, generally speaking, people will operate in three gears on a daily basis. They're either fearing something (Dangers) or they're feeling excited about something (Opportunities) or they're feeling confident about something (Strengths). In the midst of the day there's really a three-part mix of fear, excitement and confidence.

A really bad day is one where fear dominates. A much better day is one where opportunity and strength dominate. All three of those emotions, fear and excitement and confidence, can be paralyzing emotions. Everybody understands how fear can be a paralyzing emotion, but excitement can be a paralyzing emotion too. It makes you indecisive because you don't really know where to direct your attention. Excitement and strength can be paralyzing in the sense that they can make you complacent and overconfident. The job of the advisor is to take these very powerful ingredients, which are fear, excitement and strength, from paralyzing emotions to motivating emotions.

And the question is: motivating for what purpose? The answer is: motivating for whatever this person's purposes are given the three-year framework of The R-Factor Question. What we're doing is we're getting them, on an intellectual level, to say what their framework for measurement is over the next three years. Then there's a power pack of D.O.S. that they have which has these three very powerful emotions. What we want to do is take those three emotions of fear, excitement, and confidence and transform them into motivating emotions that direct the client towards his purposes.

At this point we've said nothing about ourselves. We've said nothing because the point is, it isn't about us. In The D.O.S. Worksheet, we get them to answer each of the sections individually. We do so by posing the question, "Given what you're looking at the next three years, or that picture you have in your mind, what dangers do you have now that really have to be eliminated over the next three years?"

And I will go on to frame it by further saying, "It's 2:00 in the morning, you can't sleep and something's on your mind and it's kind of worrying you. What is it?"

Things like this show up at 2:00 in the morning. The person will say "Well there's this and there's that, and there's the other."

Sometimes people don't think in terms of danger, so problems, issues, challenges, or some other words can be used, and the advisor should really be prepared to have some other words there. Continuing: so you're lying awake and you can't get to sleep, and I say, "Well what is that," and pretty soon it comes out.

All the advisor does is make note of each of the dangers that the other person shares and then feeds them back to them. Say, "Well, you told me this, this, this and you told me that." Part of the power of this conversation is that, oftentimes, this is the first time the person's ever thought about it in a clear-cut way. What you're doing is actually getting the person on the other side of the table to respond to their own information.

Then you say, "If you had to pick three of these concerns that you've given me, which would be the most important one, second most, third most." And you put other concerns aside by saying, "Would it not be true that if we eliminated these three most important ones, we'd probably eliminate all the others?"

I've found if you have ten dangers and you pick the top three and eliminate them you probably eliminate the other seven too. So that's that. Then you do the same thing with opportunities and you do exactly the same thing with strengths, so you wind up at the end of the conversation which, in some cases, can last a couple hours with a person who has very clearly defined three dangers, three opportunities, and three strengths. All along, what has been happening is that you're totally differentiating yourself from anyone else they've ever had in their life and, at the same time, you are the recipient of information that no one else in this person's life has ever received.

Not only that, but you're the first person to ever allow this person to actually see this information clearly so there's a bond that is formed in this conversation. All that said, you still haven't talked about what it is that you do. You haven't talked about money or financial planning either. This conversation will be all over the map.

Now what most advisors will say when I talk about this conversation is, "What if they bring up all sorts of information that I can't do anything about? Aren't they expecting me to help them with all of those things?"

I say, "Why would they expect you to help them? All you're doing is asking a question, okay?" And I say "Besides, in response to all sorts of questions and all sorts of answers that you don't know anything about, you can find other experts out in the marketplace and start establishing some strategic alliances so that you become the person who is a quarterback for all sorts of solutions. You're not the one that solves the problem but you are the one to direct them to someone else who solves it." I go on to say, "Would that be a useful capability to have and would that enlarge you, would it grow you as an advisor?"

*In my experience, once you attain the quarterback status that Dan describes, you have to mess up really badly before you're going to lose that client.*

Not only would you have access to your own area of expertise but access to a lot of other people's expertises. Imagine stating "This isn't my particular area of specialty but I know one of the best people in the city who can help you out. Would you like me to have her give you a call?"

All of a sudden they start to get a holistic view of what the picture is over the next three years, and you say "Okay, I'm not going to be able to come up with solutions today but, at this point, I look at this danger, and this danger, and this opportunity, and this strength and this strength, and there are five things here that I can help you out with almost immediately. What I'd like to do is go away and just ponder this a little bit."

You continue, "I'm going to need some financials from you to go along with this because these are sort of general answers we've gathered today. I'd like to get a handle on your last year's corporate standings or your last year's income tax return. I'd like to take this and put together a game plan for you based on what you feel it will take for you to make progress in the next three years considering those Dangers, Opportunities, and Strengths you've shared with me today."

At this point you, as an advisor, are at a place where you can just follow through and enter into a relationship where eventually these people are going to be introduced to your products and service proposals. Almost any advisor's success rate is going to go up 50 to 75 percent. If you don't change anything else but you just do this one thing, you will see that transformation in your business because you're letting them know it's about them.

The other thing you want is say is, "I just want it to be clear that this is the foundation that we're going to operate on. I'm going to date this — what we're doing today. Could you just sign this? I'm going to be giving you a copy and I'm going to have a copy."

The reason why you want to do that is that we've had three test cases in securities where an advisor was sued by a client. The client said that 'he came in selling me this and selling me that and selling me that.' Our client, armed with the D.O.S. worksheet signed by the client and date stamped, went in front of the judge and simply stated this is what we talked about in the first meeting. The judge looked at it and he said, "This is all about the client, it has nothing to do with the advisor. Case dismissed."

So it's been deemed as one of the best know-your-client documents in the financial services industry and it really protects you. If this is the basis for your first conversation, and this is the framework for all your ensuing discussions, you're going to have a lot of protection.

There's sort of a junction point here for an advisor because there are more and more advisors getting comfortable having this conversation. It takes a while to transition to this idea. I say that, based on the way most advisors have been trained, it's a really radical departure from the way they've done things in the past. Emotionally and psychologically, for a lot of advisors, it's a big river to cross.

Sixty percent of our clients in The Strategic Coach Program™ are in financial services of one kind or another. And the other 40 percent are from 60 different industries. Of those, almost all have come to us through a financial advisor. That's why we went after the financial services market;

because it's the nervous system of the world. They know where every-thing is. Financial advisors know. Anyone that we would want to know, a financial advisor knows. So, we've always just gone after the advisors and the advisors are referring us to everyone else. The D.O.S. Conversation works beautifully with every other kind of industry. There's no problem because, as I said, you modify the questions.

I have a jazz musician who was in for his workshop yesterday. Here's a guy really different from the typical financial advisor and he's been here with me now for 12 years. When he started, he had a six-person band competing in a real cut-throat business in Chicago. Twelve years later he's got six bands and orchestras. He now has a six-person admin-istrative staff that does everything for him. What he lives off of are all the corporate functions in the city and all the charitable functions in the city. He does Bar Mitzvahs, fundraisers and every conceivable kind of party. Last year, based on his six groups, he had no unsold nights which, in the music business, is just unheard of.

Everybody else comes in with their reels and their demos because they're there to sell music. He doesn't go in to sell music. He comes in and sits down with a client and says, "Let me ask you a question." He says, "It is now six months after your event, what has to happen during that six months in response to that event for you to feel happy with the result?"

He's taken them into the future beyond the event because, really, the event is for what happens after the event. It's for an experience that's going to occur because of the event. What the person is holding the event *for* is not what actually happens on the *night* of the event — it's what happens in the six months after the event.

He gets them to talk. He says, "What are the dangers that you have that would not allow that to happen? And what are the opportunities and the strengths?" It all comes out there and he will talk with them for 45 minutes and the subject of music never comes up.

It took him a very long time to actually wrap his mind around it. He always thought people bought music. He thought "I provide music." And then there's The R-Factor Question. But he realized people aren't buying music. Music is just one very, very small part of the total mix of what's supposed to happen that night and so, for him, instead of selling the music, if he can get them to buy into their vision of what's going to hap-pen, and he's responsible for them actually seeing that vision, the music's a done deal. And he never has to discount. What happened here? He has just altered the equation.

You are always getting them to visualize their future and then emo-tionally buy into their future and this is what the whole D.O.S. Conversation is about. Then you're going to be the person to add structure so that it actually happens. You become sort of a custom-designed guide for their best description of their future. This has nothing to do with any specialty.

Coming back to that juncture point, one of the biggest problems that financial advisors have is that they think that they are only as valuable as the product they sell. And they have a very good reason for feeling that way because as it has been the primary method of getting paid for their work. So when they sell a product and get a check, they're worth something; and when they don't sell a product and don't get a check, they're not worth anything. And this is not a good way to spend a human life.

What I'm saying is that, just in that half hour or 45 minutes, when you've allowed a person to really articulate his future through you in a way that he never has before, and you have allowed him to really mobilize and channel his emotions, you create an enormous value experience for him, and that's worth something.

Now this is the real dividing point in the industry, the tough river to cross: I'm going to ask you to charge now for this total experience starting with the first meeting. Starting in every business transaction there's a little bit of a loss leader so this may take you a while. But once you become known for doing this, you will say "Well, we're going to have the first meeting and it's going to be $500 or it's going to be $1,000 or whatever." We move advisors into a realm where they start creating a completely independent income stream away from the product set. They're going to have to do this because they're getting regulated out of existence.

I was just in Florida for MDRT's Top of the Table meeting and there were a lot of British agents there. Let me describe what has happened to the British Advisory world: I brought out *The 21st Century Agent* book in 1995. At that time, they had over 300,000 financial advisors in the UK. In 2004 they have around 40,000. They've lost 84 percent of their financial advisors. They've been regulated out of existence. And the government in Britain believes that everything that financial advisors sell, people should just naturally want anyway, so why should there be a commission?

Now the government there is waking up in the year 2004 to find out that individual investments have fallen precipitously. Savings have fallen precipitously. Pension funds have fallen precipitously over the last few years and they are saying, "What happened? Why aren't people saving anymore?" They didn't realize that it required sales people to actually wake people up to the fact that they need financial products.

The same thing is going to happen in the United States because there's a circuit that starts in Great Britain, five years later it comes to Australia, South Africa and New Zealand, then five years later to the United States and finally five years later to Canada.

But it's going to happen, and the Elliot Spitzer stuff that's been happening recently is indicative of this. Spitzer went after Marsh McClennan. Marsh had to give up $800 million in one letter. That was their entire profit for last year, and they had to give that up. It was that or have their entire executive team go to prison to save $800 million. Well, the ripple effect of that on individual advisors when a large, large brokerage company gives up $800 million in commissions is huge. That's like a tsunami going through the industry. There will probably be 5,000 fewer financial advisors next year because of Elliot Spitzer's pronouncements. That is because there are so many advisors that are just so close to the edge between making it and not making it that all they needed was another 10 percent drop in commissions or 10 percent drop in financing and the next thing they're doing is passing out carts and stickers at Walmart.

The window is closing. There's no question in my mind. I talk to 600 financial advisors every 90 days, and the window is closing. Advisors are going to be undervalued in the marketplace based on asset management fees and commissions. They're going to have to create an independent source of income, and The D.O.S. Conversation is a gateway to independent income.

**In summary:**

- The D.O.S. Conversation is the separator between the commoditized advisor and the advisor who really brings value to the client.

- It's all about the client!

- You provide clarity by finding out what the client sees as their dangers, opportunities, and strengths.

- Charge for the value that you create as an independent income stream separate from the commoditized product set.

**Dan Sullivan** is co-founder and president of The Strategic Coach Inc.

A visionary, an innovator, and a gifted conceptual thinker, Dan has over 25 years experience as a highly regarded speaker, consultant, strategic planner, and coach to entrepreneurial individuals and groups. Dan's strong belief in and commitment to the power of the entrepreneur is evident in all areas of The Strategic Coach® and its successful coaching program, which works to help entrepreneurs reach their full potential in both their business and personal lives.

He is author of *Creative Destruction*™, *The Great Crossover*™, *The 21st Century Agent*™, *Focusing Your Unique Ability*®, *How The Best Get Better*™, *How To Be A Global Thinker*™, *The Producer Group Future*™, and *Dan Sullivan's 21st Century School*™.

Dan is married to Babs Smith, his partner in business and in life. They jointly own and operate The Strategic Coach Inc., with offices in Toronto and Chicago. Workshops are also currently held in Vancouver, Los Angeles, New York, Dallas, and Atlanta. Dan and Babs reside in Toronto.

The Strategic Coach provides a structure to keep you focused, the accountability to help you stay on track and moving forward, and a plan and a path with systems and tools that give you what you need to create the life you dream of by:

- Breaking through the complexity between you and the next level of success.
- Working less and making more money
- Growing your business dramatically.
- Permanently differentiating yourself from the competition.
- Creating the quality of life you want.

For more information about The D.O.S. Conversation or other Strategic Coach products and services go to ***www.strategiccoach.com*** or call 1-800-387-3206 or 416-531-7399.

The Strategic Coach®, Strategic Coach®, The Strategic Coach Program™, The D.O.S. Conversation™, The D.O.S. Worksheet™, and The R-Factor Question® are trademarks of The Strategic Coach, Inc. All rights reserved. Used with permission.

## BILL BACHRACH

# The Trusted Advisor

*By Dave Drucker*

U nfortunately, we didn't get to travel to sunny San Diego to interview Bill Bachrach in person. In fact, the conditions for the interview were worse than ever: I sat at a vacant gate in Chicago's Midway airport hogging all of the electrical outlets within a ten-foot radius in order to activate all of my recording gear, laptops, and telephones.

Yet amid the constant patter of the loudspeaker announcing flights coming and going or moving walkways about to reach their destinations, Bill and I spent two-and-a-half hours of quality time — I finding out what makes Bachrach tick, and he delivering his unique message for the salvation and success of the financial advisor industry.

After two-and-a-half hours, I felt we had a great interview. One thing I learned is that some coaches cover a wide ground with their advisor clients; others know one thing and they hammer it home over and over again because they are so convinced their one thing is the key to it all. With Cates, it's referrals. With Kinder, it's money maturity. And with Bachrach, it's — what else — Trust.

### What is a Trusted Advisor?

I've gotten a lot of really good feedback from advisors about how their clients behave when they totally trust them. Behaviors include things like unsolicited referrals or calls requesting the advisor's opinion about things not financially related like, "I know you have teenagers and I've got teenagers… what do you think about this?"

Advisors would find themselves on a client's short list when they had good news. For example, an advisor with a client whose son was working in the World Trade Center when the planes hit the towers on 9/11 received a call from the client about 45 minutes after it happened letting him know that her son was okay, that he got out of the tower. The advisor wasn't the first person she had called, but she knew he'd want to know, and that he cared.

The nature of the relationship these Trusted Advisors have with their clients is beyond a friendship, more like a mentor — or a coach — the kind of relationship you have with a friend from whom you seek wisdom, not just somebody that you drink beer with.

The Trusted Advisor is the financial advisor who wants to be really skilled and extremely confident at communicating in a way that creates a high-trust client relationship. He's either interested in abandoning the financial service industry's traditional sales techniques or has been lucky enough to never have learned those techniques in the first place.

The financial services industry is a sales culture, so it's the *unlearning* of its sales techniques that's really the challenge. We spend a lot of time working with veterans who want to go to the next level. Advisors must unlearn what made them successful because what got them from where they were to where they are is not going to take them from where they are to where they want to go. You know, the techniques that got you a clientele of 1,200 clients and a business that you're having a challenge managing… we don't want to use those same techniques anymore. You're making a lot of money, but your life kind of stinks.

*The irony of these sales techniques that must be unlearned is that many "financial consultants" who learned them actually thought they were learning how to help clients. They drank the Kool-Aid about building that business of devoted clients.*

The Trusted Advisor must make a commitment to a way of being. There are two parts to being effective and interacting with people:

- the actual procedure — the script, method and process.

- the way of being — who you are being while you execute the process.

So, for example, if somebody has a very strong sales way of being, our Values-Based Selling® methodology would make them a salesperson using a better technique.

The first step is really to decide, "All right, I want to make sure I have a Trusted Advisor way of being." Everybody has some level of trust with their client or nobody would do business with them. But there's a big difference between being a Trusted Advisor and being a *totally* Trusted Advisor.

A Trusted Advisor doesn't handle objections. If you behave like a salesperson, you're going to have to handle objections. If you behave like a Trusted Advisor, you don't get objections. That doesn't mean you wouldn't be prepared to answer legitimate questions. But there's a big difference between somebody asking you a question and somebody giving you an objection. As a salesperson, you've got to be able to handle objections because salespeople create objections.

So what we're really talking about is not only unlearning sales techniques, but also shedding this way of being where you just kind of look, smell, taste and feel like a salesperson.

## The Initial Client Interview

The core skill of building a high-trust client relationship revolves around the initial client interview. That's the key moment where the advisor interacts with the client, so the experience the advisor creates determines whether or not the client and advisor are a good fit. It's that moment when the advisor can choose to behave in a way that helps the client make the decision to hire him, as opposed to *telling* the client he *should* hire him. Our company started with this idea of values clarification as a way of helping people make a decision and align their goals with their values.

I think fundamentally there's a legitimate chicken or egg debate as to which comes first: prospecting and marketing, or being able to create an experience where people hire you on the spot. In one meeting, you can get hired and the client is fired up about you being their advisor.

As to the chicken or the egg argument, what's more important is your ability to create that experience because then, whatever prospecting and marketing is going to be put into place to fill your appointment calendar, you know that you're really effective at truly helping people make a good decision: first of all about whether or not to hire you, and second of all about their implementation commitment. You're going to show up in the world with a lot of confidence because you know you're good. You know, the hitter who's on a roll walks to the plate with a different attitude than a hitter who's in a slump.

So I believe the core thing is whether you are really good at creating a great client experience and second, do you have things lined up so you can deliver on the promise of that experience?

If you've got a pension planner who's going to deliver a great plan; if you know that the investment policy statement is going to be accurate and appropriate for this person and it's going to be consistent with their risk tolerance and with their goals and objectives; if you know that your money managers are the appropriate money managers; if you know that your insurance resources are going to give you good, objective advice that's right for the client and not biased toward a certain product... if you know all that stuff is lined up *and* if you show up in the world with a whole different way of being than if you're uncertain and trying to make a sale, then you can create a great experience.

## Obsessions

All of this began with an obsession at the roots of which were two profound experiences.

I was an advisor working for a wirehouse, and I'd gotten back from product training in New York City to get my Series 7 license. I'd started out poor and then I came back with all my credit cards maxed out from living a life I couldn't afford in New York for three weeks. I lived in San Diego and deliberately went to work for a major firm in La Jolla because, frankly, as a naive young guy, I thought they were going to teach me how to get the wealthy people living in La Jolla to become clients of mine.

So I said to my sales manager, "Okay, I'm ready. I got all the basic training. I've highlighted all the streets on the map with all the big fancy houses in La Jolla. Now what do I do?"

And he looked at me like I was crazy and said, "What are you talking about?"

I said, "Well, I'm ready. I'm ambitious, I'm hungry, I'm eager, I'm willing to work, you know — tell me what to say and how to say it so these people will respond to me when I cold call them. And then when I get one out of a hundred to meet with me, what do I do?"

And he said, "It doesn't work that way." He said, "You've got to work in your natural market."

And I said, "What do you mean by natural market? You mean other broke 26-year-olds? *That's* my natural market."

And he said, "Well, not exactly, but people who are closer to you in age and income and, you know, people you can relate to better."

And I said, "You've got to be kidding!"

And he said, "Well, no."

I said, "I've gone through months of training and chosen La Jolla just so you can tell me to go work in the bedroom communities of San Diego?"

I mean, San Diego was really growing fast in the '80s, and people were buying houses they couldn't really afford, and they were what we called "house poor." They would move into these houses, and they'd have a BMW and a Mercedes in the driveway, most of which were either on payments or lease. So they'd have a luxury car and they'd have the maximum house they could qualify to buy. Every dime they had in cash went into the down payment on the house and then, literally, you'd walk into these houses and they wouldn't have furniture.

You know, in southern California you get your nice cars first, then you buy a house, then you furnish the house and then, someday, if you have any money left over, you save and invest, and it didn't exactly seem like a good strategy to get these kinds of clients if I expected to make any kind of a living. So I basically told my manager, "Well, Steve, you're useless, aren't you?"

That wasn't a very good career move and the next day, I was in the manager's office and he said, "We understand you have a little problem."

I said, "Well, no, I don't really have a problem." I said, "I've discovered you guys are useless, and now that I know that, I'll go figure out how to do it by myself, on my own."

So what I did was I started seeking out someone who could teach me how to get rich people as clients. And, of course, what I discovered was sales techniques, so I became obsessed with sales techniques — you know — handling objections, closing skills.

I was starting to go to all of the seminars and training programs, and I ended up at the Dale Carnegie sales class. What I liked about the Dale Carnegie class, although it was basically old-fashioned sales techniques, was that it had at least a veneer of the human relations principles from Carnegie's book *How to Win Friends and Influence People.*

I found it to be a more relationship-oriented sales system, but it was still basically a sales system. It taught us attention, interest, conviction, desire and closing. So we had some clever way to get the client's attention, to gain his interest, with an old-fashioned sale question like, "Hey, if I could show you a way that you could pay less tax and get a better return on investment, you'd want to know about it, wouldn't you?"

I had been so serious a student learning and implementing the Carnegie techniques that it was definitely showing up in my production. Then at the end of the class, I got an award called "The Sales Talk Champion Award." That resulted from a round-robin elimination tournament wherein the 50 people in the class got into smaller groups and practiced on each other. They got down to two finalists, then voted and scored them, and whoever won was Sales Talk Champion.

I remember sitting there, getting this award, and I'm looking down at this plaque that says "Sales Talk Champion" on it, then I'm looking out at the class, and I know what I'm supposed to do. I'm supposed to thank the class for creating a good environment where I could learn to grow, and I thanked the instructor for teaching us really good stuff but, what I was thinking was "Where does one actually hang a Sales Talk Champion plaque?" Certainly not where clients could see it.

That's when I realized that I was working really hard to become someone I didn't want to be. I didn't want to be a Sales Talk Champion. That wasn't my goal. All I really wanted to do was to create really good relationships with people who have some money, earn their trust so I could give them advice on what to do to achieve their goals, they would then achieve their goals, and I would get paid well for helping them.

That's what I really wanted to do, but there wasn't any training like that.

## Why Some People Trust You and Some Don't

I started asking my mentor, who was one of the instructors for that class, "So, I use all of these techniques, and they work great but, you know, when people trust me, I don't need any of these techniques."

And he replied, "What do you mean?"

I said, "Well, some people you sit down with and you just click, they trust you right away, and with those people you don't need to present the benefits, to handle objections, to use closing techniques. I listen and then I give them advice, and they say okay, and we fill out the paperwork and that's it."

And so my question to him was, "So, what's the difference? How come some people trust me and some people don't?"

And he said to me, "I don't know."

And I said, "Well, what do you mean you don't know. You've *got* to know. You're the mentor. You're the guru. I'm just the kid out here busting my butt in the field. You've got to know because if you don't know, I'm screwed." So he and I actually tried to start figuring that out, and that's what the obsession was. The obsession was to find out why some people trust you and some people don't.

And in the process, we discovered that some people don't trust anybody, so it isn't that they don't trust *you*. But all the others tend to trust people who understand them. They trust people who listen well because they're trying to help. Nobody was talking about this stuff. There were no books on it. There were no speakers, trainers or authors. It was pretty clear it was a whole different methodology that we initially created just for my use.

I mean, I had no intention of going out and teaching it to other advisors. I was just obsessed with this thing because I realized this was really the answer. This was the key but, for a while, it was way overcomplicated. Then I brought it back down to really simple:

- have a sincere conversation about what's important to people.

- define and prioritize their goals.

- benchmark their current reality.

- make a sincere offer to write a plan to help them make what's important happen in their lives.

And a lot of the people that you do that with, if you follow the process with a Trusted Advisor way of being, will be thrilled to fire their other advisors and bring everything to you.

## The Process

When an advisor with five years of typical sales training wants to undo his ways and start to have real conversations with his clients, the first thing he encounters in one of our sessions is a total commitment to Values-Based Financial Planning™ as a methodology.

Role-playing is a huge part of what we teach. Advisors will practice the six components of the initial interview as we teach them five conversations preceded by an opening. And we literally teach them that opening, which lasts about 45 seconds, and they script it out. We don't tell them they absolutely have to use our script verbatim, but what we've found is the closer they follow the model, the better the results they get. But everybody should alter it at least a little bit for their own style.

We might tell them to say, "I really appreciate you coming to our office today. The fact that you're here tells me you're really committed to making smart choices about your money." But if they want to say, "Your behavior demonstrates that you're really sincere about doing some good work with your money," that's okay too.

What we find is that most advisors open by saying, "Thank you for coming in," which is the opposite of client-centered. As soon as you say "thank you" to somebody, it becomes all about you, and most advisors never realize that. We tell them to start taping themselves so they can hear exactly what they say, and then we then teach them to examine it and question whether it's what they really intended.

When they say, "Thank you for coming in," the knee-jerk trigger might be, "You're welcome." And so we'll ask the advisor, is this really what you meant, because what's implied there is "Thank you for coming in so I have the opportunity to sell you something." That's kind of the unspoken part, and is it the message you really intend to send? Of course it's not. The advisor will say, "I'm just being polite." Sure, but your choice of words in that moment where you choose to be polite totally shifts this to being about you instead of it being about the client.

So, we teach them to say, "Hey, David and Susan, we really appreciate the fact that you invested the time to be here today. The fact that you're here really indicates that the two of you must be committed to making smart choices about your money."

In the Dale Carnegie class, what they used to teach you to do was find something about the client to compliment, but the problem with that is it always comes across as insincere. Saying "Wow, David, that's a nice tie" is a pretty "salesy" thing to do. So we avoid anything that's like that, not just because it sounds salesy, but also because it isn't congruent with building a high-trust relationship and it has no relevance to the discussion.

Instead, the advisor acknowledges the client's behavior when he says, "Susan and David, I really appreciate how much effort it took to gather together all your financial documents. I know that it wasn't especially convenient for you to drive to the office today, but you did it anyway, and the fact that you're willing to do those things really tells us that you're the kind of people who are really serious about achieving your financial goals." Now you've positioned yourself as a peer observing their behavior and seeing that they're behaving in a way that is really good for them.

 *I believe the "caring" is the crux of it. Caring is a human emotion. So the question is… are you human and do you want to interact with other people on the basis of being human? If you do, then being a Trusted Advisor shouldn't be all that hard.*

The change we're asking the advisor to make is one of both process and behavior. First of all, there's a 45-second script that we teach to open the meeting, and I just demonstrated about 20 seconds of it. The advisor therefore has some words that are different from what he's used in the past, so we help him not only change the words but also understand why those words are different.

I don't think it's impossible for anybody to change, but I do believe that there are some people who are either beyond our patience or our skills, and this is one of those moments where we separate out those advisors who have the capacity to put the client first. I think the reality is that not everybody has the capacity to put the client first, although we've seen some hardcore sales people convert.

What we find is that there are a lot of people out there who use the sales tactics they were taught but, underneath it all, they really care. So when they are able to demonstrate their caring without having to resort to those negative tactics, they change fairly easily, and then it's just a function of, "Well, I'm in the habit of saying thank you, but I can get out of that."

So, if there's an element of caring and that element of caring is sincere, then the transformation is doable, regardless of how ingrained the habits are. But if that element of caring really isn't there, and the advisor's just saying, "Hey, this is what I do to make a living," then the transformation is probably not doable.

## The Values Staircase

Another part of our process — The Values Staircase — comes from my seeking with my mentor, Doug Carter, a kind of non-sales-related and non-financial-services-related understanding of what influences human behavior.

In psychology, there is a whole body of work around values, kind of at the core of what drives people if you peel them back like an onion. I forget what the actual center of this core was, but there were values, beliefs, opinions, attitudes… there were all these things that affect the choices that people make. I think at the very center of it was instinct. So, people act on instinct primarily, possibly the worst way to make a decision.

But a value can't be false. A value is an intrinsic thing. So, when you start really studying how and why people make their decisions, it's almost impossible to not end up looking at the whole value piece. Then the problem is how to get at a person's values.

So the values question and what it revolves around are "what's important" in life. That's the question you ask to discover a person's values. Then you list everything that's important and you prioritize the things in your list. To take people through that exercise is cumbersome, so what I started working on was how to do it more conversationally because I was still looking for something I could use on the phone during cold calls.

## Doing the Ironman

When I went to do the Hawaii Ironman, I got a training program created for me by Mark Allen who had already won the race and whom I had coached informally to help him package his Ironman experience and turn it into a corporate speech for financial advisors. It was a purely self-indulgent thing, but it was part of my year in 1998 that every speech I gave, I'd try to pull a metaphor out of the air. I would say, well, I'm doing this training, and it's stretching me beyond anything I've ever done before, and here's how it relates to what I'm teaching you to do.

It was fascinating to me how this thing took on a life of its own. Some people would say, we're impressed with you as a speaker, but we hear about you doing something that is even bigger than what you're asking us to do, and that gives you so much more credibility. I thought of it as a really amazing thing to do, and I knew I would grow personally. But it really wasn't something that I thought I would ever put in my introduction or my personal resume until my bookkeeper pointed out that it might be tax deductible since I was a motivational speaker.

Another part of what we teach advisors is to build their Ideal Client Profile. I couldn't imagine working in a business where you didn't actually like some substantial portion of the people you'd be doing business with, especially if you're only going to work with 75 or 80 people. So, if I were an advisor, I'm sure I would work only with entrepreneurial people. I just have a difficult time connecting with people who will accept a paycheck for their whole life. So there's got to be a natural connection.

When I use a metaphor from something like cycling or the triathlon, chances are that's going to resonate with somebody else who has stretched themselves either personally or professionally or athletically, and I naturally tend to bond with people who are stretching themselves.

An important point here is that the goal of an advisor isn't to make the client comfortable. The goal is to tell the truth, and sometimes the truth isn't comfortable.

I know that the doctor comparison has been overused in our business, but there are a lot of things that my doctor asks me to do that are in my best interests that are not comfortable. It's not about your client's comfort. It's about doing what needs to be done to create the highest probability to get the results that he's looking for. I don't know that I ever learned that in more real terms than when I did the Ironman. I mean, there is so much about the Ironman that is not comfortable.

My handyman had been working in my house for the last couple of days, and we'd been doing stuff in the garage because it had been raining, and he looked at my bike which was hanging on the wall and said of its seat, "That can't be comfortable." And I said, "Well, actually, it's not in the beginning but, if the seat is too soft, that's actually more uncomfortable on a long ride than a hard seat." In other words, what you do is you don't look for a seat that's comfortable; you ride until your butt gets comfortable in the seat.

That's evident to me, and there are so many people out there whose whole mindset is to seek comfort. I don't think you can be an effective financial advisor if you think your mission in life is to make people feel comfortable because there's so much you have to advise them to do that isn't comfortable so they can achieve their goals for the reasons that are important to them.

If I go to the dentist and refuse to open my mouth, it's not like the dentist is going to say "Well, we might be able to work on you without you opening your mouth." If the dentist opens my mouth, he's going to do things that are uncomfortable so that I can keep my teeth, so that I have a nicer smile, so that I can chew food into my 90s. I think this comes from the sales world where the goal is to sell people what they want. You figure out what they want, and you give it to them.

## The One Thing

If I were to get advisors to do just One Thing, I would get them to do their own Financial Road Map®, write their own financial plan, and walk their talk. That, to me, is the core of everything.

There are too many advisors out there who are not earning enough money to finance their own plans. You have to generate enough business revenue so that, after you pay your business expenses, you have enough personal income; and after you pay your taxes, there's enough money to save and invest in your future as well as enough money to live a good lifestyle now.

If you ask me, a big weakness in the whole financial services industry is that no firm on the planet actually requires that the people, who go out and represent the company to clients, walk their own talk. I don't believe you have to be rich to give others advice, but I believe you should have a plan that's based on your values and your goals, and that you should be executing that plan and that, to me, is number one. In fact, I really think that you, as an advisor, should pay another advisor his full fee to take care of you.

 *I agree 100%. I have been guilty of this in my past as an advisor and I believe that being a role model of stewardship is one of the most important attributes we bring to our profession!*

The other One Thing is the client interview. You've got to be great at creating an experience where clients want to hire you, and equally as important, you have to be able to deliver what that experience promises. So, you've got to be competent. What a concept! To me, what that means is competent in the planning process and in having really good alliances and relationships because you can't deliver on this promise by yourself.

Everything we've created has come out of the conversation with the client, and we now have a complete system. We call it the The Being

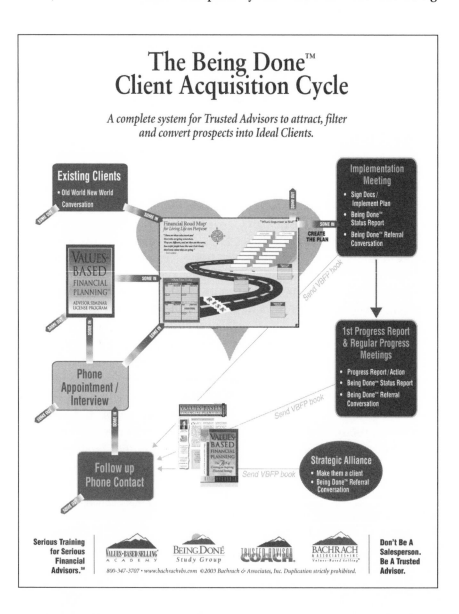

Done™ Client Acquisition Cycle, and essentially it's a complete system, the heart of which is the client interview. But then there's got to be a mechanism for filling your calendar with people who meet your Ideal Client Profile. So, we've added in the whole piece for filling the calendar, converting prospects into clients, moving existing clients to be Ideal Clients, and then keeping the appointment calendar full by referral.

That whole cycle, other than serving the client, is a temporary thing because once you're full, once you've got your 45 or how ever many clients, we are then big advocates for your having a finite number of Ideal Clients, and you should know what that number is in advance. You should know, based on what you do for your clients and how many hours each client gets and how many hours a week and a month and a year you're willing to work, that you can take care of X many people.

By contrast, the sales model also keeps one's calendar full, but the calendar never stops being full because there are no lasting relation-ships. It's just transactions. The sales model is… sit down with people, pretend to be their counselor, find their needs, and sell them products to meet their needs. If they call, service them and move on, and that's the pure sales commission model.

That didn't change much when a lot of advisors went to fees for assets under management. That's a similar model with its own magic formula. If you get $100 million of assets under management with a one percent fee, you've got a $1 million business. But again, that's not client-centered, it's product-centered, it's asset-centered.

So what I'm trying to accomplish is to create a methodology that's scalable so a large number of people can actually follow it. If you think about it, we're going to need about five times as many advisors as we have because all the advisors need to be taking better care of fewer clients so the quality of the experience for the client grows.

Does this One Thing work better for advisors employing one com-pensation model versus another? No, it's applicable to all.

But if there's one compensation model I am against, it's a pure com-mission model. You get 100 clients, you get paid four percent on mutual funds, and you get it all paid up front. You're basically getting paid for four or five years of service all up front.

When I talk to audiences compensated in this manner, I ask them, "How many of you saved three percent of this up-front commission and only spent one percent of it in the year you got it?" They all laugh, of course. They get paid for four or five years' worth of service, which they spend in the first year. So now what do they have to do in the second year? They've got to get another 100 clients to pay their four percent. And then what do they have to do in the third year? Isn't that the definition of a Ponzi scheme?

And what happens in a Ponzi scheme? Well, eventually, it collapses. You can't keep it up forever. Somebody gets their money out and everybody else gets left holding the bag. How many miserable advisors have I talked to who have 700 clients, 900 clients, 1300 clients, 3000 clients? They keep looking for some way to manage their high-volume practice; they're not focused on the real problem.

In coming up with a management system, one of the things that we see advisors try to do is cobble things together. They take a piece from over here and a piece from other there, and they try to kind of force it together to make it work. It's kind of like taking the front end of that Mercedes SL, the doors from a Chrysler and the interior of a BMW. Advisors take legitimately good pieces from legitimately good things. But they don't really piece them together very well. The Being Done™ Client Acquisition Cycle will do that for them.

So once the advisor understands that he must create his own Financial Road Map® and become great at creating an experience where clients want to hire him so he can deliver on what the experience promises, he needs a system for pulling it all together and implementing it. And that's what we give him.

**In summary:**

- Have a sincere conversation about what is important to the client.

- Define and prioritize the client's goals.

- Benchmark their current reality and write a plan that helps them achieve their goals.

- Communicate in a way that creates a high trust client relationship.

- Advisors need to walk their talk by doing their own Financial Roadmap — they need to walk their talk!

❖❖❖

**Bill Bachrach, CSP,** is the author of the best-selling book *Values-Based Selling; The Art of Building High-Trust Client Relationships for Financial Professionals.*

He is the creator of the *Values-Based Selling*® *Mastery System,* the *Values-Based Selling*® *Academy,* and the *Trusted Advisor Coach*® program for top-producers.

His latest book, *It's All About Them; How Trusted Advisors Listen for Success,* is already a big hit!

Bill is considered to be the industry's leading resource for helping financial professionals make the transition from being salespeople to being Trusted Advisors. In January of 2001 the readers of *Financial Planning* magazine named Bill Bachrach as one of the four most influential people in our business.

Bill has given well over 1000 presentations world-wide at some of the industry's most prestigious conferences including four appearances at The Million Dollar Round Table, seven appearances at The Financial Planning Association Success Form, and two appearances at MDRT Top of the Table.

The bottom line is that it is proven that producers who implement Values-Based Selling® make more money, take more time off, get more referrals, gather more assets, generate more fee income, and have an even better quality of life.

For more information about having Bill speak at your next meeting, to enroll in the 3-Day Values-Based Selling® Academy, or to invest in his learning resources contact Bachrach & Associates, Inc. at 800-347-3707 or visit ***http://www.bachrachvbs.com***.

**Tom Gau**　　　　　　　　　**Ken Unger**

# Million Dollar Producers

*By Dave Drucker*

A sk 14 different people (and we did) what coaching is and you'll get 14 different answers. Yet Tom Gau and Ken Unger feel confident in their definition: "Coaching is a program where there is accountability and follow-up." They also take pride in the fact that Gau has long been and continues to be one of the industry's most successful producers; hence the name of their program, "Million Dollar Producer." As you'll see, Gau and Unger give advisors a detailed roadmap for success, back it up with implementation systems, and watch their graduates measurably increase their production.

"D" flew solo (without me) to sit in Ken's Sacramento, California office while they conferenced me and Tom into the conversation. Tom Gau and Ken Unger explained their approach to us.

### The "Weakest Link" Theory

There are many advisors who would like to elevate their practice to the next level and many practices that could operate much more profitably. Both scenarios could benefit from coaching. We believe in a theory called the "weakest link," which says the weakest link in your office is what's going to hurt you the most. If marketing is your weakest link, then your pipeline of new people, or the ways you market to your existing people, will not be strong. If your interviewing skills are the weakest link, then that's where you'll have the most difficulty.

If you're trying to do business with a qualified prospect, say someone who's accumulated $1 million, you must bring your "A" game — there are very few people out there who have accumulated $1 million who are not at least a little savvy. You must show them you can add value by, as an example, competently reviewing their tax forms or helping with their estate plan. If you just talk about their goals and say, "I hear your story, you can trust me," we believe that million dollar prospect will say, "Let me think about it and I'll get back to you."

*I disagree. I agree an advisor must be competent. What I disagree with is how powerful the client's story is! To me the client comes first, the money comes later.*

That's assuming you *even* got in front of them in the first place!

Most people in this business overestimate their financial planning abilities. Even when we meet with our high-level coaching group, we find that they're not aware of some of the tax and estate-planning issues we train them on. These are people who hold themselves out to be very good at what they do. We're just making them better planners; as a result, they become better producers.

## Marketing

The weakest link that most advisors have is, first and foremost, marketing. That's where advisors tend to make a lot of their purchases of coaching or training systems. The question we pose is, "What are you marketing?" It's not "Are you doing marketing?"

Most advisors don't know who they're trying to attract and how best to attract them. We see advisors gravitating to systems that advertise with statements like, "Increase your production by 90 percent in just one seminar."

If a client said, "I'm going to buy this investment because I can make a 90 percent return in one day," what would most advisors tell them? Exactly! Advisors are not practicing what they are preaching.

## The Client Meeting: Setting Up a "System of Respect"

The second weakest link we find is client meetings. Many advisors don't have a strong system for client meetings. Many advisors aren't aware of scripting, and we don't mean scripting like, "Hello, my name is

Tom Gau and I would like to talk to you about a mutual fund investment." Of course not!

Scripting is knowing what to do and knowing your client. It's not scripted in the sense that, if you say this word before that word, you lose a client. The client meeting needs to be disciplined and have a timeframe.

We hold quarterly reviews with our own clients, and they are half an hour. We can hold 15 to 20 of them in one day. How? We have an agenda for what we are going to go through in those 30 minutes.

During that agenda, we update our clients' situations and share with them what's going on. Another portion of that time is to share with them environmentally (i.e., the market) what's going on. The final portion is, "Here's how it pertains to you and here are the changes you need to make."

If there is a major tax law change, we may schedule an hour per person. We'll figure that out first and then schedule everybody. What's important to note is that we have a systematic approach and we think that's where a lot of advisors struggle.

We always start meetings with personal issues that contribute to the relationship. But if someone starts giving us a 45-minute dissertation on their recent surgery, we stop them. It's like your doctor; he's friendly, but is the doctor somebody you can talk to for two hours about your fishing trip?

 *I have been accused of being too chatty. So I can see this point. Yet, I think the adage "To thine own self be true!" applies!*

We set up a professional environment where clients can share with us that kind of information, but there's got to be a limit to how much they can talk to us about that. The main thing our clients want from us is a relationship and we encourage advisors to have a relationship with their clients. But if Mrs. Jones is in for an hour and, after 15 minutes, you're falling off track, then you have to get back on track.

We call our meeting system a "System of Respect." An advisor who follows our system can spend time bonding with the client and also accomplish the necessary agenda in a time-efficient manner. One of the keys is being organized. If we're meeting for a fixed period of time, we know there's going to be about ten minutes for socializing. We don't believe you need 50 minutes for socializing; you don't have to use

50 minutes for socializing if you're running an efficient, high-level financial practice.

 *Frequent meetings are a means to production, but what if production isn't your game? Professionals charging retainers don't need to constantly be in front of their clients; they just need to "touch" them frequently along the lines of Gau and Unger's "meaningful activity" guidelines below.*

Many advisors, at the initial client interview, spend too much time on certain topics. Let's say you have a very complex estate plan. It includes a long-term care plan and a couple of different trusts. You don't have to evaluate the entire situation right then and there. We would schedule another appointment with that prospect.

Imagine if you were to walk into the dentist's office and you're in for a cleaning and it turns out you need a root canal. We hope they schedule another appointment for the root canal unless it's an emergency. Advisors can achieve both: an efficient schedule and a system of respect, where people respect not only your time but your advice.

## Meaningful Activity

If we were to give an advisor the best advice on how to increase production, we would say, "Strengthen your marketing program!" We would tell you to develop a 12-month working plan of "meaningful activity." Very few advisors have this.

This "meaningful activity" should address your three primary audiences:

1. Your existing clients. You need to be constantly marketing yourself to your clients.

2. Qualified identified prospects: people whom, through previous marketing efforts, you've already identified as qualified for you to work with, but who are not clients yet.

3. Qualified people who live in your community.

Part of our marketing campaign is our quarterly newsletter. Every quarter we write a strong client newsletter, which we invite other advisors to use. Often we are asked "Why do you write a nine- or 11-page letter? Couldn't you just write a page or two?"

To which we answer, "Don't you want a system of respect?"

*I disagree. I believe clients can find investment advice anywhere — I think a sincere connection with clients about matters other than money is key. Money is the means, not the end. Do you have to be cutesy? No. Do you have to connect — yes!*

Sending out exercise tips or feel-good stories won't accomplish this. We charge our own clients fees, and that nine- to 11-page letter is very meaningful to them.

It's not the same as buying a marketing system that has you saying to clients: "I'm handling your investments. Here are some fun holiday activities or recipes." How do you want your client to perceive you? As an investment expert, relationships are key — but you must communicate your expertise!

When you're marketing to clients, it's about meaningful touch points — and we believe there is no replacement for face-to-face contact.

Furthermore, it's not just about activity. An oft-quoted sports quip is: "Wasted activity is just a waste of time." To repeat, we believe that advisors need to have a 12-month marketing calendar of "meaningful activity" for marketing themselves.

Meaningful activity includes client appreciation events and client report cards. Every year we send our clients report cards. We want our clients to let us know how they feel about our services — so we ask them: "What do you like about our service? What do you not like?" We want them to understand that feedback is important to us so that we can discuss their concerns.

We use an approach that we call "multi-touch marketing." We show advisors how to have meaningful activity every month by picking the best options that suit the advisor's personality and practice. Some advisors don't enjoy speaking in front of groups — and they don't have to. Seminars are not the cure-all way to do business. Each advisor has his own strengths so he should build around those strengths incorporating them into a calendar of "meaningful activity."

Show us an advisor who doesn't have a strong calendar of meaningful activity for his existing clients, their prospects and the community, and we'll show you an advisor who's going to have a very weak economic future.

## Views on Selecting a Coach

There are a myriad of coaching programs available to financial advisors. When determining whether or not you should sign up for a coaching program, we believe you must first figure out the type of coach you need. Do you need someone who is industry-specific or someone who helps you in more generic areas? "Million Dollar Producer" is very industry-specific.

It's easy to be a high producer in a bull market, but there's a different philosophy out there now. We're in a confusing market. In a bull market, lots of people talked about going from $400,000 to $800,000. In a difficult market, many producers that became top players are not top players anymore. You have to adapt your business model to this new environment.

Ten years ago it was a commission world. Now it's a fee-based world. The question isn't, "Did you substitute the word 'fee' for 'commission' in your marketing materials?" The psychology of the client now is very different. If you're holding seminars, what are you doing to really separate yourself and can you back it up? You know, can you not just read from a script — can you offer a total package?

> **Five-Star Tip: Do Your Homework and Due Diligence!**

## Be Realistic

What gets in the way for many advisors are unrealistic goals. This is a typical conversation: We'll ask an advisor "What would you like most to have gained from a coaching program?"

They'll say "I'd like to have $100 million under management," to which we'll respond, "Okay, how much do you have right now?"

Their answer will be something like "$19 million."

And we'll ask, "How long have you been in the business?"

"Twelve years," they'll reply.

"When would you like to have $100 million under management?" we finally query.

"Well, I figure if I'm in your coaching program for a year, I'll have it by the end of the year."

Pregnant pause... then we'll say, "Imagine a prospect walks into your office and says, 'I'm 55 years old and I have $40,000 in my retirement plan, but I want to retire on a $40,000 income for the rest of my life in four years.' Is that realistic?"

Can that advisor bring in $10 or $15 million in new money? We have helped others do that but for that advisor it might be a stretch. You have to be realistic. It's not about accomplishing the impossible. We know that if you draft a disciplined, pragmatic plan, then you can increase your production from 30 to 100 percent. Can it increase 500 or 600 percent? No, that's just not realistic.

## Three Keys to Achieving Your Goals

In what other business can you make as much money as you want and help people too? Better yet, you get to determine when you want to work! You have to do three things:

1. Utilize some form of meaningful marketing in order to get in front of people.

2. Schedule regular appointments. In each session, use scripts to assist you with establishing a business relationship with the client.

3. Service the client.

Now ask yourself, "How can I do these three things in the shortest period of time without pressure?" The shortest distance between two points is a straight line.

## The One Thing

There are two rules for being successful in this business. Only two rules! If you follow these two rules, you'll make more money than you could ever imagine. The first rule is, always be meeting with clients.

Think about it… what should a financial advisor be doing with his or her time? Always meeting with clients! When you meet with clients you make money.

The second rule is very simple: always remember rule number one!

 *Many of the other coaches in this book would say having the right conversation with the client — to really know the client as as individual before offering advice — is The One Thing. Gau and Unger take a different approach and will appeal to a different type of advisor.*

Do you know the average number of client appointments a financial advisor has per week? Only Seven! We know from experience that that should be about 18 to 20 appointments a week. Amazingly, only five appointments a day equals a million dollars of gross income.

## More Time or More Money

At the beginning of our Boot Camps we ask "Would anyone here be happy if they doubled their production? Would they consider it being successful?" Most advisors raise their hands.

We also ask, "If you kept the same level of production but you only had to work half the time, would you consider that to be successful?"

Most answer, "Absolutely. I want time off to enjoy life. If my production level is the same but I only work half the time, I'm interested."

The interesting thing is, as advisors embark on doing this work, we hear, "My production is over one million now, but it's not because I tried. It's just because I'm getting more efficient. I'm better at what I do and I'm working far less."

It all depends on what your goal is!

**In summary:**

• Identify your business's "weakest link."

• What are you marketing and who are you marketing to?

• Have a systematic approach to client meetings.

• Develop a marketing plan of "meaningful activity."

• Always be meeting with clients.

**Tom Gau** is an active, in-the-trenches financial planner who produces over $3,000,000 a year while working only nine days a month. How has he accomplished this? By working smarter, not harder, and he is willing to show you how to do the same thing! His proven systems and techniques have already allowed thousands of financial planners to significantly increase, and double or triple, their production.

**Ken Unger** is a 24-year veteran of the securities industry. For the last five years, Ken has been our industry's leading coach for million dollar producers. He taught thousands of experienced financial advisors how to market investment- and retirement-oriented programs. Ken has held hundreds of seminars and has successfully trained and motivated some of the industry's largest broker-dealers and producers on a variety of topics, including efficient practice management strategies and effective sales and marketing ideas.

Tom and Ken's Two-Day Boot Camp is considered the industry's finest training session. Their 2004 book, *The Keys to High-Level Production*, has sold over 60,000 copies.

For more information, write to info@mdproducer.com and/or visit ***http://www.mdproducer.com/index.html***.

*If we go on the way we have,*
*the fault is our greed,*
*and if we are not willing to change,*
*we will disappear*
*from the face of the globe.*

—Jacques Cousteau

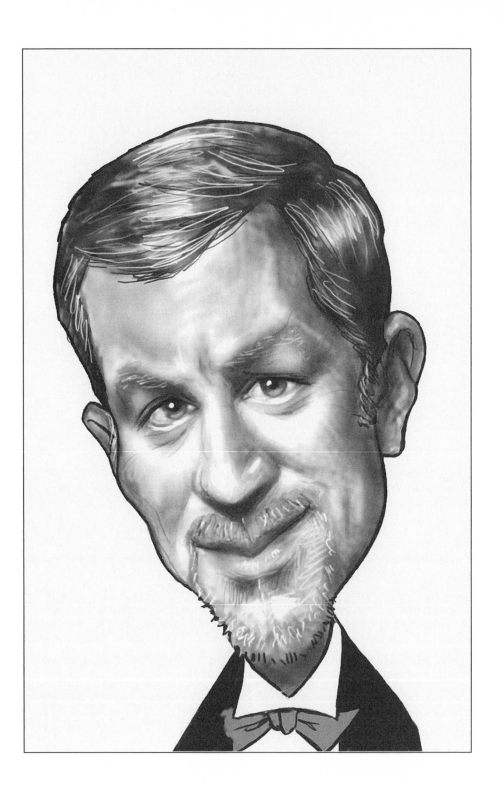

## DAVID GRAU

# The Wisdom of the Marketplace

*By "D" Shannon*

I t's another drizzly day in Portland, Oregon as I drive my rental car to Business Transitions' Offices. Bleary-eyed from a late night arrival the day before, I hazard the Portland rush hour traffic with more ease than I'd figured on. I park, exit and walk to the building and scan the foyer sign for the suite number and floor.

Looking around as I exit the elevator, I realize this is the first interview I've done without Dave along. I open the suite door and am greeted by people who feel like old friends. Having listed and sold my business through Business Transitions' FP Transitions website this spring, I talk at great length with every one of the principals and staff members of the firm. Each had held my hand, offered encouragement and given guidance on some phase of my experience.

After a brief tour of the offices, I sit down with David Grau and we dial up Dave. He's also a friend of the firm as he, too, listed and sold his advisory business through Business Transitions in 2001. During some friendly banter, Dave warns Grau about being left alone with me for prolonged periods. All three of us give and take like college sophomores and, with enough caffeine in us to stop an elephant's heart, we begin a fascinating conversation amongst old friends.

❖❖❖

## The One Thing

No matter how much you like your work, you can't practice forever.

I've worked with over 550 sellers and I can tell you from firsthand experience that very few advisors retire at age 65 or even according to any pre-designed plan. Actually, more advisors retire or move on to another opportunity at around the age of 55 than 65. Regardless, your eventual exit from this profession should be an event that you control. You wouldn't leave your clients' futures to the hands of fate!

Advisors need to plan for the future of their own practices when it comes times to leave, whether due to retirement, choice or catastrophe.

 *That is precisely what I did. At the age of 53, with 20 years in the industry, I needed to get out to do something different… move on to the next chapter of my life. There are a lot of us out there; some just haven't realized it yet.*

The idea is simple. To take care of your clients, first look after yourself and plan for your future, including the possibility of your accidental death or permanent disability. You need to have either a succession plan (selling to an employee or partner) or a transition plan (selling on the open market). Learn the difference and how it affects your firm's value.

Good news — you don't have to surrender your lifestyle to take care of your needs and your clients' needs simultaneously. That's right — you don't have to merge your practice or hire employees if you don't want to. Whether you're a sole practitioner or a partner in a large firm, the open market process has created opportunities and values that have never existed before. All you have to do is learn how.

## Built in the USA

I used to be a regulator of the securities industry. After passing the bar, I entered into the practice of law representing the financial advisors I had previously tormented. My government friends said that I turned to the "dark side." For me, the lights were never brighter. I had the opportunity to work with other independent, entrepreneurial business people who shared my passion for helping others and making a difference.

 *Who knew they let nice guys become regulators? I thought you had to eat at "Bada Bing" and have three fingers!*

In my law practice, I frequently helped advisors buy and sell their practices. But even as recently as five or six years ago, this was a very rudimentary process. Other than endorsing business valuations, industry experts had done little to promote succession planning and transition planning options at a national level. Each deal had to be custom-drafted and buyers found quietly and confidentially — one at a time.

I'd get a call from one of my RIA clients on a Saturday night and he'd tell me about a new opportunity in his life or, sometimes, that he was very ill and needed to sell his practice. I would start calling my other RIA clients and we'd try to find someone who was willing to take on 100 new clients with $45 million in AUM on a moment's notice and actually pay something for the practice and the opportunity. Buyers thought they were doing sellers a favor.

The first question these buyers would ask is, "Do people really buy these things?"

The rules weren't clear, value was an unknown factor, and no one knew if the clients would even stay. There were also liability concerns.

"Can I get sued for decisions the old advisor made five years ago?" Buyers would ask.

People didn't know the answers to these questions and they didn't know for sure if they could transfer the loyalties of the clients. As a result, we routinely sold practices like this for 80 cents on the dollar on a five to 10 year earn-out with little or nothing down. That had to change — and it did!

We formed Business Transitions around 1997, migrating through various forms and stages. Five of us were the founding members: Bill Grable, Rick Thomas, David Goad, Tom Brattain and me. Each of these visionaries contributed to the concept and the first versions of the inaugural Transitions website (there are now eight Transition sites). We made a lot of mistakes, but we got the important parts right.

Collectively, we all had a hand in creating an open market forum that will forever change the landscape of financial services practice valuation. We helped to bring standardization and predictability to these deals. It may be my picture on this chapter, but I'm standing on the shoulders of Bill, Rick, David and Tom and a great staff of people whose tireless efforts make it all possible.[1]

---

[1] Please indulge me for a moment — good companies aren't about any one person: A special thanks to Bill Grable who assembled the Transitions team and believed in this concept, and me, through thick and thin. They say you shouldn't go into business with a friend. I broke that rule and prospered. Bill is a CPA, but unlike any CPA I've ever met. He thinks like an entrepreneur and he's not afraid to push the edge of the envelope — in fact, he revels in exploring things. Bill is the creator of much of what is "Business Transitions" and came up with the concept of "Unplanned Transitions" (more on this follows) during breakfast. Also, thanks to Jeanie Bueermann, our longest-tenured employee who is our Director of First Impressions. Jeanie is the voice behind our 1-800 number; she makes us more than just a website.

Once the concept was created and brought to the market, a funny thing happened. Advisors took over and the entire concept evolved into an "open source" type of architecture. From my point of view, the best thing we have done as a company, beyond creating the Transitions websites, is to just get out of the way.

We learned that our best function is to simply observe and report. We don't guide the market — we just tell people what it did last year, what it is doing now, and what it is capable of doing. From that point on, the wisdom of the crowd created its own solutions.

We launched our first website, FP Transitions in January 2000. Initially, buyers, sellers and the magazine writers that covered the industry looked at the open market idea, and anything with a dot.com in the name, as a novelty. I think the expectations were for a very short, but exciting business life.

The data coming out of the marketplace from buying and selling activity was still raw and too thin to rely on. Advisors didn't really trust the Internet as a tool to buy or sell a practice. Very few sellers over the age of 60 used our services. We tended to have young buyers and young sellers who were smaller practitioners — many of whom didn't do so well as older advisors during the volatile markets. Our entire staff honed its skills on this younger group and we'll always be thankful to them.

In our third year things changed dramatically. We learned to let the market find its own path and create its own sense of value. We stopped trying to sell valuations and we learned the difference between succession planning and transition planning. Then things just took off like a rocket!

The size and quality of our listings jumped. Older sellers began to list their practices for sale. Older sellers meant more mature client bases. Mature clients meant better practices with higher cash flows and better value. Better practices attracted highly qualified buyers. These buyers created successful transitions, often retaining 95 percent to 98 percent or more of the acquired clients. This, in turn, attracted more and better sellers and critical mass was achieved.

And that's how the Transitions open market system was built.

## The Best of Times — The Worst of Times

On a Thursday morning we listed a practice for sale in southern California. The seller was a sole practitioner in his early 60s, and had just been diagnosed with inoperable and terminal cancer. He wasn't ready to retire, but it was time to go. We listed the practice at 10:00 a.m. that Thursday, along with the details of the transaction. By Friday morning the next day, 24 hours later, the seller had 17 inquiries. On Sunday, two days later, one of these prospective buyers flew in from Denver to meet with the seller. After some due diligence, they used one of our form contracts and signed a letter of intent. Thirty days later the deal closed, at full price, with one-third cash down, and the balance on a promissory note, secured and personally guaranteed.

It seems ridiculously simple, but that's how it works. Some deals, when circumstances require, have been completed in as little as 48 hours, with excellent long term results for both the seller and the seller's clients. If an advisor can accomplish this with no planning, imagine what can be done with some advance thought.

The gentleman in the example above, had he waited, would have had 30+ choices of buyers to interview. All are independent advisors who have started and run a business on their own and who want to grow. The strong demand by these buyers puts a seller in a very good position not only to obtain great value, but also to find the best qualified successor to step in and help his clients. In virtually every instance, the seller passes on the highest bidder in favor of the advisor best suited for his or her clients.

*I was extremely fortunate; my best buyer was also the highest bidder.*

There is hope if you are a sole practitioner and you don't have or want to have an employee or a partner to succeed you. Listed quickly, financial advisory practices often receive 90 percent to 100 percent of their value — even with no advance planning! With 30 buyers per listing (on average), it isn't a question of *if* the practice will sell rather for how much and to whom.

I'm frequently asked, "Would I be better off if I had a partner or employee to hand the practice off to?"

Not really. Working with over 550 sellers I've observed the answer firsthand. The number of clients successfully retained by a partner or employee, measured one year after closing, is almost exactly the same as when selling to an outside, third-party buyer. However, partners and employees generally don't pay as high a multiple of value as an outside buyer. Nor do employees or partners put down an average of 33 percent in cash down with the balance paid over the next three to four years, secured and guaranteed.

For years, "experts" have held forth on how advisors will lose value if they don't have a "real business" or take on employees or partners. We now have more data on this subject than anyone in the country and the data is very clear: Bringing in a highly-qualified, successful business owner to succeed you is almost always a better value proposition than an internal sale.

## Unplanned Transitions

A woman walked up to me after one of our conferences and asked for one of my business cards. She said, "I'm going to staple this business card to my Will. It's going to be my succession plan. My husband will be glad to know the problem of what to do with my practice after I'm gone is solved."

I was humbled at the praise and awe-struck at the responsibility.

Another advisor told us that he instructed his attorney to add a provision in his Will that his practice should be sold on the open market to the highest qualified buyer available immediately upon his death. As more and more people said things similar to that, we realized that sole practitioners weren't about to take on a partner or hire employees to solve this problem, at least not en masse. It just isn't their way.

As a former sole practitioner myself, I understood that kind of thinking.

So we got to thinking and came up with a new idea to address this need — Unplanned Transitions. This new transition planning tool provides advisors a method to create and update their own "Just-in-case" seller listings, with quarterly, automated prompts to keep the listing current. The program even includes a sample client letter to let clients know about this important step, and instructions to the executor or personal representative to activate the listing in the event of the advisor's untimely demise or permanent disability.

We made the service available and ten advisors listed their practices for sale in our Unplanned Transitions system in the first ten days — just in case. The first person to list was 27 years old and had just purchased a small practice through our NAPFA Transitions site. Here's what he had to say:

*David,*

*I just listed my practice in Unplanned Transitions. I am 27 years old. I think your sample client letter for Unplanned Transitions says it best: "practice what you preach."*

*In my case, you couldn't have launched the service at a better time because I just completed my estate plan. When I called my attorney to make the change, the ink wasn't even dry on my Will yet! Timing is everything.*

*The estate attorney who did my documents is also someone who refers business to me. Being that we have clients in common, it made me feel good to show him that, as a sole practitioner, I was planning ahead and looking out for the long-term interests of my/our clients. Combined with my good work, I hope my planning for my own future will help our relationship, which could eventually lead to more referrals. I hope that everything continues well for you and your business. So far our transition rate is at 100 percent. My relationship with the seller grows stronger and stronger each day! I couldn't have asked for a better deal for my long-term success as an advisor.*

*Thanks for helping to make it all happen!*

*Warmest regards,*

*Greg Fernandez*

This is an excellent example of how looking out for your own future impacts all those around you. Look after yourself and have a succession plan or a transition plan. Only by taking care of you and your families' needs can you completely look after your clients' financial goals.

## Succession Planning vs. Transition Planning

One of the key points in distinguishing between these two terms revolves around having a "business" as opposed to a "practice." A business generally has multiple partners, qualified employees or family members ready to step into the void created by a departing advisor. A practice, on the other hand, relies heavily on a single person — the sole practitioner, to shepherd the client relationships and generate cash flow.

At one of my speaking engagements, I met an advisor with $370 million in AUM. I asked her how many partners she had, and was surprised to learn the answer. "I'm a sole practitioner. I have seven great employees, but I'm the only shareholder."

This advisor went on to say that she had read my column in *Financial Planning* magazine about the difference between succession planning and transition planning, and agreed on the difference. "I'll never have a partner," she said, smiling. "Done that before!"

"Succession Planning" is really a traditional concept describing a strategy that culminates in the transfer of ownership to the next generation. In practice, it is a strategy for businesses to transfer or reallocate an advisor's clients in the event of his or her retirement, death or disability, usually to a natural, internal line of qualified candidates, such as partners or family members.

"Transition Planning" describes a strategy for the actual transference of ownership, in an open market, and for subsequent, long term client retention. This term originated as sole practitioners began to sell or transfer their books of business, or practices, in the open market to the best qualified candidates available, and usually without the benefit of a succession plan of any kind.

In working with over 550 sellers, as this book goes to press, we have learned that succession planning is just not relevant to sole practitioners. Maybe it should be, but this first generation of sellers tends to be closer to age 55 than 65, and most are not retiring. They are moving on to a different line of work.

As a result, one of the problems with planning for your own future is timing. Very few advisors exit the profession according to a pre-set plan. And even if you have a plan, you, or your life, tend not to follow it.

 *One of my favorite quotes is* "Life is what happens while you are making other plans." *John Lennon*

Transition planning was created for the practices out there that do not have and never want to have a "real business." These practitioners do not want a successor in the form of a partner or well-qualified employee to enter ownership and take over at a predetermined time in a predetermined fashion. Transition planning, however, does have the advantage of producing quick results and high value as we saw in the example above with the distressed sale.

Sole practitioners used to fear the time it would take to exit their practice. They had no useful information to guide them on what to expect. The typical buyer had to be a friend or family member because the risk of clients finding out and leaving on their own was too great. Imagine how valuable you appear, as a seller, asking a buyer to buy your practice. The value proposition goes out the window!

These fears still get a lot of press... so much so that many sole practitioners still think their practices have little value. Oh, how times have changed!

Bottom line — the value of your practice and its liquidity have changed forever. Without any work on your part, the open market has proven that your practice is liquid and transferable, and that your clients can be well served by a outside buyer.

Want to learn more? Read about the methods and opportunities, the successes and failures, in each of our two, annually-published Transitions Reports. The knowledge alone will change the future of your practice.

## Partial Book Sales

We received a call from an advisor in one of our early years as a company with an interesting proposition: "I've got a hundred clients and the bottom 20 are below my minimums and for me they're not very profitable. I hate to just give them away. Would anybody want to buy them?"

I didn't know the answer but, as a company, we were intrepid enough to find out. We listed this partial book sale and, low and behold, it sold very quickly and easily.

Shortly afterwards, we opened up a special "Partial Book Sales" section on our websites. One partial book listing received 82 buyer inquiries. The marketplace quickly realized that a partial book sale offered smaller, younger practitioners an affordable acquisition option. In many cases the sellers mentored the buyer, as well.

Partial book buyers typically get to work with the seller for at least six months. More often than not they continue the relationship with the seller and acquire additional clients as the seller reduces the size of his or her practice over time and as retirement approaches. I think that partial book sales are a tremendous planning option for the sole practitioner, as well as a great way to grow a practice for a younger advisor.

Consider what one advisor did: We watched her — beginning at age 60 — sell off 20 percent of her book on our site, followed by similar sales the following years. She didn't want to retire but she also didn't want to work 60 hours a week. Slowly, gradually, at her own pace, she reduced the size of her practice while generating additional revenue from the sales (most at long term capital gain tax rates).

The buyer of the first group of clients realized that if he did well he would have a good chance at acquiring additional clients. And it worked!

Buyers of partial books are usually younger than our average buyer — often *much* younger. But they bring a lot of energy to the relationship and their technology skills are better than the seller's.

Buyers tend to pay more down for partial books because they are very affordable — as much as 50 percent in a cash down-payment. Partial book sales draw a lot of interest because sellers often agree to mentor the buyer and to provide office space in which to meet and work with the newly acquired clients.

We also see partial book sales being used to reshape books. This is a great way to look after your own goals and make sure your clients are guided by an advisor who matches up well with their needs.

As an example, imagine you're a fee-based practitioner and you want to move to a fee-only business model, yet you have 20 commission-oriented clients. You can sell those clients to a fee-based or commission-based practitioner who can deliver the services these clients expect while you move toward your goals.

## Option Agreements

If you're not quite ready to retire, but you have an employee who's anxiously waiting in the wings, consider using an option agreement to sell your practice. This is a great strategy to take control of the future, lock in your practice's value, and create your own legacy.

An option agreement provides your employee with the right to buy your practice at a specific time in the future (often one to three years) and at a predetermined price and terms. Unlike a buy-sell agreement between two partners or shareholders, which is more of a "what if" scenario, an option agreement provides a specific plan, price and timetable. When the time comes, the plan is executed. Employer and employee agree on the exact timing and terms in advance.

The buyer/employee usually pays a price for the option by writing a check to the seller when the option is signed — in the amount of $5,000 to $25,000 — depending on the assets and cash flow of the practice to be acquired. A good rule of thumb is 2.5 percent of the agreed-upon purchase price.

The employee is not buying the assets at this time — he or she is buying the right to buy the assets at a predetermined point in the future. In most cases, the option price is credited towards the final purchase price if the buyer completes the process. All of the "purchase agreements" are negotiated, agreed to, and signed at the time the option is purchased and entered into.

If the numbers don't work out, or the practice isn't in the same condition when the time comes to exercise the option, then the employee/buyer either doesn't exercise it. He may rely on the purchase price formula to do its job and adjust the price and terms. As an employee/buyer, you have bought a choice and an opportunity.

Better yet, as an employee/buyer, you've outmaneuvered your competition before they've even gotten started and had the chance to bid on the practice — a smart first move for a new, independent entrepreneur!

With an option agreement, there are no surprises to either side. Isn't that the way a professional planner would have it? This process results in continuity and predictability and value, for the buyer, seller and the clients, who must tacitly approve the whole arrangement by staying put for the next five to 10 years.

It's living, written proof of what advisors preach.

From the time the agreements are signed to the closing of the transaction, the seller is the employer and the buyer is the employee — business as usual. However, starting the day after closing and every day thereafter, the buyer is the employer and the seller is the employee. Now that has to be awkward for a while!

The seller still has 50 percent of the contingent purchase price to motivate him to play a key support role for up to one year after closing. During this "economic marriage," the parties really learn to work together. And, most importantly, it is the clients who benefit.

Clients often meet face-to-face with the seller and the buyer, even before the option period. This makes for a very comfortable transition and, when the seller finally fades from sight, the clients are well acquainted with the buyer who has quietly, and professionally, been placed in front of them.

## Practice Continuity Agreements

If you have a partner or you are one of several principals in your advisory firm, you probably have, or are considering, a buy-sell agreement. That's good business planning. If you haven't done this, you should.

If you're a sole practitioner you probably have not given serious consideration to a practice continuation agreement. We have now worked with over 500 sellers and 10,000 buyers and less than one percent of the people we speak to have a written practice continuation plan.

Here's a quick overview: For advisory firms with more than one owner, a buy-sell agreement details how ownership transfers if one owner dies, retires, or becomes disabled. It is an agreement between partners of a partnership or between shareholders and their corporation as to the terms and conditions of a future sale of the partners' or shareholders' interests. It also ensures that sellers or their beneficiaries get a fair price for their interests.

For advisory firms with only one owner, the sole practitioners out there, a practice continuation agreement (or continuity agreement) is the sole-practitioner's equivalent of a buy-sell agreement. A continuity agreement provides that, in the event of an owner's incapacity, death or retirement, another advisor or advisory firm will step in and run the distressed practice during the period of incapacity or, in the event of death, conduct an orderly sale or possibly acquire the practice for themselves.

A continuity agreement typically provides for a means of determining the fair market value of the seller's business and in certain instances to provide the funds necessary to carry out the purchase.

The important difference between a buy-sell agreement and a continuity agreement is that the buy-sell is a sale to an insider who is usually involved in the business on a daily basis. In the continuity agreement the sale or continuation services are provided by an outsider who probably has little day-to-day working knowledge of the client base he or she is going to take over.

There are two main types of continuation agreements: One is the one-to-one agreement undertaken with another advisory practice. The other is the group agreement where several different advisors may act as successors to each others' firms, and clients are given the choice of several surviving firms to choose from.

The seller should prepare a manual with a complete set of operating documents including a list of the types of services offered, key employees and all the pertinent information necessary to function successfully. A continuity seller's staff should also get to know the continuity provider(s) since the provider may be their new boss.

Don't forget about including your employees' thoughts and participation in the development and implementation of the continuity plan. From the clients' perspective, the assistance of the disabled or deceased advisor's staff during and after the transition phase can make or break the entire process. If you have a licensed staff member, he may be the best continuity provider you could hope to find, especially if what you need is a temporary fill-in rather than someone to buy and operate the practice.

Finally, you need to keep your continuity agreement up to date. Calendar an annual meeting with your continuity provider to discuss the plan and the steps needed to successfully implement it.

Remember, The One Thing is to plan for your future and what happens to your clients if you can't be there.

For taking the time to read this chapter, we'll provide you with a free copy of a continuity agreement — Just give us a call!

## The One Thing Again

I think it bears repeating: Advisor, plan for the future of your own practice. Only by taking control and understanding the great options you have can you fulfill your role as a professional financial advisor. Practice what you preach and create a plan. Take the time to learn about the following planning tools for a professional financial advisory practice:

- Partial Book Sales

- An "Unplanned Transitions" seller listing

- Option Agreements

- Continuity Agreements

No matter how much you like your work it has to end sometime.

In the meantime don't let anybody tell you that you have to sacrifice your lifestyle to take care of your clients! You can follow your passions and still plan for yourself.

Plan now for the possibility of an accidental or sudden death or disability and tell your clients about your plan. Tell your employees about your plan and involve them in the process. You owe it to your family, and you owe it to your clients and their families. It is the final step in a complete financial planning system.

## A Final Note

Don't fix what's not broken. I learned this one the hard way.

My wife, Penny, has been in the real estate profession, both commercial and residential, for a long time. In fact, she contributed many of the ideas for assembling the Business Transitions systems from the multiple listing systems, to form contracts, to escrow services. In my infinite lawyer's wisdom (I now proudly consider myself an ex-lawyer), I thought I'd return the favor by fixing her business for her so that she had more time off, became more profitable and separated her business relationships from her friendships.

My attempt did not go well.

Penny likes being friends with her clients. For her, it's not all about business. In fact, from my point of view, most days it's not at all about business! But she loves what she does for a living and she is happy doing it. She is not willing to sacrifice her current level of happiness and her friendships to make an extra $20,000 a year, or to take an extra week of vacation. From her point of view, she has the perfect job, and there is nothing that needs to be fixed.

If you like what you do, don't waste time and money trying to be something you won't like. Do not let experts and consultants sell you on a new lifestyle using scare tactics and fear-peddling to change who you are. When you are ready, the open market has a buyer for you and the buyer will be someone who thinks and runs a business just like you!

**In summary:**

- Know you have value.

- Know the difference between Succession Plans and Transition Plans.

- Partial Book Sales are a unique tool that can work to the advisor's and the client's advantage.

- Option Agreements are helpful in creating your own legacy.

- A Continuity Agreement can provide a means for determining the fair market value of an advisor's business if something happens to the advisor.

- Advisors need to have a plan in place for the future of their practice when it comes time to leave.

**David P. Grau, JD** is the president of Business Transitions, LLC, the largest transition planning and succession planning company in the U.S. for financial advisory practices. David is now the country's leading expert on the subject of buying and selling advisory practices. David writes a monthly column in *Financial Planning* magazine, and was named "one of the most influential people in the profession" by *Financial Planning* magazine in their 2004 Movers & Shakers survey.

David has worked with over 550 sellers and 10,000 buyers of financial advisory practices. He is one of the five original founding members of what has grown into the Business Transitions group of companies (four) and web sites (eight). He is a regular speaker on the conference circuit, presenting 30 to 40 seminars every year. David has been quoted or profiled in periodicals such as the *Wall Street Journal, Financial Planning* magazine (cover story), *Investment Advisor, Dow Jones Newswire,* the *Business Journal* (cover story) *Bloomberg Wealth Management, Financial Advisor, Registered Rep, Investment News, Journal of Financial Planning, On Wall Street* and others.

David is a graduate of Purdue University with highest honors and Northwestern School of Law. He is a member of the Oregon State Bar, and is a past board member of the Oregon and SW Washington Chapter of the Financial Planning Association.

Most importantly, David has been married for 26 years to his high school sweetheart, Penny, and has two grown sons — David Jr. is a straight "A" student in his junior year at Oregon State University (Go Beavers!), and Ryan is serving in the U.S. Army based in Dexheim, Germany, having completed a year on station in Baghdad, Iraq.

For more information about Business Transitions and how you can implement your plan look for the annual FP Transitions Report. It comes out on March first, every year. The RIA Transitions Report comes out on September first, every year.

To receive your Transitions Report go to ***www.fptransitions.com*** or call 1-800-934-3303

*Nowadays
people know
the price
of everything
and the value
of nothing.*

—Oscar Wilde

# Don't Miss the Big Trends

*By Dave Drucker*

Mark's interview was another we did by phone. Mark Tibergien is a partner in a CPA firm, as most readers already know, and he's very vocal about advisors' need to be better business strategists and managers. For all his dire warnings, though, Mark has a wonderful sense of humor and a very human quality that one may sometimes miss in his writings. We believe it came through quite clearly in our interview.

## Don't Follow the Herd

When I look at what's happening with advisors, the thing that I think is critical for every advisor to recognize is that they don't have to follow the herd. There is comfort in doing what other people do, but the key for everybody is to consider their approach to business from four critical perspectives.

The first is a personal definition of success. That to me is the one non-negotiable; that if you're doing things that don't fit within that definition, then nothing else matters. If you can resolve that question, then you can start building a business model that addresses the other critical perspectives.

*Again, this is a message that Mark doesn't often share with the trade press. We feel fortunate that he's sharing it in this book because everything does start with you. Your business should serve you, not the other way around.*

- The first of these is to figure out who is your optimal client, and how do you respond to this client.

- The second is to determine who else competes for those clients, and how do you best demonstrate your competitive edge to differentiate yourself from your competition.

- And the third is to build on your core capabilities, the strengths of your practice or yourself in order to achieve your definition of success.

So I start with the premise that most people who are entrepreneurs, and that's all the people who are independent advisors in this business, tend to start their business either because they have a passion for helping individuals achieve financial independence or they have a technical skill and this was a natural way for them to make a living using that skill.

I think, though, that when I look at the horizon for the business of financial advice, there are several things that are causing distress and it doesn't mean that they're unsolvable. I'll just kind of go over them generally.

## Four Trends in the Business

- **Managing the Top Line**

It's very clear that we're dealing in an environment where, especially for fee-only or fee-based practices, advisors are going to experience a slower rate of growth from existing clients. So I think the first thing is that it gets difficult to manage the top line because most advisors have a physical limit in terms of how many relationships they can manage. Ninety percent of their growth is going to come from existing clients to the extent their fees are tied to assets under management or to hours or to projects. There's a governor on their ability to grow the top line unless they change their business structure.

- **Rising Cost of Doing Business**

And at the same time the top line growth is being governed, their cost of doing business is rising at an even faster rate. We've already seen that in terms of compensation to any staff they have, but the new regulatory climate has put a great amount of stress on a lot of firms. The new need for a chief compliance officer that just came out… that's a cost, however they deal with it. These things clearly have an implication for the business.

- **More Demanding Clients**
  The third part of this is that we're dealing in an environment where clients are more demanding. I think the level of anxiety clients are experiencing about their personal and financial lives is causing them to demand more attention and more service from their advisors and, as a result, it continues to put more pressure on advisors to be more efficient in how they deliver services. And this is putting them at a crossroads as well.

- **The Nature of the Competition**
  The final big trend from a business perspective is the nature of the competitive landscape. Community banks are the single biggest buyers of advisory practices today. It's pretty clear that there's a trend toward consolidation via merger, where practices are getting bigger. The kinds of things that Mark Hurley predicted are coming true in a moderated sort of way. What I think the challenge will be for a lot of advisors is to figure out how to differentiate themselves in the market, not so much for their existing clients, but in order to capture new opportunities. What are they going to do to really make themselves appealing to new clients?

  I think these are the forces of evil conspiring against people in this business that advisors are going to have to confront.

## Tailor Service to Your Clients

So I think that there are several things that advisors should do. The first thing I mentioned is that they have to think about what business they're in, and what we're finding is that the practices that are managing to overcome these issues have an advantage. They are defining who their optimal client is and consequently they are able to define their client service experience.

I just hung up the phone with a prospective client. He had so many different approaches to his business that I couldn't keep track. But the one thing he said he wanted to do is deal with affluent clients and I'm thinking, well, that doesn't do it for me. I don't even know what that is because there are so many other nuances to affluent clients.

Is it a client that works in a business? Is it a doctor? Is it a retiree? Is it an old person, a young person? What are some of the things that you

know depending on their life cycle, their occupation, their risk toler-
ances, their emotions? If you could replicate those clients, what would
they look like?

Why these things are so important is that, by knowing the unique
characteristics of your optimal client, you can build a client service
experience that is tailored to that client. And I think that's really a pretty
critical way in which you keep up the efficiency of your business. If your
decision is not to add staff, then what you're going to have to do is say,
"These are my parameters; I need to be clearer about who I'm serving
and how I'm serving them. I have to figure out how I'm going to manage
my growth organically if I'm not going to add in-house capacity to do it."
So I think that really makes a big difference.

## Speaking of Margins

Doing all of these things will improve your margins. When we look
at the financial performance of a business, we pay quite a bit of attention
to the gross profit margin. When the gross margin is declining, that's
usually a function of things like:

- are you pricing your services right?

- are you productive?

- do you have the right service mix?

- do you have the right client mix?

You can manage your costs all you want but if you don't fix these
four elements of your business, then you will still have profitability
problems.

Think of it this way: when we organize a financial statement, revenue minus direct expenses equals gross profit minus overhead expense
equals operating profit. The direct expense is what is paid to professional staff as fair market compensation plus any related bonuses and incen-
tives and benefits that comes out of it. If it were a manufacturing company, that would be the cost of goods sold. Overhead is everything else
like secretarial staff, administrative staff, depreciation, technology, rent,
marketing — all that stuff is overhead.

*One way to increase your profit margin is through
virtual-office tools and techniques... but that's
another book.*

When we look at an advisory practice, the practice that does under a million dollars of annual revenue spends over 40 percent of its revenue on overhead, rent, utilities, and marketing. That's a lot. In fact, you'll find that number is even higher in most practices. Yet it should be about 35 percent of revenue.

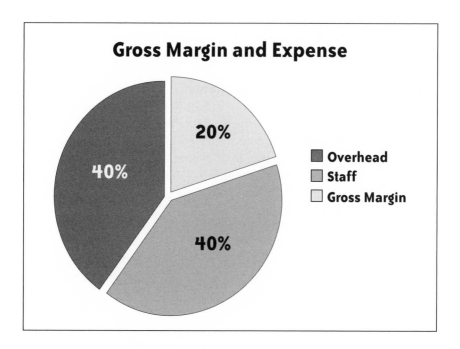

**Gross Margin and Expense**

40%

20%

40%

- ■ Overhead
- ▨ Staff
- ☐ Gross Margin

But most practitioners have difficulty getting it below 40 percent because there are certain expenses they must incur, which is one of the compelling reasons for people to think about merging. When I look at advisors' gross profit margins, that number should be close to 60 percent and the reason is that the most a typical advisor can spend on professional staff is about 40 percent of revenue.

So, literally, the way the model should look is a hundred percent to revenue, 40 percent for direct expense, 60 percent gross profit, 35 percent for overhead, and 25 percent to the bottom line. So if you're running this like a business, what this is basically saying is that your direct expense is the cost of labor and the operating profit is the reward for ownership. The reason an independent advisor makes more than his wirehouse counterparts is that he's getting a reward for the risk he's taking for running a business.

If you're a top producer in a wirehouse, you can take 40 percent instead of 65 percent, which is what it would come to. The reason is that, as an employee of a brokerage firm, you're not taking a business risk — you're just an employee.

So when I look at that gross profit margin and I observe it over time and I see that it's actually declining, the symptoms of it are typically what I mentioned before: the pricing of your services, the productivity of you and your professional staff — meaning how effectively are you dealing with clients, are you generating enough revenue to recover that cost? And are you dealing systematically with services that are right for the actual client? Then the fourth point is client mix.

## Managing People — Including Clients

In the last survey we did for the Financial Planning Association (FPA), what we found was that there was a clear demarcation between those practices that had 80 percent of their clients in their sweet spot and those that had 20 percent of their clients in their sweet spot. If you believe the 80-20 rule applies to you, what that tells you is that 80 percent of your clients are not in your sweet spot and they're being subsidized by the 20 percent that are.

- **Determine Your Optimal Client**

Some people have figured this out and said, well this is crazy, I'd rather have 80 percent of my clients in my sweet spot so that I have a more efficient practice. Those people who do it, their revenue goes up three times over the others, and their gross profit margin obviously is much higher as well.

I think that is a big part of it, but I think it would be too simplified if I said that that was "the one thing." I think knowing who your optimal client is will certainly help you to build the right strategy but I don't look at an advisor strategy as necessarily revolving around the client.

An advisor strategy really revolves around any one of eight things and the drivers are what do they want to be known for? Do they want to be known for the market they serve or the service they provide or the way in which they create business? What is the combination of differentiators that will help them to capture more business and knowing one's optimal client is key to that. But that's not the only strategic choice advisors should make.

- **Strategy and Organization**

Number two is that the best advisors have created leverage and capacity, meaning that through a combination of technology and people, what they've recognized is that they're doing things they shouldn't be doing and must figure out a way to better leverage themselves.

Now, how you organize your business really depends on what your strategy is. If you decide, for example, that your business is geared around the 401(k) plan market, that's going to result in an entirely different organization than if you decide you're going to serve strictly individual clients. Your processes, your protocols, the type of people you hire, your reporting, all of that. What you have to do is say, "Once I'm clear on that strategy, I can now create an organization that supports that strategy. I can hire the right kinds of people and employ the right kind of technology to get there."

It ain't what you make — it's what ya keep*! I believe that, as investment advice becomes more and more commoditized, advisors will have to offer unique experiences that clients can't obtain elsewhere to combat eroding profit margins.*

- **Profit Management**

The third component is having an attitude about profit management. It's not only an attitude about cost control; it's an attitude about management, both the gross margin and the operating margin. And that means advisors monitor and measure what's going on in their business so that they can react to it and manage it accordingly. They have to be looking at leading indicators to understand what changes they have to make.

## Business Skills Are Important

The one absolute truth is that if running a successful advisory practice were easy, everybody would be doing it. And it isn't. I have an immense amount of respect for people who've taken the risk to try it, but what they have to do is work to improve their business skills, just like they work to improve their technical skills.

Have I seen any change in advisors' willingness to do this in the ten years since Moss Adams has been active in supplying performance data to the industry? Yes, I have. I've noticed a material change even in how people express themselves. Now, when I speak on these subjects, people don't look at me like I have three heads, and that's a victory in and of itself.

I think people in this business are intellectually curious. One of the great qualities of financial advisors is that they're intellectually curious and, to a degree, they also have a competitive element to them. I think because they are problem-solvers by nature they have an inclination to say, "There's no reason why we should tolerate mediocrity. We have to find another way to do it." I think that where the crisis occurs for many of them is their lack of confidence in their ability to manage their business or grow it to another level. I think there is a high level of insecurity over that.

At one time I was recruited to the Seattle office of a company that provided investment management services. Part of my job was calling on wirehouses to sell portfolio management services to their brokers. My boss said, "You know, Mark, you're going to struggle in the first five or ten years of this business because there are a couple of things you need to succeed." He said gray hair was one and hemorrhoids were the other. I said, "Why is that?" And he said, "The gray hair is to look mature, and the hemorrhoids are to make you look concerned."

*I believe the number one attribute an advisor must cultivate is confidence in what they can do and what they can't do — and as the serenity prayer says "the wisdom to know the difference!"*

## Chronic Problems

So I kind of laugh about that because some people in this business, finally, after 15 or 20 years of struggle, are esteemed in their communities and are thought of as major league advisors. Once they reach that pinnacle, they say, "You know, I really don't think I want to grow my business. I don't think I want to be dealing with more clients." So by the time they can finally capitalize on their investment, they say, "Oh, I don't want to do this."

There's a great deal of irony to all of that. "How can I make more money? How can I hire good people? How can I better leverage my time?" All these things that advisors have been complaining about for 20 years are still chronic conditions. I think that people would like to solve these problems but aren't confident that they can.

A lot of people have grown practices where they're surrounded by people and they say, "How in the world did this happen? I mean, how did I end up with all these people around me who are just a collection of misfits, in a way?" Not that they're bad people, but it's just kind of an odd strategy that people have in hiring and putting people in positions.

## Human Capital Strategy

So one of the things that we found to be an important characteristic of a best practice is that it has to have a human capital strategy in line with its business strategy, meaning that how it selects people, what jobs it puts them in, how it matches them for their jobs, and how it rewards their behavior, is all a part of its business strategy.

One of the mistakes made in business is the belief that everybody wants more money. I believe that people want to satisfy their intellectual curiosity. Financial reward is important, but so is personal fulfillment, and part of that is making sure that the individuals you have in your practice are consistently challenged to do better. I see that as both an opportunity and a hurdle for advisors. How do you develop a human capital strategy that is in line with what you're trying to do in your business?

So I think that the whole people side of the business is going to be a real area of emphasis for advisors going forward. It's the nature of the work, the nature of the worker, and the nature of the workplace. What I hear on the street is people saying, "How do I find good people?" I can't tell you how many times I hear people ask that question. And they say, "Once I find them, how do I keep them?" It's really hard to keep people unless you have a career path for them.

In fact, I think a funny thing that goes on is that you hire good people and then you try to keep them down. Often times when I go into a practice I'll find that there is a very, very large gap between the owner of the practice and everybody else in terms of efficiency, technical ability, and so forth. "You know, I just don't have confidence in so and so to do the kind of work that I need done." And from a business perspective, that's so bewildering; I think, "Man, if you don't have confidence, how come you still have him in your company?"

And so I find how people are resolving that question just a little bit disconcerting. In fact, I had a situation recently that was kind of interesting and it was a conversation along these lines.

The advisor was expressing his discomfort with the people who worked in his practice, people who had been there for a long time, and I said, "Let me ask you a question. When you're retired and you're no longer licensed and you're no longer able to deal with your own financial matters, how likely are you to hire your former colleagues to help you with your personal investments?" And he said, "Not a chance." And I said, "Do you hear yourself? I mean, how do you think your clients feel?"

## The Client Service Experience

The Client Service Experience is a concept that I've used that for a long time. I kind of learned that somewhere deep in my past. When I started selling professional services, what I was taught is that you should never sell intangibles as if they are a product, but that you have to create a new experience for the buyer. It's that whole idea of making a connection with the client that touches them emotionally. So the term "client service experience" — I can't explain how other people are using it — but it's a phrase that I've often heard around the idea of selling intangible services.

Over time, this is probably what will distinguish the traditional financial advisor from the mass market organizations such as banks. One is client-centric, the other is product-centric. One sells the relationship, the other sells the goods. Some clients will prefer to deal with one over the other but, in either case, their perception of value will be based on this "experience."

The Client Service Experience is a good phrase for advisors when you think about it because what they're offering is an experience. Whenever you look at client satisfaction surveys, the issue for clients is not really so much whether you're achieving performance goals, but whether you're listening to them and do they feel that you're responsive to their needs. Are you anticipating their issues? I think when you're serving individual clients, a part of what justifies their need for you is whether or not they perceive that you're valuable to them.

## In the Beginning

I grew up in a little town in Upper Michigan and, you know, most of the people who grew up there never get out. Mostly because they don't want to. It's a slow pace, and a low-stress environment. What's funny is, if you talk to other people in the rest of Michigan, they kind of think that the Upper Peninsula is a welfare state. So one of the things that compelled me along the way was the desire to do some things that weren't part of the normal experience of kids growing up there.

I can tell you that to confuse me with an intellectual would be a gross error. For my very first job, I was hired by a radio station in Michigan to read their obituary reports on the air. The town I grew up in was Gladstone and mine was the biggest high school class in years. It was as though some mad night in 1952, all the parents got hot and heavy. But the town... well, if you ever saw the movie *Grumpy Old Men*... we had nine months of winter. I played on the golf team and we played in the snow. That's how cold it was.

So I worked for the local newspaper as a reporter. I actually started out as a journalist working for the local newspaper and radio station when I got the obituary gig. I had to rush to the office early in the morning and call all the funeral homes to find out who kicked the bucket the night before.

It was funny because I had to be really somber, which was really hard for me because I was pretty young. Every time I'd come across a

funny name, I'd get the giggles and that really annoyed the funeral director who sponsored the show.

They finally bumped me up to where I had to read the news and the
first story one morning was about a prostitution ring in Wisconsin that
had been broken up the night before. I got in late because it was New
Year's and it was my obligation to celebrate so I was late to work.

I didn't have time to rewrite the news; I just pulled it off the wire and
started reading. The first thing I said was that a Wisconsin night club had
been raided, but there was a typo in the story. I got to the name of the
Madam, which was Sally Suckup. Well, that just sent me into convulsions.
Overall, I wasn't made for radio. I have a face for radio, but not the necessary control.

I guess all of that has qualified me to be a consultant. As they say, if
you can't do, teach; if you can't teach, consult.

## The One Thing

For The One Thing, I have to go back to my opening premise, and
that is that it's human nature to follow the herd. I understand why that
occurs, but I think that when advisors develop a business model, they
should be asking themselves some questions:

- What are my capabilities that I can build on?

- What is my optimal market?

- How do I differentiate myself from people who compete for those
  clients?

- What is my personal definition of success?

Whatever business strategy you adopt, you must consider all four of
those perspectives. If you're one-dimensional in how you approach your
business, then you're going to be one-dimensional in how you operate
your business. I think that people need to force themselves to broaden
their view of how they operate.

**In summary:**

- Know your definition of success

- Identify your optimal client

- Determine who else competes for these clients and differentiate yourself from them

- Tailor service to your clients.

- Build on the core capabilities and strengths of you and your practice to achieve your goals.

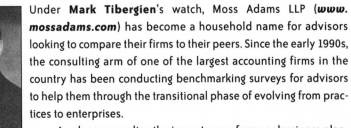

Under **Mark Tibergien**'s watch, Moss Adams LLP (***www. mossadams.com***) has become a household name for advisors looking to compare their firms to their peers. Since the early 1990s, the consulting arm of one of the largest accounting firms in the country has been conducting benchmarking surveys for advisors to help them through the transitional phase of evolving from practices to enterprises.

As planners realize the importance of proper business planning, Tibergien says Moss Adams will continue to add staff and additional services. He hopes to add other specialty consultants for planners to his team in the near future.

Moss Adams LLP / 1001 Fourth Avenue, Suite 2700 / Seattle, WA 98154

*Things will get better—*
*despite our efforts*
*to improve them.*

—Will Rogers

## TRACY BECKES

# The Effortless Outrageous Business

*By Dave Drucker*

Tracy Beckes is different from any other coach in this book. She's a "business coach" who works with clients "from the inside out." While Tracy works with a diverse clientele, she specializes in helping financial advisors create thriving practices that support an ideal lifestyle. Tracy's "interior" approach allows her to work with advisors at every stage of development.

I met Tracy when she spoke at a fee-only NAPFA (National Association of Personal Financial Advisors) conference about four years ago and was attracted to the uniqueness of her coaching style. Tracy gets a fair amount of exposure as a speaker at NAPFA and FPA (Financial Planning Association) events but, compared to some of our other coaches, she's less well-known.

The reason, she explains, is that her intensive coaching style allows her to work at any one time with a relatively small, exclusive set of advisors; too much exposure means too much business that can't be addressed by Tracy's intensive coaching approach.

D and I interviewed Tracy by phone on a Sunday morning when she was "fresh" and relaxed. The following discussion offers insight into how Tracy developed her transformative approach.

❖❖❖

## Coaching Advisors

I have been around advisors for nearly two decades and I consider them to be some of the brightest, most gifted and talented professionals. They're a truly exceptional group. Most advisors have a highly-developed skill set: the ability to look at complex issues in a comprehensive way, to connect with people, earn their trust, and support their dreams. These skills position them to create an ideal business and life more easily than most people. They have the strategies and the knowledge to move businesses forward in remarkable ways; yet, at some point, many advisors find that something gets in their way.

Some advisors realize they are out of balance and see that their relationships and health are suffering. Others come to the gradual realization that they don't have to work as hard as they are, but can't figure out how to shift into a different way of operating. It's not uncommon for successful advisors to sense that their initial passion for their work is slipping away, leaving them drained, uninspired, overwhelmed with details and lost in drudgery.

And there are other advisors who know they are capable of operating at a higher level and delivering better service, but can't find the time to streamline and refocus their energy or establish a framework that takes some of the pressure off. The challenges are different for each person, but my clients all find their solutions through the same profound process.

## The Holistic Approach

In order to operate at the highest level, advisors must first uncover the true source of what's preventing them from effortlessly moving forward. Each one of us operates from what I call "default source-code programming," the core-level assumptions and beliefs that are so ingrained in us that they are taken for granted. This programming influences every aspect of our lives, from our style of communicating to our relationship with money, from the environments we create to the goals that drive us, and even how we take care of ourselves. Examining our ideas and beliefs can radically improve our experience of every area of our lives.

Advisors hire me to address a wide variety of situations in their lives and businesses. The effectiveness of coaching is the ability to develop an individualized approach for each person. When someone comes to me with a desire for a better quality of life, we consider many aspects of their current situation, such as the hours they work, the quality of relationships they engage in, and their level of compensation. The approach for each advisor is highly customized.

Some people want to explore how to get clear on the next phase of their life. Others want to work on specific aspects of their business, such as profiling their ideal client, improving communication skills, hiring and training key employees, developing effective engagement standards or, in some cases, just getting support while they go through the succession-planning process.

An increasing number of people are addressing "quality of life" issues, searching for ways to incorporate more happiness, satisfaction and fulfillment into their life. Almost everyone is looking for ways to stop working for the business, and get the business to start working for them.

As advisors explore this process, they start to realize that all areas of their life and business are interconnected so, when you work on one area, other areas are affected as well. When you examine a person's relationship with money — or time, or their health, or any other dimension of life — and work to uncover the underlying issue that keeps that person from moving forward, you start to see a kaleidoscope effect. When one piece moves, everything starts to shift. When you take time to really learn from one aspect of your life, those lessons can effortlessly transfer into other areas as well. The process frees up energy to create better results in all areas of our lives.

*Perhaps more so than any other coach in this book, Tracy is concerned with making sure the advisor's personal and professional lives are optimally balanced.*

I have had clients triple or quadruple their income over the course of our coaching relationship, but very few of them initiated coaching for the purpose of making more money. Since most of the people I work with are well-established professionals who have been in the business 10, 20, even 25 years, they know how to run a successful business. Many are financially independent and they're looking for something else, like an increased quality of life. But since everything in our lives is interconnected, progress in one area inevitably spills over into other areas as well.

## The Power of Being Complete

The process of coaching starts with an evaluation of a client's current situation and the objectives they are looking to achieve. With that information, a coach customizes a specific approach that will create the most value for the client. That strategy usually addresses many areas of the client's business, but one common aspect is "incompletions."

"Incompletions" is a coaching term to describe anything that you have not responded to or handled fully. They are the tasks that stay on your To-Do List and cycle through your mind, calling for your attention and contributing to the feeling of being overwhelmed.

It's very common for people to live with the stress of incompletions, and learning how to manage them can lead to a dramatic breakthrough for many advisors. The typical professional averages 170 interactions per day, personally and professionally, in a variety of forms, including conversations, e-mails, voice mail, faxes, and so on. The average, fully-engaged, successful professional has 200 to 300 — and in some cases up to 600 — hours of backlogged work. This includes handling client situations, reading journal articles and exploring different projects.

I think of our generation as a pioneering generation, because never before have we had to manage so much information and negotiate so many demands on our attention. The speed of change and the impact of technology have given us a tremendous amount of information to track, assimilate and respond to. At times, it's very stressful. It can be overwhelming. The sheer number of commitments and projects that professionals juggle would shock a previous generation, and yet this is the nature of our everyday lives.

 *I think this point is so salient! And it's why I really don't like the term "multi-tasking"! I argue for doing one thing well at a time until it's finished!*

We attend to the things that are the most important in our lives, and everything else gets put off, simply because there isn't time or opportunity to address everything as it arises. As the list of incompletions builds, so does the stress level. If people don't create a reliable and effective system — outside of their head — to manage this barrage of information, they can pay a huge price on many levels. Their ability to focus and fully engage is compromised by the distraction of tracking all the loose ends. They spend time and attention worrying that something important may have fallen through the cracks. And inevitably, something does.

One of the most powerful things a coach can do is support a client in tracking and responding to the incompletions in their life, clearing out the things that are draining them, and handling the issues and problems that are consuming precious life energy. It doesn't matter if you're a financial advisor, high-level executive, an athlete or an entertainer — incompletions can take a significant toll on your life. When you free up the energy consumed by a long list of incompletions, you're able to effortlessly focus on what you most want. Handling incompletions creates clarity, energy and creativity that will support growth in your personal and professional life.

## Coaching in Action

Coaching is one of the most effective ways to create what you most want in your life, regardless of where you're starting or where you're going. It's a collaborative partnership that can quickly build the skills and strategy to achieve what you most want for your life and it provides the consistent support that helps people stay committed to their goals.

For example, I've been coaching a woman for over five years, an elite advisor with a wildly successful firm. Many of her clients have placed over $20 million in assets under her management, and her visionary ways have created success in other areas of her life as well. She's one of the most intelligent, capable women I know.

*When I sought to move from the advisory profession to the writing profession, working with a coach (mine was both a writer and a licensed psycotherapist) was one of the wisest investments I ever made.*

She asked me to help her reevaluate how she interacts with her staff. She was too close to the situation to be able to see it clearly, and since she's often several steps ahead of other people, there was a growing challenge with interoffice communications. An immediate breakthrough came when she learned to set boundaries around her time to minimize employee interruptions. This structure allowed her to focus more energy in her areas of strength and contribute the most she could to the firm.

At one point, I described to this woman an effective way to manage incompletions by using an external tracking system. Since she's such an organized person, there wasn't a lot of value in that for her personally, but she immediately recognized that her *staff* could really benefit from the material. She shared some of the system at a staff meeting and her employees were very interested. I offered her a tutorial, tips, tools and resources, and the firm conducted a full off-site session based on the material. They then spent three days in the office without any client appointments, giving everyone a chance to apply what they learned, and an opportunity to develop those skills at a much higher level.

Over time, this advisor mastered the process of evaluating a situation and working through to a solution. At one point, we had an hour-long session where she guided herself through the process of evaluating a challenge and identifying an opportunity to move forward. One step at a time, she asked *herself* the questions that I was about to ask, finding her own way from inquiry to insight. By the end of the hour, I applauded her mastery of the process.

She responded by saying that the process was incredibly useful, but that the solutions were actually not the most valuable aspect of coaching for her. She relied on our regularly-scheduled sessions to step back from her life and business and take an objective look at the way she was operating. That is a key value for all of my clients: the opportunity to check in with themselves and be sure they're on track. People really appreciate a chance to escape from the whirlwind pace and dialogue about the way things are going. An objective sounding board helps us stay grounded in a balanced perspective.

## Early Influences

I started developing the concepts of the Effortless Outrageous Business when I was 11 or 12, while I was working on local farms. Even then, I had an inkling, a strong sense that work didn't have to be a chore, that maybe work could be pleasurable *and* profitable. I was driven to figure out how to create that for myself.

A couple years later, at the age of 14, I heard Bruce Jenner, the 1976 Olympic gold medalist, speak at a sports banquet. There was one small detail of his story that fascinated me: he worked for just three days each month selling insurance, and took the rest of the month off to train for the Olympics. A few years after that I met a woman who sponsored an annual Renaissance street fair, working just three months each year and making enough money to spend the rest of the year on her hobby, which was running a small, independent bookstore. I was inspired. They were operating from a very different paradigm and had created a work environment that was in service to other aspects of their lives.

In high school, I started reading — *Think and Grow Rich, The Power of Positive Thinking* — every book on personal development I could find. When I got to graduate school, my interest in creating an ideal business expanded. As I worked toward degrees in marketing and finance, I found myself in a business decision-making course. I spent hours in the career research library developing a model that would assist people in creating the career and the life of their dreams.

I conducted extensive research to identify the main areas and components that contribute to career satisfaction, research that continues to influence my coaching today. My passion for learning and my deep, driving curiosity about how to create an ideal business have resulted in a collection of over 800 audio recordings on personal and business development.

The work that I do today is a synthesis of my life experiences. I was raised in a family of entrepreneurs and that influenced my ideas and beliefs about business, as did my extensive research on entrepreneurial success and satisfaction. Combine that with my experience in corporate America, the business development aspects of the MBA program, my history of working with advisors and nearly two decades of exposure to this industry.

In addition, when you include extensive personal-development work and a holistic perspective on business development, as well as my comprehensive training in high-level coaching and relationship skills, you can see that the scope of my training is both broad and deep. This colorful montage of experience has come together as a passionate commitment to the understanding that business and life can be both effortless *and* outrageous.

## Marketing for the Advisor

I have an undergraduate and graduate degree in business, with an emphasis in marketing and finance. When I studied marketing, the primary formula was: figure out what the customer wants, and then manufacture a product to meet the customer's needs.

What most advisors don't understand is that this only applies to marketing products, not professional services. To be truly effective, an advisor has to identify when they're operating at their best, and then attract clients that resonate with them. This is the essence of my entire philosophy and approach.

To reorient your way of operating around this philosophy takes some practice and reprogramming. It requires that the advisor first take time to get clear on when they're at their best and what aspects of their life support them in operating from that paradigm. What kinds of people, environments and activities bring out their best work, raise their energy level and inspire them to achieve more? What daily rituals of self-care need to be in place to foster consistently good health and high energy? What kinds of goals and relationships will build a structure that propels them forward effortlessly?

The process requires that the advisor adopt a key understanding: that sometimes it benefits everyone to be a bit selfish. It asks the advisor to put more attention on his or her own needs, based on the concept that one can only truly be of service when one's own needs are met.

In general, advisors are a very caring group of people. They want to do what's right for the client. Many will even do so at the expense of themselves, not realizing that when they push themselves too hard to meet the needs of the client, in the long run, everybody loses. They lose, their clients lose, and their families lose. If the advisor isn't thriving, the probability of sustaining and delivering a high level of service over time diminishes significantly.

A business is a reflection of the people in the business. A business thrives because the people in the business thrive. It can't be the other way around.

## Being Different

My approach is very different from that of most business coaches. I use an "inside-out" philosophy that honors the interconnectedness of all areas of life. There's a depth to it that other coaching programs can't get to. In addition to traditional business development strategies, my work with clients incorporates transformative perspectives and tools that empower people to make internal shifts that result in lasting change.

Over the course of 10 years, I co-directed a two-year graduate program at the Hendricks Institute, which was operated by Drs. Gay and Kathlyn Hendricks, two of the nation's top coaches in the realm of interpersonal relationships. Their action-based, forward-looking orientation to coaching taught me to get to the source of what's going on — the essence of the issue — so that people can address the problem, not just the symptoms. By grounding these insights in action, people can take focused steps to move their lives forward in ways that will pay off for many years to come.

I also spent over two years traveling around the world, visiting 27 countries, which broadened my perspective and enhanced my ability to support clients.

My intention is to bring the best, most respected ideas and strategies to the client and help them apply these concepts to their own specific situation. The power of what I do lies in customizing my approach for each person.

## One Size Fits No One

Instead of relying on a set curriculum, I evaluate where a client is in his or her development and then pull from a wide variety of ideas, concepts, strategies and tools. My background allows me to look at all aspects of their business and life and then support them with a plan that addresses their individual needs.

What I offer clients is the opportunity to set up their business and life in a way that supports them in operating at their best. That process is different for each person, but we start by asking questions that elicit what is really important to them, such as:

- What would an effortless, outrageous business look and feel like for you?

- What are three to five goals that you're going to use to measure the quality of your life?

- If you had $1 billion or more, would you keep doing what you're doing?

After giving a speech at a recent industry conference, I met an advisor who had built a large financial planning firm. He enjoyed my speech for one specific reason. A few years prior, he had been diagnosed with a serious illness, and it caused him to take a step back and evaluate his life.

Once he identified what was most important in his life, he decided to sell his firm and devote his time to raising his children. He really wanted to be with them, more than anything, and he was willing to reorganize his life to do it. He was so excited by the fact that I was asking people the same questions that it took a life-threatening illness to get him to ask himself.

### The One Thing: Figure Out When You're at Your Best

You have one wild and precious life — how will *you* live it? It's a question most people have considered, but coming to clear, detailed answers can be a challenging proposition. At the core of my philosophy are some very simple — but extraordinarily powerful — questions that will help you identify specific ways to design your own phenomenal life. Ask yourself:

- When are you naturally at your best?

- When do you feel most energized?

- What kinds of activities are you doing, what kind of people are you with, and what kinds of environments are you in when you feel most alive, most fulfilled?

*A like-mind connection: Tracy asks similar questions here that George Kinder asks clients in his chapter. Both seek what is the innermost desire.*

To ask these questions over and over throughout your day will help you uncover your natural abilities, your innate rhythms, your ideal environments and most suitable activities. Once you're clear on what energizes you, you can begin to reorient your life around the people, environments and actions that inspire you and propel you forward.

The process of creating an Effortless Outrageous Business has three parts: the first one is identifying when you're at your best; the second is being able to honor impeccably when you're at your best; and the third is teaching your clients how to access your best.

Every Effortless Outrageous Business is a unique creation because it is an authentic reflection of the advisor. One advisor might want a simple, stable, consistent business, while another advisor may want a lot of flexibility. The key is to develop a business that supports your own definition of an ideal lifestyle.

A business that authentically reflects the advisor is a key component of professional satisfaction because it supports a commitment to operating in the most powerful, effective way possible. When you learn to manage your life energy like it's the most precious resource you have, when you stop wasting your time and attention and focus on what you really want to create, life can be extremely fulfilling.

As I work with clients to discover when they're at their best, I believe the wisdom lies within the client. The coach's job is simply to draw it out with effective questions. When the answers come from the client, their chances of implementing them, making sustainable changes, and living a more fulfilling life are increased significantly. The process of coaching is one that empowers people to make conscious choices that support the life they truly want to live.

**In summary:**

- Identify what you most want in life.

- Identify what's preventing you from effortlessly moving forward.

- Learn how to manage the "incompletions" that compete for your attention.

- A coach can provide consistent support and strategies to help you achieve what you most want in life.

- Reorient your life around when you are at your best to help you achieve your goals by

    1. identifying when you are at your best

    2. honoring impeccably when you are at your best

    3. teaching your clients how to access your best

❖❖❖

**Tracy Beckes, MBA,** is the founder of Tracy Beckes and Associates, Inc., a Washington-based firm that specializes in helping advisors create thriving businesses and vibrant personal lives. Widely recognized as a pioneering business coach, she is consistently sought after by premier financial planners for her transformative business approach and unique coaching style. Tracy's clients streamline and simplify their lives, focus on what is most important, master effortless productivity and create prosperous businesses that nourish the soul. Ultimately, they learn to use their business as a tool to live an extraordinary life. Behind Tracy's contagious enthusiasm is deep wisdom and years of education and experience that have won her the respect of the financial planning community.

| | |
|---|---|
| Email | tracy@tracybeckes.com |
| Toll-Free | (888) 633-9446 |
| Website | www.tracybeckes.com |

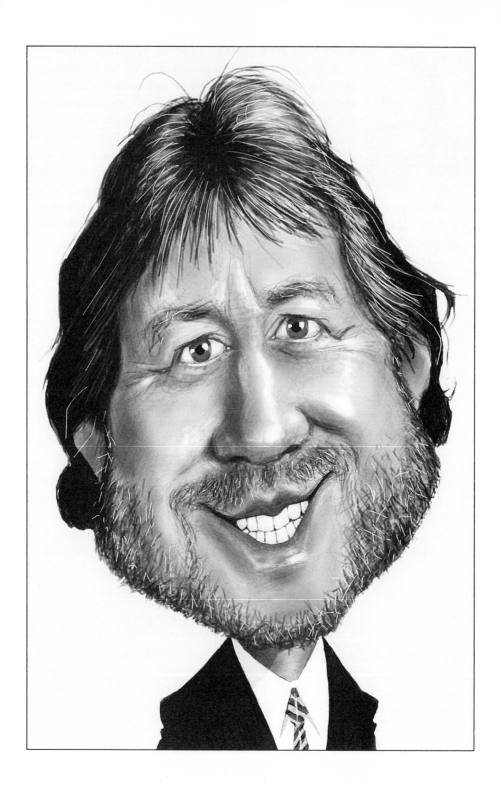

## JERRY REITER

# Document Everything

*By "D" Shannon*

**There is no surer way to misread any document than to read it literally.[1]**
*Learned Hand*
*Recalled on his death 18th of August, 1861*

I confess: I did it. I joined Financial Advisors Legal Association (F.A. Legal) years ago because I was scared. The following anecdote is completely true but, I'll warn you now, it reads like fiction.

It was August 2nd and I was packing for our annual pilgrimage to the Outer Banks, where we haul the kids and dogs to the beach for relief from the sweltering dog days of D.C. My office is on my farm so when the phone rang, I reluctantly agreed to take a client call, in between shoving more suitcases atop our Ford Excursion.

The caller said, "'D,' it's John[2]. Got a moment?" Without even a pause for my negative response he blurted, "I'd like to rent your farm while you're at the beach."

Not much causes me to sputter, but I did. "What in the good Lord's name do you want to rent my farm for, John? You can't possibly grow something in two weeks and we don't have room for livestock with the drought!"

---

[1] Simpson's Contemporary Quotations, compiled by James B. Simpson, 1988.
[2] Changed to protect the guilty.

"Well, "D," it's like this: see, I've never told you this, but my wife and I are swingers. We want to rent your place because our business income has dropped due to the recession and we figure we can throw a heckuva swinger's party at your place! Shoot! We'll give ya 25 percent of the gate!"

Now I'm really sputtering. "Ahhh, umm... I DON'T THINK SO!," I said, as I fully realized what this guy was asking!

I continued. "AND ANOTHER THING... YOU'RE FIRED AS A CLIENT!"

That was only the beginning of the nightmare. Months later I received a call from an insurance company. "Mr. Shannon?" began a nasal voice that could only belong to someone in compliance. "Mr. Shannon? This is Ms. Yackity-Yack[3] with Big Box Insurance Company. We have received a complaint from John Blowhard that you have allegedly sold him an insurance policy as a retirement plan." Her voice dripped with condescension.

I'm now sure I know where the unemployed KGB agents went to work after the fall of the Soviet Union: to the legal and compliance departments of the large insurance and investment houses!

To keep this crazy story brief, I spent 17 months trying to prove my innocence. The insurance company was poised to withdraw approximately $10,000 of well-earned commissions from my checking account. No one at Big Box Insurance Company returned phone calls or emails. Yet wave after wave of complaint forms and legal threats ensued. Finally, through a side channel, I got Big Box's chief legal counsel on the phone.

"Hello, this is Vladimir Lenin[4]", the voice on the other end of the phone said. (I knew it!)

I piped up. "Umm, Mr. Lenin, this is "D" Shannon calling about the Blowhard complaint."

There was a long silence, followed by a big sigh. "Mr. Shannon, this conversation NEVER happened — understood?" He continued. "Mr. Shannon, we never had a doubt as to your innocence here at Big Box. In fact, we think you did a textbook case of planning for the Blowhards. Frankly, we couldn't admit it because we were under investigation by the state of Virginia for failing to file notices of adverse underwriting. Upon receipt of his fraudulent claim, we realized that Mr. Blowhard's file was one of those that we hadn't filed the form for. So to protect ourselves, we had to let you dangle. We're in the clear now so you don't have to worry."

I began to think seriously about threatening to make this guy walk with a limp and then stopped before I spoke because he was either

---

[3] Changed to protect the criminally dull.
[4] Okay, Okay ... so I'm taking this too far! I swear the guy had a Russian accent though!

a) ex-KGB or b) an attorney. Frankly, I'm not sure which of the two bothered me more.

I spent thousands of dollars protecting my good name, I lost sleep many a night, and now they tell me it had nothing to do with me... that it was all about John Blowhard lying to see if he could scam me for greenmail. And it was about Big Box Insurance Company protecting itself from its own mistakes.

I joined F.A. Legal within a month after that fraudulent claim was filed against me. I realize now that, while more colorful than most, my story was far from unique. Many of you reading this have the same scars on your back. I'll tell you "The Rest of the Story," as Paul Harvey says, after Jerry tells you his story.

## F.A. Legal — The Beginning

How did F.A. Legal begin? Well, it all started back in 1989. I had sold my syndication companies and began providing consultation to the insurance and financial industries under a company called Higher Plateau. Higher Plateau provided due diligence and compliance oversight training for financial principals and certified continuing education for all financial professionals. We primarily taught litigation prevention and product due diligence and were fortunate because our curriculum was endorsed by many financial institutions nationwide.

We trained CPAs, compliance officers, financial advisors and broker-dealer principals. These financial professionals would enroll for two-and-a-half-day educational symposiums. For convenience, these symposiums were taught in various parts of the country and boasted certified instructors with specific expertise — including law. Attorneys would speak on various issues, one of which was how attendees could protect their practices. Interestingly, advisors kept asking us at the end of the conferences, "Where can we find an attorney?"

Now finding an attorney is like finding a cow in a cattle stampede. What they were really asking is, "Where can I find a good attorney who's qualified to represent me in this business?"

*I have a list of attorneys I'd like to put in a cattle stampede!*

That was the true question — and one that was tough to answer initially because there are so many legal nuances to the financial services business. Because this was such an important issue, in 1994, Higher Plateau began to include lawyer referral for attendees.

At that time, we also toyed with the idea of actually defending advisors by forming a professional association, designed to provide legal defense and consultation to the financial advisor. We felt that power in numbers would be a major benefit in this area. The need was apparent, so we dedicated two years of research to analyzing the market and refining the concept. Actuarially, the concept was researched from two different angles. At the same time, we conducted voluminous interviews and surveys with our attendees and other financial advisors. Because it was necessary to offer membership in all 50 states, we also devoted a lot of time to reviewing the various state regulations that govern legal associations to make sure we complied with them.

To make a long story short, Financial Advisors Legal Association was officially launched in 1999. It's now one of the fastest growing associations in the country and operates in all 50 states and Canada.

### What We Do

We're not rocket science; we're simply filling a need by providing legal defense, consultation and educational tools to individual financial professionals and broker-dealer firms. A quarterly newsletter and business resources are also part of the package. Our services are provided for an easily affordable annual membership fee.

Considering the cost of legal defense, our members receive tremendous economic benefit. After a small retainer, we defend our members against claims from clients and customers. This is a huge benefit because previously, an advisor was faced with the Hobbesian choice of paying $18,000 for legal representation to defend a $10,000 claim. Faced with such a choice, many would, regretfully and with grinding teeth, opt to pay the lesser amount and have a mark on their record for the rest of their life, even though they were innocent!

In addition to legal defense, F.A. Legal provides legal phone consultation and litigation prevention tools to members at no additional cost because we believe, wherever possible, in eliminating potential legal problems before they occur.

We expend a lot of energy and expertise on educating our members. For example, we created the *e*Defense Manager, which is a step-by-step tutorial on how a financial professional should set up his practice to enable him to prevail in the event of a legal attack. It was structured from over 1,000 interviews with financial advisors, similar to you, "D," who have experienced litigation and found out what worked and what didn't,what forms were missing, and what they should have done better.

Sadly, many of these interviews were with innocent advisors who have been unjustly penalized.

Bottom line: our *eDefense Manager* is a street-smart tutorial based on what you need to do with your clients from A-Z. It is a web-based tool that is updated in real time, so that when there are legislative changes, our members receive a "legislative flash." For example, when the Patriot Act was first introduced, there were a lot of compliance issues and systems that needed to be incorporated. We sent notices out to our members about what the Patriot Act was and how it would affect their practices and gave them a step-by-step system on how to implement it. This was done six months before the enforcement date. It is our mission to keep our members "ahead of the curve."

 *Believe me when I say I was perplexed about how to implement the Patriot Act and privacy laws simultaneously. F.A. Legal gave me a path to follow.*

We do this for selfish reasons because if one of our members is sued, we want them to be well prepared so that they'll prevail. Our research has shown that the majority of claims filed against financial advisors are fallacious, yet over 90 percent of those claims are settled because advisors either can't afford to defend themselves or were unprepared. Our legal phone consultation is a major benefit in this area. Because financial litigation demands specialized legal counsel, many advisors don't know where to start or who to call for help. Our members don't experience that problem because we can hook them up with qualified legal counsel within 48 hours or less.

Since F.A. Legal's inception, we have consistently tracked the increase in claims filed against financial professionals, looking back as far as the late '80s. We've determined that the average pace of complaints filed has increased by some 20 percent each year. The largest increase took place in the last 12 months, with over a 25 percent increase!

While I don't know if this pace will continue, I don't see it falling. We are also seeing a massive increase in legal defense costs. In 1999, when we first formed the Association, the average cost to defend a claim was $18,000. Today it's $42,000!

What's causing this acceleration? There are many reasons, but first and foremost is that lawyers are advertising, in all forms of media, for clients to sue their financial advisors. These lawyers are playing a numbers game because they know that the majority of financial advisors are either unprepared or will settle a claim for economic reasons, no matter how ludicrous the claim.

There are over 1,400 websites that advertise for clients to sue their financial advisors. This is compounded by billboard, TV and radio ads. This campaign has fermented a very bitter wine. Today, clients are looking to their financial advisor not just for advice, but also for blame. Forget fairness; litigation is now about economics and everyone is a victim.

No single category of advisor, be it insurance agents, brokers, CPAs, or fee-only planners, is exempt from this problem. If you're advising other people on financial issues — making recommendations and getting compensated — then you are a target! Some statistics show that financial advisors are the #1 target of litigation, even over doctors!

Today, you must be able to back up and prove, in arbitration or in court, what you say or recommend to a client. Litigation is emotional, and when things become emotional, objectivity pretty much goes out the window. During a litigious confrontation, emotion will trump objectivity every time. Unless you have provable, objective facts to override the emotion, you're in very hot water. In other words, the client will lie to get his money back.

 *As a one-time arbitrator for the AAA, I can assure you that clients will bring all kinds of erroneous calculations before arbitrators to support a claim. You're then at the mercy of the arbitrators and whether their prior experience gives them the tools to decipher those numbers correctly.*

And unless you can document your statements and recommendations, it doesn't make any difference what you say; it's impossible to prevail. Arbitrators, for example, have a tendency, just like juries, to "divide the baby," so to speak. They want to make everybody happy. Illegitimate claims, ludicrous claims are being settled that shouldn't be settled at all. These claims are going to arbitration just because the advisor either can't afford to defend them or has not properly documented his client relationship and planning recommendations. The advisor can't prove it so he settles — or worse yet, he's forced out of the business.

Needless to say, times have changed. The financial professional today lives in a different world than even three years ago. Today, they'd better be able to assert, document and defend their client recommendations or they will not prevail under litigious attack. The number one reason a financial professional will go bankrupt or be forced out of business is litigation.

I suspect that you, as a reader, are wondering, "Jerry, is there anything I can do to protect myself?"

I absolutely believe there are specific and definite steps you can take, and that's what our Association *is* all about. We've developed easy-to-use and extremely affordable systems that our members can use to protect themselves. Our *e*Defense Manager is the most comprehensive system available.

This simple step-by-step system is considered by many to be a "gold standard" system. The *e*Defense Manager gives advisors five easy-to-use modules that cover client evaluation, documentation, due diligence, communication, client education, and how to protect your financial practice. It gets into specifics and teaches you, for example, how to evaluate clients and when and how you should fire a client.

## The One Thing

I don't care if you're an insurance agent, fee-only planner, or whatever — you are one of the most litigious targets of any profession in North America! So with that said, The One Thing that a financial advisor needs to do is to document.

There is a common denominator that characterizes successful financial advisors with the lowest incidences of litigation. They document everything and annually reassess their clients' risk tolerance, along with their goals and objectives.

Whether you want to admit it or not, financial advisors are pretty much focused on sales and marketing. You have to acquire and retain clients and you can only do that through a marketing solicitation effort. However, like most sales people, financial advisors, as a group, don't document. You don't write things down. You don't keep track of the details of client meetings. You don't take notes.

 *And third, proactive advisors document every meeting, every phone call, every client interaction in a Client Relationship Management (CRM) software program.*

Additionally, the financial advisor has to perform diligent research into the various products and services he recommends. These recommendations require that you have a very strong intellectual side. Like doctors, you are required to continually educate yourselves in an ever-changing environment.

The difference is that doctors don't have to go through a marketing dance — but they do have to document. If you walk into a doctor's office, you'll see files and files that document every aspect of the patient (client). When a doctor interviews you, he's taking copious notes. He checks your file and checks it again. You'll be asked what your allergies are and what medications you're taking; these questions won't be asked just once, but probably three, four or more times.

 *I have had three fraudulent claims made against me. The only reason I prevailed was because I had files that were seven inches thick from documenting* everything!

Unlike doctors, financial advisors are not trained to document properly. Every financial advisor knows he needs to document better, but he often lacks the discipline to do it. To alleviate this problem, you need to transform yourself from a mindset of *needing* to document to *wanting* to document. We motivate our members through paranoia, case studies, and stories to get them to understand the critical importance of proper documentation. We focus on getting them to develop good habits. We do this through systems that are pretty much "brainless" for them to learn and to follow. Our focus is to get the financial advisor to *want* to document. Doctors do this habitually and so should you!

However, this is easier said than done.

There's a huge difference between *knowing that you need to take action and wanting to take action.* For example, years ago I knew that my wife and I needed long-term care insurance. But we didn't buy it back then because it wasn't important enough to us at the time. However, my mother-in-law recently went through back surgery and, unfortunately, came out of the surgery paralyzed from the waist down. Compounding her problem was the fact that she had let her long-term care insurance lapse just eight months prior to her surgery!

With her long-term care having to come out of our pockets, we experienced the consequences of *not taking action.* We went from knowing that we needed long-term care insurance to really wanting it! I looked at my wife and said, "We need this. I want to get this for us now!" Within 30 days we obtained long-term care insurance.

There's a huge mental transition from *need* to *want.* But when a person is motivated, this transition can come quickly. For many, motivation is stimulated by fear. Maybe a colleague gets sued or a client calls and threatens to sue. Maybe a regulator knocks on your door or the door of an advisor you know. Whatever it is, the move from *need* to *want* can be triggered quickly. My advice is to achieve some peace of mind by moving to a mindset of *wanting* to take action <u>now</u>.

Needless to say, joining F.A. Legal is a major first step. We can help you make this transition. You never know when a bad thing, like a car accident, cancer or a heart attack, will happen. Statistically, for a financial professional, you *will* be involved in a litigious attack; it's not a matter of *if*, but *when.*

Finally, I am asked all the time why litigation between advisors and clients is so venomous. Here are my observations.

To begin with, most people regard their financial information as highly confidential and personal. Some of the information a client will share with his financial advisor isn't even shared with his spouse. As an example, most people will share information about their sex lives and the personal intimate details of their marriage with 11 times more people than they will their financial affairs. So when a financial advisory relationship is broken, emotionally, it can be worse than a divorce.

In addition, clients get more emotional when they lose money than when they make money. At F.A. Legal, we see the emotion come out because your former client is thinking, "I trusted you with things I wouldn't trust with anybody. I told you what I make, I told you what my goals were, I told you all my aspirations, my fears, I told you how I wanted to educate my children, and look what you did to me!" In short, you get all the credit — and all the blame.

You must understand this from a client's emotional viewpoint. It's why you are the number one litigious target. It's why you must prepare. It's why our Association is growing. We are filling a need; a need that imparts peace of mind — a need that can protect your family — a need that can save your livelihood.

## "The Rest of the Story"

"D" Shannon: My (ex) client's wife-swapping story is true (although I'm a little fuzzy about the KGB part). F.A. Legal guided me step-by-step through the morass. Jerry himself gave me reassurance. I'd have to tell you that, to me, the most important benefit of their service was knowing that I was not alone.

In today's world, most broker-dealer attorneys have a very different agenda from yours. They're out to protect their client: the broker-dealer! Your innocence or guilt is not as important to them as their fiscal health.

Your errors and omissions (E&O) carrier also has a bottom-line mentality. Most times they make very disturbing calculations that are all about spending the least amount of money necessary to make it all go away.

You, on the other hand, want your good name protected. You live in the community where you practice. You go to church or synagogue there. Your children go to the local schools. In short, the agenda you have is justice and fair play. This *may* put you at odds with your broker-dealer and your E&O carrier, both of whose primary motives are monetary.

F.A. Legal, to me, did three things very well:

1. F.A. Legal helped me navigate the mess with the fallacious claim by the wife-swappers. I successfully beat that "greenmail" attempt thanks to their guidance and suggestions.

2. Once I successfully beat that fraudulent claim, I thoroughly plumbed their *e*Defense Manager and implemented it with my assistant. Their system helped me beat two other claims. While not as tawdry as the first claim, I prevailed in situations where my innocence was clear from the start. In fact, I almost begged the opposing side to hurry up and get to the "discovery" phase because I had such clear and compelling documentation.

3. Finally, and most importantly, my confidence was intact. Nothing bothered me as much in my years as an advisor as being accused of wrongdoing when I had done a great job for the client! I now know that nothing can stop the increased litigious nature of our society. However, I never lost sleep again. I never lost sleep because F.A. Legal's systems allowed me to have a demonstrable process that captured each conversation and documented each decision and implementation.

"Needless to say, I'll always be a member!"

**In summary:**

- Document everything — it does not take more time!

- Invest in systems — you'll be glad you did.

- Fire clients when necessary.

- Take your clients' financial and emotional pulse annually.

❖❖❖

**Jerry L. Reiter, CEO / Chairman**
**Financial Advisors Legal Association, Inc.**

**Jerry L. Reiter** has over two decades' experience in the financial services industry and related fields. His expertise covers the spectrum of investment structure, securities law and due diligence procedures related to the securities industry and investment programs.

Jerry began his career in oil and gas exploration and development. In 1983, Jerry sold his oil and gas companies and established a consulting company under the name Higher Plateau, Inc., which became an internationally recognized company specializing in certified continuing education, due diligence training, and contracted due diligence consulting to the financial community. Higher Plateau's continuing education certifications encompass the Certified Financial Planner (CFP) Board of Standards, National Association of State Boards of Accountancy (NASBA), National Association of Securities Dealers (NASD) and various other national and international financial professional advisory associations.

In 1996, Higher Plateau expanded to include attorney referral as part of its services to the financial community. In 1998, after training over 5000 financial professionals, Higher Plateau morphed into the Financial Advisors Legal Association, Inc. (F.A. Legal), a member-based organization offering legal referral, litigation prevention, certified continuing education and legal representation to the financial services community. F.A. Legal has become one of the fastest growing professional associations in North America.

Jerry has authored articles on the pertinent issues facing today's financial professional which have been published in *The Wall Street Journal, Financial Advisors Magazine, Registered Representative Magazine, Investment Advisor Magazine, Horse's Mouth, On Wall Street Magazine, Agent Media News, Advisors Edge Magazine (Canada)* and the *Dow Jones Newswire.* He is also routinely contracted as a keynote speaker for major events involving the financial community, including the Financial Planning Association, the National Association of Insurance and Financial Advisors, and the Society of Financial Service Professionals.

For more information about F.A. Legal, go to ***www.falegal.com*** or call 800-261-0633.

# Get a Life!

*By "D" Shannon*

I hadn't visited Boston in years. My first wife and I dated there, so I used to be very familiar with Logan Airport and the main arteries. But that was in 1986 and, 18 years later, I was clenching $3 for the toll collector in my teeth as I drove with one hand and gripped the MapQuest® directions in the other.

"Man, these people drive fast up here," I thought, as I slowly wound my way to the exurbs of Boston where George Kinder lives and works. An hour passed as the traffic slowed and the bright Fall day came alive that November mid-morning. Getting closer, I noticed the lingering Fall colors, stacked stone walls and pastoral byways punctuated with quaint barns. It all reminded me why I enjoyed New England so long ago.

I pulled onto the gravel drive to which George had directed me, crossed the train tracks, and found myself outside a collection of small camp cottages centered around George's home and surrounded by a lake. I gazed across this Thoreau-like setting and noticed a beaver dam nearby. The brisk clean air was invigorating, the pine straw under my feet was fragrant and the sun warmed me as I walked to the side of the house and knocked on George's door.

George's broad smile greeted me warmly as we began a fun, interesting and potentially life-altering interview.

❖❖❖

## The Road to Financial Planning

*"The mass of men lead lives of quiet desperation."*
A statement from *Walden*, by Henry David Thoreau

I was born in Wheeling, West Virginia with a middle-class back-ground. My dad was a small-town lawyer and my mom was a stay-at-home mom and a Christian teacher who became president of the Ohio Historical Society. We were not wealthy nor did we have inheritances or anything like that. My parents knew the value of a good education and worked hard so that their four sons could get good educations. I went to Harvard in the late 1960s and, while there, became interested in being an artist — specifically in writing poetry and painting. I also became fasci-nated with the world's religions.

After graduation, I took a couple of years to do meditative internal work and practice the world's major religions. I started with Christianity and then moved on to Judaism and then Sufism, Taoism, Hinduism, and Buddhism. I plumbed the meditative practices of each. Harvard was intellectual, but I was interested in the experience of these religions, in getting an understanding of the profound experiences they are known for — being born again, attaining Nirvana, ending suffering.

I dove into the practice of the various religions, practicing each tradition intensively for several months. I lived near where I am today in Littleton on a farm and I did a lot of writing and painting. I did spir-itual practice out in the fields of that farm for as much as six hours a day. That was what was profoundly important to me — that and my creative life.

One of the things I learned early on was I couldn't find anybody who was willing to pay me for my poetry or my prayers and meditation, so I had to come back and get a day job! Looking back, I see that I've come back to the same place, doing similar things here in Littleton 30 years later.

Having decided I needed to make some money, I went back to school for Accountancy and ended up with the bronze medal in Massachusetts for scoring third highest in the state CPA exam that year. I thought about joining a CPA firm but balked at it. Even then I feared a lack of integrity in the corners that were cut in accounting, and I didn't want to work 60 or 80 hours a week and not have a life.

So I started filing tax returns on my own in the mid-1970s. Clients came in with problems that I knew I had the solutions for somewhere in the 15 volumes of tax accounting manuals I had purchased! I became quite good at helping them with their taxes and started off charging less than H&R Block.

Then clients started asking me, "What do I invest in?"

I didn't know and suggested they find an advisor. The same client would come back the next year and tell me about limited partnerships they'd bought and how they were going to save on taxes. However, they were horrible investments! And the fees were atrocious! They had been sold a bill of goods.

I got ticked off that they were being taken advantage of so I started to read about financial planning. At roughly the same time, the National Association of Personal Financial Advisors (NAPFA), a group of fee-only advisors, was just getting off the ground. I joined NAPFA in 1984 when it was a year old or so and began to attend their conferences and educate myself about financial planning. That's how I evolved into a financial planner.

## How Life Planning Was Born

We've gone through three periods of crisis in the financial planning profession. The first period was 1973 to 1974 — the oil embargo shock. Word on the Street was that 90 percent of money managers gave up; just quit with the crash of the market in those years. Out of the frustration and disappointment of the mid-seventies something good was created: financial planning and the CFP designation were born.

*I love George's historical narrative on our evolution! Nowhere else have I found it so well explained!*

The second period of crisis was in the early '80s. In 1982 the market crashed again. Moreover, stocks had gone nowhere for 13 years. Just as in the mid-'70s, people were saying equities are dead. Capitalism is dead. And the market was awash with a plethora of limited partnerships.

There were horrible abuses by these so-called "tax shelters" with as much as 30 percent in upfront fees. Middle income people, typical clients for me in my tax practice at the time, were buying these partnerships. Then these partnerships began to die — they were totally going south. Once again something positive was created out of bad experiences; out of the limited partnership abuses, NAPFA and the fee-only movement were born.

At the end of the '90s came the third period of crisis. We had the Internet bubble burst, the Enron scandal, and all the other scandals that have come up from [New York Attorney General] Elliot Spitzer. Once again I think we saw a crisis of confidence in the advisory community.

I personally think that most people in the profession are really good people. When it's revealed to us, as good people and as advisors, that our products and our systems are failing, and that we as an industry are failing the consumer and the broader public, then I think a crisis of confidence occurs.

Good people question, "What is it we're doing here?"

And it becomes important to these same good people to then change what they're doing and in so doing, change the industry. Out of this third crisis, Life Planning was born.

Look, can I say something radical here? The reality is that we've been living in a truly profound economic crisis for decades. It's like the emperor with no clothes, because nobody's willing to speak about it. Our economic system is broken. It doesn't work. For 50 years the western world, the developed world, has produced, per-capita, three times the wealth of its grandparents; yet all the studies show that we're no happier than they were. If that is not an economic crisis, then I don't know what is. You might say it's a spiritual crisis. Well it's that, too. Or you might say it's a political crisis. No question. But it's not identified as a crisis of any of these kinds. Why not?

Because to acknowledge this crisis, our political leaders, our economic thinkers, and our spiritual figures would all have to admit that they have failed us — failed us abysmally.

There is one small group in America that takes this crisis seriously; one small group that's determined to do something about it. They call themselves Life Planners. They understand their province as being the place where money and meaning collide, where they intersect. And their intention is to restore meaning to our economic lives, one family at a time.

In 1994, Dick Wagner and I started discussing what we now call "Life Planning." We gave a talk to Certified Financial Planner (CFP®) designees about the soul of money. It drew such a strong response that we decided to arrange a weekend retreat at a YMCA camp in the Rocky Mountains the following year. We invited anyone we thought might be interested and 34 people showed up, not knowing what would be discussed or who would be there. We named it the Nazrudin Project after the Mullah Nazrudin, who came up with unconventional solutions to problems. From Nazrudin discussions I became inspired to write my book, *The Seven Stages of Money Maturity*, and began speaking more and more about Life Planning.

Just as financial planning was a reaction and movement in response to the mid-seventies crisis, and NAPFA was a reaction to the crazed partnership debacles, Life Planning has grown out of the current crisis of confidence born of the scandals and uncertain markets we've seen recently. I think that each of these developments is a movement toward greater trust, dignity and efficiency for consumers. Clients today are not paying as much but are getting more.

I think that 10 years from now, Life Planning will be the industry standard for how you do financial planning. It's growing geometrically right now.

I remember the first speech I gave to a large audience, just over 1,000 people, and it was at a big Institute of Certified Financial Planners (ICFP) conference. This was probably around 1999, just as *The Seven Stages of Money Maturity* was coming out. Bob Veres later wrote that he thought 10 percent of the audience walked out on me and that was probably accurate. For many people there, it was too far out on the edges.

Now what's happening is that we give our two-day *Seven Stages* workshop on a regular basis prior to the Financial Planning Association (FPA) convention each year and we're setting records every single year for attendance. And every year someone comes up to me and says, "You know, I was there in Dallas (at that ICFP conference) and I was one of those who walked out on you. Now I'm absolutely a true believer in this material."

In the early adoption phase of a new way of doing business, the old guard reacts strongly against it because it threatens their business model. That is true of Life Planning but in this particular situation, we're not only threatening their business model, we're talking about a much more personal way of working with a client. We are threatening their way of being.

 *Of course, Life Planning isn't a threat to advisors who have always delved deep into their clients' psyches just because they intuited that was the right thing to do. It's threatening to the quants and the wirehouses who are either unable to do it, or are always playing catch-up to the most recent, and better, ways of doing things.*

It's threatening because Life Planning is a relationship business, not a sales or information business — not your traditional "financial" business. We, as Life Planners, know who the client really is — and that's where the efficiency comes in. We create the kind of relationship where the client really trusts the advisor but also, where the advisor is subtle enough, sensitive enough, thoughtful enough in the questioning process to really understand what's profoundly at the heart of the client. What is it that's most important to accomplish in his or her life?

And what is profoundly threatening for some advisors is that you can't do this for others if you haven't asked these questions of yourself. You can't be a great financial planner without doing some inner work yourself — without challenging your own integrity to live your life's dream.

### What is Life Planning?

Life Planning addresses the fundamental question, "What are the most important things in your life that you want to accomplish?" It gives you the road map to get there.

In the financial planning culture, one of the things that my book led to was the realization that really everything, almost everything, has to do with money. We need the settings, the space and time, to be able to be the person that we want to be. So that's a money question — space and time.

Over the past 10 years I've spoken, written and taught about what I believe is the evolving science of transcending money — as the primary conversation planners have — to a discussion of the more sacred topic: our clients' very lives.

I've illustrated this science here in my Five Phase Life Planning Process.

### EVOKE

EVOKE™ is an acronym for the process I've have developed to put the client's primary focus, their Life's Dream, at the heart of their plan. But it's

## The 5 Phase Evoke™ Life Planning Process

| Phase | Planner | Relationship | Client |
|---|---|---|---|
| **E**xploration | Genuinely Interested | Creating a Bond | Anxious → Relaxed |
| **V**ision | Sensitive, Inspired | Bond Confirmed, Alignment | Receptive → Inspired |
| **O**bstacles | Challenging, Reassuring | Bond Tested, Alliance Deepens | Inspired → Anxious → Committed |
| **K**nowledge | Traditional Financial Planning | Partnership | Committed → Confident |
| **E**xecution | Coaching | Mutual Trust and Accountability | **Accomplished** |

THE KINDER EVOKE™ MODEL
© 2004 Kinder Institute of Life Planning

really about listening. How do we listen for what the client has gone through — for where they're excited, for where they're scared? How do we listen for that and then respond in an empathic way that helps the client feel connected with, like they're going forward with, something. So:

## E

"E" stands for Exploration. The "E" is really the first interview or the first segment of your interview process. In that first client meeting, what I'm training advisors primarily to do is to listen. Use real tough questions like, "Why are you here?" "What did you want to accomplish in our work together?" And (my personal favorite) "Anything else?"

Instead of looking down at a "fact finder" or financial profile questionnaire, you simply engage the clients as fascinating people and explore what's on their minds and in their hearts. We use open-ended questions and appreciations, never boxing a client in or narrowing their conceptions to simple "yes" or "no" responses. In this way we relax together, build a relationship, build trust.

## V

"V" is for Vision. Working with your client, you create a compelling vision of his or her future. My object in the "V" phase is to light their fire — their torch. I'm going to carry that torch for this client for the rest of my life. Every time they come in I'm going to relight their torch.

So I want to know, "What is their torch?" I get at this by asking three questions:

1. If you had all the money you need, what would change in your life? How would you live it?

2. Your doctor says you have a fatal disease that won't make you sick but it will kill you in five or 10 years. How would you change your life?

3. Your doctor tells you that you are going to die in 24 hours. What are you going to miss having done in your life? Who did you *not* get to be? What did you *not* get to do?

 *These questions really got me in my gut! I'd challenge you to take out pen and paper now and answer them!*

I've asked thousands of people these questions now. I've had certainly 500 or 600 people who've shared their answers personally with me. And it's rare — it's less than five percent of the population — who say, "Everything's perfect just the way it is."

Wow, less than five percent of the population! It tells me that everyone has something there that they mourn not having done! Whether we call it "a life of quiet desperation" or a "secret sorrow," there's something there for every one of us that we're missing.

And this is the profession, financial planning, that can make it happen — that brings it alive. So my advice is: listen, listen, and listen! Most people have not had the space to ever voice their "secret sorrow," to voice their innermost dream, to lay out what their greatest regret would be if they left this world tomorrow.

It's going to be what's deepest. It's going to be what they would most regret if they were to die within 24 hours. That thing, that secret sorrow, is what is keeping them from living a vital life, a fulfilled life, a life that is flourishing. Typically we find the deepest dreams fall into four categories: family, spirit, creativity, and place or community.

It could be not having written the novel they've dreamed of; it could be not having been there for the kids' birthdays and events; it could be not having quit the medical profession to become a rabbi; it could be not living more in nature. Any and all of these have come up. It's different for each of us and your job is to listen, to find out what this secret sorrow is and to carry this flame going forward for their life.

How do you light the fire for them? Right in that moment when you discover what's most profound for them, what their secret sorrow is, you say, "We're going to make this happen!"

You'll tell them that whatever is most profound for them will be the focus of their financial plan. Whatever they've just given you by way of revealing to you what's most profound to them, your job then becomes, "I'm going to make sure this happens! I'm going to use every trick I know in financial planning to help make it work. How does that sound to you?"

They are so moved by your connecting with them on this issue. And this is really where they needed to go with their financial plan. It's not about the second home. It's not about the retirement plan. It's that reconnection with their spouse and kids. It's about writing the great American novel or about becoming a rabbi. It's about whatever they would most regret not having done!

## O

The third phase is "O" — which stands for Obstacles. The third phase, in a way, is the most exciting and the most critical phase. In the second phase you've asked the three questions of your client. But what you really did was light their fire around what is most profound and deepest for them.

You take this profound dream of theirs, be it playing in a rock and roll band, or writing a novel, or simply spending more time with the kids. You probe some and discover that your client figures that they need 20 to 30 hours a week to dedicate to doing it, to making it happen.

The obstacle is that they're working 55 hours a week now, including their commute, with maybe five hours a week max that's left to spend on writing. They confide to you that they need another 20 hours a week to really have a go at this. Now they've got a much more challenging problem.

Remember, when we lit their fire in the vision phase, we said, "We're going to make this happen!"

As far as I'm concerned, this is the focus of the financial plan that you do for your client. The questions that we're addressing are classic financial planning questions.

Our primary focus in the '80s and early '90s was, "How do we accumulate the assets to get to retirement? What are the rates of return that we need to achieve to retire? How can we minimize the taxes to make all that happen?"

 *The budget is the primary focal point. I have thought about that statement a lot and agree wholeheartedly — cash flow baby, cash flow! It's all about cash flow!*

It's not that those issues go away. It's just that we're now looking at their life's dream which, in planning terms, argues for the budget to be a much more important focus than we've made it in the past. We ask the client, "What do you think the obstacles are to making this happen?"

You may find out that it's the spouse, for whatever reason, who's blocking the move to fewer hours working and more hours writing or playing music. You may find out that it's their employer who can't shift gears and be more flexible with their schedule. Who knows, it may be their parents or their kids. In reality, there may be conversations that are necessary, but it always comes back to the client.

So we ponder, "What is the reality here?" And as you inquire, you'll find that you are getting some of the psychological pieces, even though you're not going to be doing therapy. But you're also going to get, "How can I afford to write the novel? I need to be working a 35-hour week instead of a 55-hour week to be able to do that, but I need the 55-hour income!"

 *One of the most frequent objections to doing Life Planning is that we, as advisors, aren't qualified to be therapists. How is having a down-to-earth conversation with your client doing psychotherapy?*

When that happens, we bring out all of our financial planning tools, techniques and bag of tricks. This becomes very exciting as we go back and forth between two fundamental relationships to the client. One is around their anxieties — they're anxious about making the move — and the other is around their inspiration — they're inspired by our lighting the fire. As they get scared and think that living their ideal life is impossible, saying, "There is no way I can make that shift!," we empathize with their struggle and we keep relighting their fire! We keep coming back to, "This is really exciting, your dream of writing this novel!"

We already know about the novel in some way so, when they get anxious, we pick out what they're excited about and hold it back up for them. We've already thought with them about where they'll be writing it, what time of day, will they use a typewriter, laptop or handwrite it, and so on. As they get anxious, we inspire them with all the things they've envisioned that excite them. We're going back and forth between inspiring them and empathizing around where they get anxious. This is the emotional piece that cements your relationship.

Meanwhile we, as financial advisors, have in the back of our minds a dozen different scenarios as to how they might accomplish this. So you might be thinking, "Hmm, maybe we sell the house in Wellesley, MA and move back to St. Louis, MO where their family lives? That could work... yeah, the real estate values are so much higher here and the difference could provide a lot of cushion for this transition!"

Budget issues tend to be the obstacle, so we wrestle with all the different ways of saving money or saving time. We pepper them with suggestions and ideas. And it's not that we have the final idea. We don't know. What we're trying to do is to stimulate inside of them the vitality to go home and think about different alternatives themselves.

It's in the obstacle phase that we play with different scenarios using our traditional financial planning skills. The budget comes much more to the foreground than what we'd focused on previously as we wrestle with various scenarios that allow our client to light the fire of his dream. We alternate between empathy and excitement as we keep that fire lit and burning bright.

Confident in the process, we are alert, present, centered, courageous and exuberantly creative.

## K

"K" is for Knowledge. It's where we do the traditional financial planning work, the difference being that we know that what we're aiming for is what the client really wants. As Elvis Costello says, "Our aim is true."

## E

"E" stands for the Execution of the plan [comes after "D," who is one of the authors of this magnificent book]. All those problems advisors have in getting their clients to draft their wills or fund their insurance? They don't happen in Life Planning. If you know what the client wants and you design a plan guaranteed to deliver the life they've always dreamed of, how could you possibly have a problem with execution? All the problems of the past had to do with not knowing your client and then trying to sell someone you didn't know on something they didn't need, didn't understand, and didn't want.

### The One Thing

I believe that The One Thing that you, as a financial advisor, should be doing for your client is: *deliver their life.*

Deliver the life that they want, the life that they dream of living. Deliver that to them by working the financial planning numbers and wrestling with the obstacles in such a way that it produces that life. No one else can do this. Not a stockbroker, not a priest or a minister, not a therapist. The financial life planner is the only one with the skills to make this happen.

When the client comes in for an annual review, we focus on what's still missing in his or her life. What do they still not have that they want in their innermost heart? Then and only then do we look at the financial planning numbers: How are we going to get there? What's the timeframe? What are the time and money budget sacrifices that need to be made to make this happen?

Clients are much happier with this approach and much less suspicious of who you are as compared to, "I thought you told me I should get a 10 percent rate of return!" It's a much healthier relationship and the advisor feels it as much as the client does.

**In summary:** EVOKE

- E = Explore — Use an open ended conversation that builds trust and relationship.

- V = Vision — Light their fire and carry that torch of their life by asking these questions:

  1. If you had all the money you need, what would change in your life? How would you live it?

  2. Your doctor tells you that you have a fatal disease that will kill you in 5 or 10 years. What immediate changes would you implement in your life?

  3. Your doctor tells you that you are going to die in 24 hours. What are you going to miss having done in your life? Who did you not get to be? What did you not get to do?

- O = Obstacles — It is in the obstacle phase where we play with different scenarios using our traditional financial planning skills.

- K = Knowledge — It is this phase where we do the traditional financial planning work, the difference being that we now know that what we're aiming for is what the client really wants.

- E = Execution — Know what the client wants and design a plan guaranteed to deliver the life they always dreamed of!

 Nationally recognized as the father of the Life Planning movement, Harvard-educated **George Kinder** is the Founder of the Kinder Institute of Life Planning and Director of Life Planning at Abacus Wealth Partners. He has been a practicing financial planner and tax advisor for nearly thirty years.

Kinder's book, *The Seven Stages of Money Maturity*, is considered by many to be the seminal work in the burgeoning field of Life Planning. Available in most English-speaking countries, it is now available in German and Japanese editions.

In 1975, Kinder earned the Bronze Medal (third place) on the National Uniform Certified Public Accountant (CPA) exam in Massachusetts. In 1995 he co-founded "The Nazrudin Project," an influential think tank of national financial advisors dedicated to exploring the human and spiritual aspects of money and personal finance. In 2000, *Investment Advisor Magazine*, the largest circulation magazine for financial advisors, awarded Kinder its Portfolio Management Award, which is given to those who have "contributed significantly to the art and science of portfolio management."

In 2002, *Mutual Funds Magazine* listed Kinder as one of the "Top 100 Planners" in the country. *Investment Advisor* named Kinder one of the 25 most influential people in financial services in America in May 2003. In January 2005, based on a poll of their readership, *Financial Planning Magazine* named Kinder one of the six most influential financial planners in America. The other five planners had all studied with Kinder.

Kinder has appeared on radio and television programs across the country. His investment strategies have been featured in *The Wall Street Journal*, *The New York Times*, *Newsweek*, *Business Week*, *Fortune Magazine*, and other national publications. He has spoken at many national conferences, including Charles Schwab & Co., Inc., the International Association of Financial Planners, the Social Investment Forum, the Institute of Certified Financial Planners, the National Association of Personal Financial Advisors, and the Financial Planning Association.

His two-day *Seven Stages of Money Maturity*® seminars have been widely attended by financial advisors and the general public. His five-day *Training in Life Planning* has attracted many of the leaders in the financial planning industry. His website provides a list for the general public of hundreds of advisors across the globe who have studied with him and who do Life Planning.

Kinder currently divides his time between his offices in Massachusetts and Hawaii.

For more information, go to ***www.kinderinstitute.com*** or call (877) 7STAGES.

## DAVID J. DRUCKER

# The Virtual Financial Planning Firm

*By Dave Drucker*

## Success by Different Routes

"D" and I started in this industry at the same point and went in very different directions. It's somewhat important to understand this because the segment of the industry in which one spends most of his time usually colors his view of what it means to be successful and the practice management strategies that will get him there.

This is, by the way, a point that some coaches "get" and others don't. I believe it's each advisor's job to define "success" for him or herself. Success is a personal concept that ties directly into an individual's values. Some coaches realize this and take an approach that permits their advisor clients to achieve success as those advisors define it. Other coaches define success *for* the advisor and give him methods of achieving it. These imposed definitions, we have found, tend to be geared toward making more money, and the accompanying coaching methods geared to systems that provide more clients.

By contrast, alternative — more "holistic" — coaching approaches tend to help the advisor understand his values and his personal strengths so he can fashion a business that will serve those values; money is an important but secondary consideration. Ironically, these methods almost always *lead* to more money because the advisor, enlightened by the coaching he has received, creates his own new services, client relationship systems or operating methods that generate added revenue.

Getting back to my point, though, "D" and I met each other when each of us was feeling our way around the industry. I had already pledged allegiance to a strict fee-only approach to planning a) having had no sales training and distrusting large financial organizations, b) having worked for many years as a financial analyst in an advisory role to senior management types, c) wanting to use my MBA (in Finance) to run my own business, and d) believing that fee-only = professionalism. I still believe in that equation, by the way, although I don't believe one *must* be fee-only to be a professional.

Having established a successful, if very young, fee-only firm with a partner in Washington, D.C., I counseled "D" on our way of doing things. "D" tried to duplicate the fee-only way and found it difficult. I practiced in a large metropolitan area where plenty of wealthy and educated clients were beginning to learn of, appreciate and seek out fee-only services. "D" practiced in a small town where fee-only planning was virtually unheard of. Hence, I stayed with my approach, and "D" searched for a different way. I'll let "D" tell the rest of his story in his own chapter but, suffice it to say, after 20 years or so in the industry, we both achieved our personal definitions of success by somewhat different routes.

*Only if you count being broke and no food in the cupboard as "difficult." Hey! I like catsup on crackers!*

## What I've Learned: The Conversation

My "One Thing" is influenced by my experience as an advisor from 1981 to 2001 (when I sold my practice, all except for five clients); by what I've learned as a writer for the industry's top trade publications; and by what I discovered writing this book. The last piece, though most recent, was highly influential because rarely do any of us get to sit in front of so many thoughtful people within such a short period of time — people who are all focusing on the same question:

> *What is The One Thing advisors need to know to succeed*
> *in this profession we call financial planning?*

My goal as a young financial advisor, at the same time learning a profession and running a new business, was to develop standardized systems that would permit me to serve the client in a way he would perceive as customized. Standardization with a customized feel, that is. I decided that was the way both to make money and give clients what they wanted.

My systems dictated the initial course of the client relationship. I would gather the data required by my proprietary questionnaire, I'd manipulate it in my financial planning program of choice (usually a homegrown spreadsheet), and I'd make recommendations to my clients based upon my analysis. If I "clicked" with the clients, they'd stay around a long time and a relationship would grow.

Eventually, with my long-tenured clients, I'd get to know more about their personal likes, dislikes, values, and their pasts — information that, I found, allowed the relationships to go deeper and somehow contributed to clients staying with me longer. The longevity part of the equation was especially important to me since, towards the end of my advisory career, I was tiring of initiating new clients to my service. I no longer wanted to grow my business, but simply to work it. I just wanted to do the best job I could do for my 50 high net worth clients so they would stay with me forever and I wouldn't have to market for new ones.

What I would do differently now, as a result of all that I've learned working on this book, is to reverse the sequence of activities with clients. I would invest much time up front in what more than a few coaches call having the "Conversation," those deeper talks with our clients that give us the real information we need to meet their expectations and which, not coincidentally, bring us closer to them.

 *One of the things that I love about Dave is his integrity! Not many people have the courage to say "I'd do this different if I was doing it again!" That is a mark of wisdom!*

The Conversation takes time, so it isn't for every advisor. If your success strategy is to maximize client contact and, therefore, sales opportunities, the Conversation will probably be seen as excessive, unproductive, too touchy-feely, or all of the above. But the Conversation gives the client an incredible experience, probably more than he expected, and adds so much value that he'll likely view the fee you charge as more than reasonable.

What is the Conversation? The Conversation is the difference between saying, "I've constructed an estate plan for you that ensures you'll pay no estate taxes," and "When you die, the trust we've created for your mentally handicapped son will ensure he gets everything he needs without blocking his access to federal or state funds."

The Conversation is the difference between saying, "The investment portfolio I propose for you is equally weighted between equities and fixed income to match your risk tolerance and the rate of return needed to all but guarantee you a comfortable retirement," and "The investment portfolio I propose will provide you income to live on and working capital to start the new business you've always dreamed of."

The difference is that of preparing a competent plan that addresses the client's fundamental needs versus a plan based on a discovery of the client's *true* goals. One approach emphasizes money and the other, self, or very personal concerns, much like the orientations into which advisors divide themselves.

The two approaches have different economic effects, too. In the first scenario, a client will stay with you as long as you demonstrate competence and competitive investment returns. In the second scenario, the client is yours forever because you've touched him at a deep level and you've truly understood his needs the way no other advisor has before. The difference is in the degree of client turnover and its attendant costs. It's the reason why money-focused advisors must work with hundreds of clients, while self-focused advisors work with dozens.

## Client Selection

Client selection has a significant impact on success, too. My "ideal" client was usually a retired couple that fit the description of "The Millionaire Next Door" from the book of the same title by Thomas J. Stanley and William D. Danko (Pocket Books, 1996). These were payroll employees or small businessmen and women who had accumulated wealth in the $1-3 million range through hard work and modest spending. They were typically less than impressed with depreciating consumer goods or lavish homes. (Unlike clients of my own generation, they had no interest in luxury cars and other signs of conspicuous consumption.) They took their wealth seriously, but were willing to delegate its care to a trusted advisor. This profile reminded me of my own parents and, hence, I generally found we shared similar values and they were likable and easy to work with.

I was motivated by issues of self more than money. Money has always been important to me because I have a family to support and a "retirement" to prepare for (something no one could possibly be more keenly aware of than a financial advisor).

I decided to take my vision of how one might operate virtually to create a whole new business model for myself and the planning profession, to improve my own profitability and income, and to further strengthen client relationships so I would know my income was secure.

## The One Thing

So I guess I'd have to say that my One Thing has been to conceptualize and construct a Virtual Financial Planning Firm that has enabled me to live my preferred lifestyle, make good money, and earn the respect of my clients by providing them with a one-man, high touch financial management service. I'm not a Million Dollar Producer but, then, I'm not a producer; I'm an advisor.

For those who have no concept of what I'm talking about, you can short-cut your education by getting a copy of my book *Virtual Office Tools for a High Margin Practice* (Bloomberg Press, 2002) or a subscription to my newsletter *Virtual Office News* (*www.virtualofficenews.com*). Maybe a little more background will explain it better, though.

## My Background

After working alone for several years while earning my CFP, I joined with a partner and, eventually, a handful of employees to create the Washington, D.C. firm of Malgoire Drucker Inc. We worked 14 long years to build a stable base of high net worth clients paying us fixed retainer fees to oversee their every financial planning, investment management and, sometimes, personal need. This was no easy task because we insisted on taking the fee-only route.

One of the reasons so few people went this route, besides the lack of commissions with their attendant vision of getting rich quick once one discovers the secret to becoming a "top producer," is that there was no blueprint for this practice model. One joins a wirehouse or independent broker-dealer (again, aside from the commissions) because these organizations offer a turnkey business model. We had to figure out the fee-only model through trial and error.

Getting to a point of stability and continuous growth, which took almost ten years, was gratifying but taxing. As someone who has always prided himself on his organizational skills, I found as our client numbers grew rapidly that I was losing control of my time and life and unable to solve the puzzle of how to *regain* control. Part of this was my partnership, I discovered later — not my partner, per se — but the dynamics of partnerships, in general, which require that certain high-level decisions be unanimous.

## From D.C. to Albuquerque

At the 14-year point, and having then lived 47 of my 50 years in the Washington, D.C. area, I was also feeling stressed by my environment.

Washington in the '50s was almost a sleepy little town. Washington in the '90s was an overpopulated, polluted, ever-expanding, automobile-congested, overly humid, low-quality-of-life place to live; in my opinion, at least. I had to get out of there.

My family and I had vacationed four times during the '90s in the Southwest and, on our last visit, found a house and bought it. I went back home, told my partner I loved her but couldn't continue in the partnership for personal reasons, and we set about designing a plan to carefully extract me from the practice without upsetting anyone's clients or income.

I would keep my D.C.–area clients (roughly half the firm's clients) and pay my partner a certain sum of money for two years to help support our staff who, in turn, would continue to support me, from afar. Meanwhile, my partner would add enough new clients to her side of the ledger to provide the revenue to eventually support the entire staff on her own. By then, I would presumably have a new system of support as well.

The plan worked beautifully. In fact, it became the beginning of my realization that a virtual financial planning firm — a firm with no employees, only outsourced relationships; a firm with no paper, only digitally scanned images; and a firm relying as much as possible on the convenience of email and the Internet to perform all of its critical functions — was possible. Thus was born the concept of the virtual office, for me, at least. (I didn't dream up the idea. Others were using the same tools as I to create very similar operations. I was just one of the first people to write about it.)

My family and I moved to Albuquerque, a place much like the sleepy little town D.C. once was, replete with laid-back lifestyle, a friendly new culture to learn about and enjoy, a change of scenery, 330 days a year of sunshine, and intersections that never took more than one red light to get through. (Native Albuquerqueans complain of the heavy growth that's taken place over the years, and what they now consider to be traffic congestion. They have absolutely no idea how good they've got it.)

### A New Concept Emerges

My options, business wise, were to recreate the "traditional" style of firm I had in the D.C. area, or to expand on this phenomenon of virtual (non-payroll) workers. I chose the latter. Ever since adopting my daughter and working from home so I could care for her in her infancy, I had warmed to the notion of working in sweatpants and frayed T-shirts with a dog or two by my side (and no employees). And so my virtual financial planning firm came closer to perfection.

My next job was to scan my many files onto my hard drive and eliminate the paper. Then I could retrieve many years' worth of client data in seconds rather than minutes or hours. I got an 800 number, a website and reliable email server, and my far-flung clients could reach me anytime. In fact, they actually had an easier time getting a hold of me 2,000 miles away then they did when I was 20 minutes away.

I was also discovering that, not only was this business model terribly convenient, allowing me freedoms on the job I'd never before experienced, but it was economical, too. The virtual assistant I hired to do my administrative work, the outsource firm I hired to run Centerpiece, the compliance expert I hired to re-do my ADV — all were far less expensive than employees because I only paid for the time I used.

With all of these discoveries, the concept of an entirely new, lean and mean, operating entity emerged. From that came a book, and from the book came a newsletter. And now we've got an entire industry that's either making similar conversations or looking seriously at whether they should do so.

So, am I saying The One Thing every advisor must do to succeed is to run a virtual office? Essentially, yes. There are a lot of different *ways* to operate virtually so I'm not advocating a strict set of systems. Sole proprietors tend to do it differently from 10- or 20-person advisory firms. But do I think everyone should maximize their efficiency by using *some* combination of virtual tools and techniques? Absolutely. I'm as convinced of that as Bill Bachrach is that you must be a Trusted Advisor, or that Dan Sullivan is that you must find your Unique Ability.

## A Dysfunctional Culture

The U.S. brokerage industry, with its combining in one entity the manufacturing of investment products, the distribution of those products, and advice on product selection, defined the financial planning industry for its first 10 or 20 years of existence (depending upon the year one considers it to have begun). This has been problematic for reasons most clearly expounded by Harold W. Gourgues, Jr. who, during most of the '80s published a particularly insightful monthly newsletter for financial advisors — *The Gourgues Report.*

Gourgues, a former broker, explained the failure of the brokerage industry to provide real financial advice through his belief that the investment manufacturing, distribution, and advisory functions must be separate in order for each function to have integrity.

That this is true in the brokerage industry isn't news to anyone except, possibly, consumers. Those working in the financial services industry understand that brokers, as advisors, are compromised by the requirement that they sell their employers' products and other inventory whether or not such products meet their clients' needs.

Again, remember that this is the paradigm with which the financial planning industry began. Why is it significant? Because, for advice to have integrity, it must serve the interests of the advisor only if, at the same time, it serves the interests of the client. Brokers, by definition of the institutional rules to which they are bound, are incapable of providing advice with a high level of integrity. So financial planning, as a real profession, had to move away from the stockbroker paradigm.

## The Beginnings of a True Profession

And, fortunately, it did. The fee-only planning industry took root in the early '80s and helped define the professional advisor and the advisory industry by showing consumers and all manner of financial advisors and brokers that real planning could be done with significantly fewer conflicts between the advisor and his client. Although fee-only planners remain a small percentage of the total advisor industry, they have helped grow the profession and move a large segment of the industry in a more professional direction.

Those brokers who, over the past 25 years, decided they wanted to be the "real deal," have migrated out of brokerage firms to independent broker-dealers, a segment of the industry that has seen geometric growth partly — and ironically — attributable to the fee-only movement.

So what makes up the financial services industry today are planners representing all of these stages in the historical evolution of the planning industry. On a spectrum of compensation, advisors range from strictly fee-only (deriving income only from clients, never from products) to fee-based planners (deriving income from both) to commissioned wirehouse representatives.

But what the coaches in this book are telling us is that compensation doesn't matter. By their programs and systems and philosophies, they are telling us (whether they all realize it or not) that the spectrum is defined by advisors' values and priorities, which are clearly reflected in their regard for clients.

At one end are those advisors for whom clients would be a total nuisance if they weren't the ones with the cash. At the other end are those advisors who so revere their clients they feel it's a crime to make a decent living serving them. In the middle of the spectrum is where the profession lives and grows, where the advisor knows he must establish a relationship of mutual respect with his client to achieve his definition of success — whatever it might be.

*I loved it when Deena Katz, exasperated, said,
"When are we going to move past the compensation
conversation?" Dave points this out and I echo it!
Let's get over it!*

## Coaching and Strategic Perspectives

The best process by which to establish mutual respect with one's clients and build one's business isn't something on which coaches, consultants and visionaries readily agree. As far as I can see, the advisor must choose between two possible perspectives to find the right coach, and those are "money" and "self."

If money is the starting point, the advisor's main priority is to maximize his income and he's willing to do whatever is necessary to make that happen: work long hours, work with almost any client, and work in any location that gives him access to clients.

If self is the starting point, the advisor's main priority is to discover his unique ability and personal values (to borrow concepts from Dan Sullivan, George Kinder and others in this book). With this knowledge, the advisor can grow a business in accord with his skills and values, designed to enhance both his job satisfaction and the value he can add to the client's experience.

- **Money**

The advisor adopting a money perspective is often younger, working in an environment in which he is referred to as a "producer," and may or may not believe that strong client relationships are central to his goal of maximizing income. This advisor is less concerned with finding a niche or creating a unique advisory proposition than he is with becoming a top producer within his chosen environment (usually a wirehouse, a national branded institution such as Edward Jones or, in some cases, an independent broker-dealer). He believes a system exists to double, triple or quadruple his income, if he could just find the coach to whom that system belongs.

So systems are what coaches catering to the money-focused advisor tend to provide: systems for marketing and referrals, for closing clients, and for maximizing the advisor's opportunity to sell products and services to clients. These may take the form of frequent drip-marketing campaigns or getting in front of clients as often as possible if that's when sales primarily occur.

But where *do* clients fit into the equation for these advisors? We said earlier that mutual respect between the advisor and client is necessary for the advisor to be successful, but what does that mutual respect look like in the case of the money-focused advisor? Very simply, the client must respect the advisor's knowledge, his time, and his ability to improve his client's financial life. The advisor must respect the trust the client has placed in him, as well as the client's need for unique solutions and real planning, not the product du jour that so many advisors who work primarily in transaction-based relationships foist on their clients.

Does this advisor derive anything from his job besides money? As a byproduct, and particularly if he enjoys the people aspect of his work, he may form close relationships with some of his clients which will enhance his enjoyment of his work. But doing so isn't a prerequisite to maximizing income.

- **Self**

The advisor adopting a self perspective is often a bit older, calls himself an "advisor," and believes his clients' needs must be the focal point of his planning efforts. While income is important to this advisor, it is a byproduct of his efforts, not the focus of his business strategy.

This advisor is likely to seek out a coach who will help him find his strengths, fashion his business, and characterize his "ideal" clients in concert with those strengths. Likely to be the fee-based representative of an independent broker-dealer or an independent Registered Investment Advisor (RIA), this advisor seeks a coach who will guide him to self-discovery and, with it, greater job satisfaction and improved client services.

Systems catering to this advisor tend not to be the operating systems so eagerly sought by the income-focused advisor, but exercises that make the self-focused advisor think in new ways about what he offers clients that is uniquely his own. Because this advisor is more likely to earn fee income, client meetings aren't sales opportunities as much as they are the means to help clients discover their own values. By crafting a financial plan that honors the client's values, this advisor brings the client closer to his dreams in a way the money-focused advisor may never be able to.

The client's respect for this advisor is a direct result of what the advisor has helped him achieve, which is just as likely to include personal growth as it is enhanced financial well-being. The advisor respects the client as a person with whom he has bonded due to a sharing of values and life principles.

Does this advisor derive anything from his job besides self-discovery? Ironically, advisors who achieve personal growth through self-directed coaching strategies also achieve higher income — often much higher income — say the coaches to these advisors.

## Who's Who and Who's Best?

Which type of coach is better, again, is a function of your definition of success. Which of these approaches "speaks" to you? Are you young, perhaps single, comfortably beyond "rookie" producer status, eager to move "to the next level," enamored with the material signs of success, someone who enjoys working with clients but who enjoys the paycheck it brings you even more? Sure, this is a gross stereotype but, if all or most of it fits, then you should probably be taking advice from those with marketing and operating systems that can give you a quick boost in income.

If you've been in the business a while, have your own company, make good money (although more wouldn't hurt), believe your clients are wonderful — in fact, your greatest source of work-related satisfaction — and you feel tremendous gratification from making a difference in their lives beyond simply straightening out their finances, then you probably need to be listening to a self-directed coach, consultant or visionary.

Which coaches are which? You'll find the answer in this book.

## Self or Money?

So what's my focus — self or money? It's both, actually. I believe in the old-fashioned capitalistic notion that one profits from business when he anticipates and satisfies the demands of his would-be customers. I anticipated that clients would want fee-only planning at a time when the notion of providing investment advice on anything but a commissioned basis was considered lunacy. I developed systems to provide high-touch service and advice so efficiently that I could compete with anyone. And I used those systems to enhance my life, to relocate my family from a high-stress, high-cost area of the country to one that meshed naturally with who we are. Along the way, I created a financial planning business that served all my financial and personal needs.

Ultimately, I sold that business in 2001. Remember, sole practitioner practices — according to many experts — have no value. Yet I sold mine for almost three times what commissioned advisors (and most CPAs, for that matter) are able to get for their books/practices.

Am I wealthy? No, merely comfortable. I must still work, which is fine, because I've built a new business that pays me well to do the things I love, including participating in new ventures as they emerge with friends and industry partners. Being self-employed and doing what you love and getting paid for it — that's my definition of success.

**In summary:**

- Define your vision of success.

- Understand the difference between working from the perspective of money vs. the perspective of self.

- Integrate systems that deliver personal service and advice efficiently.

- Anticipate and satisfy the needs of your clients.

- Use virtual office systems to improve profitability and to increase compensation and leisure time.

**David J. Drucker, MBA, CFP°** is the co-author of *Virtual Office Tools for a High-Margin Practice: How Client-Centered Financial Advisors Can Cut Paperwork, Overhead, and Wasted Hours* (Bloomberg Press, 2002), and editor of the monthly newsletter *Virtual Office News*. He is also the co-author of *The Tools & Techniques of Practice Management*, released in December 2004 by The National Underwriter Company.

Drucker writes on practice management issues for other professional advisors as a contributor to *Bloomberg Wealth Manager, Financial Planning, Research*, and *Financial Advisor* magazines, and as a monthly columnist for both the ***MorningstarAdvisor.com*** website and the *NAPFA Advisor*. Drucker is a member of the American Society of Journalists and Authors, serving on its finance committee, and a member of the American Institute of Certified Public Accountants' Personal Financial Planning Section Editorial Advisory Board. He also serves on the Rydex Funds' Skip Viragh Award Advisory Board.

In addition to his writing, Drucker is a fee-only financial advisor who started his own advisory firm in the Washington, D.C. area in 1981 after working as a financial analyst in government and private industry for over ten years. Drucker still manages the financial affairs of a limited number of high net worth clients as President of Sunset Financial Management, Inc., an Albuquerque, New Mexico state-registered advisory firm.

A principal in the firm of Practice Merger Consultants, Ltd. (***www.practice mergers.com***), Drucker helps other advisors prepare their practices for merger and/or acquisition. This includes helping them identify and negotiate with potential, well-matched merger/acquisition candidates, assisting them in structuring merger/acquisition contract terms, and showing them how to use strategic technology to improve the profitability of their merged entity.

Drucker is a member of the Financial Planning Association and the National Association of Personal Financial Advisors (NAPFA), and has served in a variety of NAPFA regional board member and conference planning roles during his many years of membership. He was named by the readers of *Financial Planning* magazine to its 2003 list of "Movers, Shakers & Decision-Makers," and by *Worth* magazine as one of the Best Financial Advisors in the U.S. every year from the beginning of the *Worth* survey in 1994 through its 2001 listings when Drucker cut back his financial planning activities. In May 1996, he was given the NAPFA Distinguished Service Award for his contributions to the fee-only financial planning community. He is the original author of INTEGRATE financial planning software used by him and other financial advisors nationwide, now developed and distributed by PlanWare, Inc.

Also a virtual office consultant, Drucker shows other financial advisors how to replace traditional, inefficient office systems with virtual office systems (outsourcing, paperless office technology and other virtual tools) to improve profitability and increase the owner's compensation and leisure time.

Drucker's community service activities include his weekly volunteer work with the Animal Humane Association of New Mexico's (AHANM) Junior Humane program for children ages eight through 18, for which he received distinguished service awards in 2001 and 2002. In 2003, he was recognized by Helping Everyone Reach Out in Community Service (H.E.R.O.I.C.S.) for his volunteer efforts with AHANM. Drucker is also a volunteer worker with "Project Second Chance," a joint program of the Animal Humane Association and the New Mexico Youth Diagnostic and Development Center, in which youth offenders are made responsible for the care of shelter dogs to promote the rehabilitation and growth of both species.

Certified Financial Planner® is a federally registered mark of the Certified Financial Planner Board of Standards, Inc.

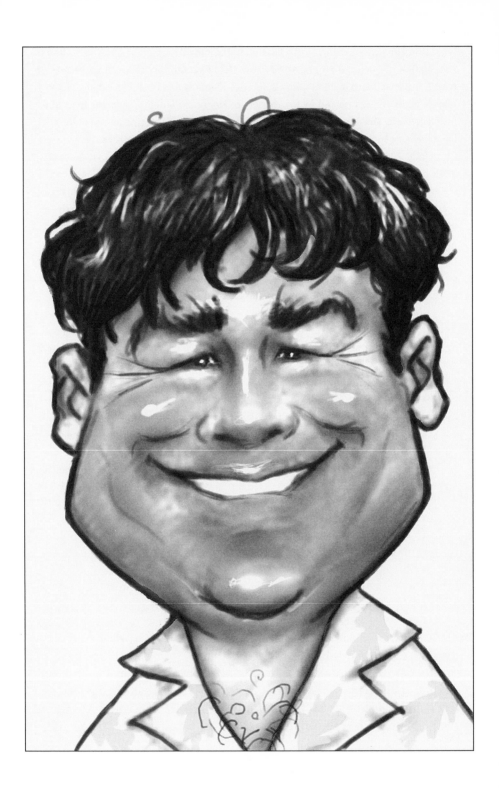

# "D" SHANNON

# Never Forget

*By "D" Shannon*

*When you come to a fork in the road...Take it!*
*Yogi Berra*

I am writing my chapter during the Christmas holidays. I am simultaneously trying to refinance my farm, remodel my garage, fight a "paperclip" war with the guy who bought my advisory business, and shepherd five children and a semi-crazed wife through the holidays. It's Christmas Eve, I've had a total of 30 minutes' sleep, and I have zero money in my checking account. I'm not in a bad mood; not at all!

Well, maybe an intense mood. More accurately, I want to make someone walk with a limp! Believe me when I say that I have a "naughty and nice" list and I'm checking it twice... a minute!

Now, if you don't know much about me (or haven't divined this from my previous writing), I need to warn you — I am irreverent, sharp-tongued and rarely mince words!

So here's the Compliance General's warning: Caution! Reading this chapter may be injurious to your mental health! You may begin to ask too many questions, you may become a skeptic, and you may (and I say *may*) begin to laugh out loud at some of the absurdities in the daily life of a financial advisor as a direct result of reading the rest of this chapter.

So stop and ask yourself: is it worth the risk?

Do you really want to become an independent thinker? Are you willing to question what you've been told are the tenets of faith as an advisor? Are you willing to start anew with a fresh sheet of paper and stop making a living and instead, make a *life*?

If your answer is "No!," then put down the book, back away from it and call the thought disposal unit from your compliance department.

However, if you have a glimmer of "Yes!" welling up inside you, then read on.

## Let Me Back Up Some

Many of you don't know who "D" Shannon is or where he's come from. Let me tell you briefly.

I am you.

More accurately, I have done what so many of you reading this book do. I have been a fee-only planner in NAPFA. I have sold life insurance and qualified for the MDRT. I have run leads for health insurance. I have been a "captive" producer. I have been an independent. I have been one of the top producers for the largest independent broker-dealer.

I have had clients complain about me and have lost sleep over it. I have held the hand of a dying client while sitting on the edge of her bed. I have wept with clients when they lost a child. I have laughed and danced at a client's child's wedding. I spent hour after hour calling my clients in the immediate aftermath of 9/11. And I have lain awake at night wondering how I was going to make the next day's payroll. I, dear reader, am you.

I think it would, therefore, be instructive to tell you how I came to this business in the first place:

I had my first brush with financial services when I was four years old. It was actually my fourth birthday and like any other red-blooded boy, I was fixated on two things that cold February day: Playing in the snow and my birthday party! I paid little attention to the man who sat in the living room with my parents, talking over coffee.

Mercifully he soon left, but with an angry look on his face. Then we got down to the important stuff — chocolate cake and party hats! To this day I remember my Dad lighting sparklers and putting them into the snow fort he'd made for me that afternoon.

I remember it so well because it is the last memory I have of my Dad. He left the next morning for someplace he and my mother had never heard of before he got his orders: Vietnam. My father was a chopper pilot in the 114th Aviation Company. He arrived in country on March 10th. He was dead by March 15th.

The man in the living room had been a life insurance salesman my father had sought out on receipt of his orders. My father really wanted to know that his young family would be okay if something happened to him. Dad had asked to take out, my mother told me later, a $100,000 life insurance policy. That was big money in 1964!

The reason the man in the living room was angry was that my Dad had taken his physical and passed, but hesitated about taking the whole life policy. My father balked at paying $97 a month for the policy when he only made $337 a month as a First Lieutenant. Who could blame him for being unwilling to pay nearly a third of his salary for insurance? So Dad didn't buy it.

What I now know, based on what my Mom tells me, is that the insurance agent never told my Dad that he could have term insurance and convert it to whole life later when he made more money. I'll never know what a positive difference that policy would have made in our lives.

My second brush with financial services was more painful because I was more cognizant of the consequences of bad advice. I returned home from military service honorably discharged because of a blown knee. My dreams of serving my country and being a pilot like my Dad and grandfather were gone. When I came back home I noticed that my grandfather's behavior was, well, strange.

Along with my mother and grandmother, Papa (my grandfather) had practically raised me. My grandparents' home in Lynchburg, Virginia was "home" to me. So when I returned home in 1984 I noticed Papa's peculiar behavior. For example, he was blowing the leaves with his electric leaf blower. Now that's not so weird — but blowing to one side, then back across, then back to the other, then back again for hour upon hour... well, that's pretty unusual.

Another thing: Papa was frugal — he used to cackle that he was "tight as bark on a tree." So I was surprised to see him hand a waitress his wallet in a restaurant and tell her, "Just take whatever you want!"

Papa could no longer tell a dollar bill from a ten.

This went on for nearly a year. Finally, in 1985, I convinced my grandmother to let me take Papa for a physical. I sat in the waiting room reading a *Look* magazine from 1953. I looked up to see the doctor standing over me.

"Mr. Shannon?" he asked as I nodded. "Can I talk with you back in my office?"

After we settled into his office he continued. "Mr. Shannon, I can't tell you for sure, but I think I know what's happening with your grandfather. I've never seen this before, but I believe he has something quite rare called Alzheimer's disease."

The world seemed to end in that moment.

I hope you have never had this sort of discussion. I really don't remember much of what else he said. Frankly, I don't know how I drove Papa and myself home.

Stunned, shocked, numb… all describe what my grandmother and mother and I felt. We didn't know what Alzheimer's was. In 1985, Alzheimer's was not a commonly known affliction — there were no support groups, no caregiver training, no literature, nothing, nada, zip, zilch, zero! We struggled initially to figure out what this meant. After all, he *looked* healthy. He still played a wicked golf game, regularly shooting sub-par. He could drive his car and at times seemed perfectly fine.

And yet he wasn't.

So began the second brush with financial services. To make a long story short, Papa's accountant, his banker, his broker, his lawyer, and his company's controller all drew blanks when we asked for advice. They simply wanted to transact, to do taxes, to be left alone. I began trying to find books, magazines, *anything* that would offer us a clue about how to help my grandparents through this gathering storm.

I started reading *Money* magazine. It simply left me feeling empty because I wasn't a ca-billionaire like the smarmy couple on the cover. I took an adult education course in financial planning; it was better than nothing but still, frankly, shallow. I started night school in the local college evening MBA program and found a part-time professor standing at the front of the room reading from the text in a monotonous droning tone.

Nothing helped.

I applied for full-time MBA programs within a three-hour drive of my grandparents' house. I got into Duke University's Fuqua School of Business, the University of Virginia's Darden, and Wake Forest's relatively new Babcock School. I couldn't afford Duke, UVA had lost my application, and Wake offered me a fellowship. Simple decision: Wake Forest, here I come!

The first year in a top MBA program is rigorous enough. Mine was tougher because I left every Friday afternoon at the end of classes and drove three hours back to Lynchburg, returning Monday morning at 5 a.m. to make 8:30 classes. I felt my full-time job was to support my grandparents and my part-time job was studying.

In my second year, as a result of Papa's growing anger and depression, he had hit my grandmother and knocked out two of her front teeth. Quickly conferring with my Mom, she and I decided, over my grandmother's objections, that we had to place my grandfather in a facility. Within a week we identified one, made the arrangements, and began the process of having my grandfather declared incompetent.

The worst day was the day that I helped Papa quietly into his Oldsmobile. I took his urine-soaked Lazy Boy and strapped it into the open trunk. He didn't know how to talk anymore but as I drove him away from his home, tears streamed down his face because he knew... he knew he was never going back home.

My grandmother was so angry with my mother and me for taking him away from her that she rarely spoke to me again.

My grandfather's business partners in his industrial distribution company manipulated my grandmother into taking pennies on the dollar for his share of the company. She accepted $187,000 for what I now believe was worth $1.1 million.

My grandfather lived five more years in the facility. My mother strongly urged me to stop going to see him in the last few years so that I'd remember him for the robust little man he had been. During the last year of his life, my grandmother lived on $198 a month.

### What does all of this have to do with your reading "The One Thing"?

It's quite simple. I never forgot.

I never forgot what it felt like when my grandmother asked me to go to the bank[1] and find out how much money we had. I'll never forget the look on her face when I told her it must be the wrong bank because we didn't have a fraction of what she thought.

I never forgot what it felt like to be powerless to help the people I loved so much because of the lack of money.

I never forgot what it felt like as a four-year-old to watch as movers whisked you and your things away from your home because there was no money with your Dad dead.

 *I believe the best advisors are those whose personal experiences drove them to do this work. My own story is not as dire as "D's," though my parents did grow up in the depression and lost most everything they'd accumulated up to that point in their lives.*

I never forgot any of that every time I sat down with a client over the 16 years I practiced as an advisor.

---

[1] My grandmother had never written a check in her life until this point and had never dealt with their money.

I walked out of my MBA program with my diploma and quite literally went to the 4th[2] NAPFA National conference the same day. On the day the conference ended, I flew back to Winston-Salem, NC, packed, and drove to Portland, Maine to set up a fee-only planning business with no contacts and only a credit card for money.

And because I never forgot, I kept going even while I struggled. I failed miserably as a fee-only planner, but I kept going.[3]

I signed up to be a telemarketer for LL Bean after all my clients quit in the wake of the New England banking debacle of 1989. But I stopped at the front door, turned around and kept going — because I never forgot.

When I struggled as a life insurance agent I kept going because I never forgot the look in my grandfather's eyes as I left him the last time I saw him.

When my general agent told me, "There's a little larceny in every sale," I never forgot. I remembered the hushed conversations about my grandfather in the kitchen with my Mom and grandmother about what we were going to do and, somehow, a "little larceny" never factored into our plans.

I never forgot. Please, I beg you, never forget either.

## The One Thing

I have attended countless financial advisory conferences, sales congresses, sales meetings, motivational talks, etc., etc. Since 1988 I have heard the following major themes discussed at each:

1. Product features and benefits

2. Financial planning techniques

3. Sales training

4. And more and more compliance "driver ed" lectures

These may be important topics; they're just not the *most* important topics! That's why I (and I suspect, you) have learned as much in the hallways of these meetings as I have inside the conference rooms.

Oh sure, an exciting speaker comes in as a keynoter and gives us the "big picture;" but frankly, in 16 years, I've heard little that has changed my clients' lives. The few exceptions are the people who are included in this book.

---

[2] I think it was the 4th — I'm sure one of you folks in NAPFA will correct me if I am wrong.
[3] Failure is when all you have to eat are potatoes and you run out of butter and salt.

The people Dave and I invited here have, at times, stirred the pot. They zigged when the world zagged. Tell me George Kinder doesn't resonate with people, even though he initially alienated some. Try to convince me that Dan Sullivan doesn't possess one of the clearest minds about where our industry is and where it's going!

It's rare that you'll find people with the integrity to discuss their own business, warts and all, like Deena Katz. I could name each of our participants with many a redeeming quality that sets them apart from the norm. I'd wager that you'd find their rooms packed if one of our participants was speaking at a conference and the other room featured the topic, "Estate Planning: Boom or Bust?"

Simply put, Dave and I asked these people to become involved in this project because they think, write and speak about topics *exclusive of* the aforementioned four topics.

So what is my One Thing? It's **V6**.

What the heck is **V6**?

In 1994 I was at lunch with a really nice fellow who was the regional rep for a life insurance and annuity company. His name is "Tom" and he's a class act. Tom asked me, "How do you seem to do this (financial advisory work) so easily, when so many seem to struggle?"[4]

I thought about it for a second and took the paper napkin from my lap and wrote down the following list:

1. Product knowledge

2. Financial planning skills

3. Sales skills

4. Marketing

5. "Get your head on straight!"

I turned it around to Tom and began to explain. "Tom, I've watched what the 'Big Box'[5] firms I've worked for, and with, have spent their money on to train me. I've also read what they've told me their 'mission' is. They ain't the same thing."

I continued. "Tom, these are the priorities, in order, of Big Box's values, as witnessed by the time, effort and energy they put into training their sales force. It doesn't matter whether you're captive, independent or fee-only; it's still the same.

---

[4] Success is a relative term. At that time I was successful because my rent was mostly on time and I then ate macaroni and cheese and cube steak instead of the aforementioned potatoes without salt or butter.

[5] 'Big Box" is my current term of art for all the large financial services firms.

"Their mission statement usually has some mush words that sound good about caring deeply about their public and that their people are their greatest resource. Horse-feathers![6]" I said with passion. "Do we need products — yep! Is financial planning important — yep! Tom, these just aren't *the* most important things!" I continued.

"Don't get me wrong, Tom," I said as I pointed with my pen at each item, one at a time. "The people at these Big Box firms are some of the best I know. But I don't think that any of my clients ever fall asleep thinking, "Gee, I sure hope "D" sells me an L-98 whole life policy tomorrow!'

"Now, Tom, what I found by luck or by pluck was that the actual order of what's important for an advisor can be found by flipping this list upside down," which I did by turning the napkin upside down for him.

"Watch this," I said.

I then wrote a different list:

1. Head on straight

2. Marketing system

3. Sales conversation

4. Financial planning skills

5. Product knowledge

"These priorities are in the exact opposite order, Tom, and are what top advisors do that separates them from everyone else," I said.

Continuing, I told Tom, "The best advisors know that the number one thing they need to do is to be passionate, purposeful and congruent about their vocation. An advisor must absolutely believe that he or she creates tremendous value in the lives of his or her clients and, in that process, creates tremendous value for himself and his family.

"If an advisor has this core set of beliefs, if he's that passionate about his work, he's purposeful in what he does, and he's totally congruent about being a role model of good advice, well, Tom, then he couldn't help but be wildly successful, even if he didn't have the remainder of the list working all that well," I said.

"Stop and think about it, Tom," I went on. "If an advisor has great marketing that supplies him with a never-ending supply of good prospects for his services, *but* he's a basket case mentally without any belief in the value he brings, then he'd struggle and not do that well at all! An advisor who's on fire about his work will thrive even *if* he's weak in marketing, Tom. So my list is the priority of values that I see in top advisors."

---

[6] Okay, I'm busted! So I used, shall we say, a more scatological term?

"The sacred cow that I'm moving lower on this list, Tom, is financial planning skills," I said. "There are tons of CFPs® who will fight me to the bone because I place planning skills lower than the first three values. Again, I'd argue that you can be an awesome financial planner *but* without a steady stream of prospects, without a good opening conversation that naturally leads prospects to want to hire you, and without a strong conviction that what he, the CFP®, does is important and necessary work — well, that particular advisor would be smart… and broke. More importantly, Tom, that advisor who's brilliant technically but deficient in all the other areas will deprive the world of his vast talents!"

We continued talking and wrapped up lunch, but I kept that napkin and thought more and more about it over the years.

## V6 Today

As my business grew, I realized that I'd left a value off my list — Systems. Today the list looks like this:

1. Have your head on straight: be passionate, purposeful and congruent.

2. Have a systematic approach to running every aspect of your business.

3. Have a marketing system that delivers a never-ending supply of the right prospects to your door.

4. Have an un-sales conversation that's all about the client and that helps him understand who you are and what you can do to help him.

5. Be technically proficient at financial planning.

6. Know the product universe you recommend.

Why do I call it **V6**? Simple! Six Values = **V6**.

As I progressed through my career I noticed something within the context of **V6**. The more successful[7] an advisor becomes, the more likely he'll delegate the lower priorities (items 3 through 6) and focus on providing clarity, direction, leadership and a role model of stewardship.

In fact, I believe the converse is also true. The less successful an advisor is, the more likely it is that he or she focuses mostly on products and planning.

---

[7] I do not believe income is the *only* measure of success. But I do believe it is a good measure because it indicates the level of confidence your clients have placed in you.

What is not true is that top advisors can be complete idiots financially and clueless about the products and services they recommend.

 *This discussion reminds me of Bill Bachrach's chapter. Bill talks about "unlearning" sales skills. If only we didn't learn all the wrong lessons to begin with.*

We all start our careers trying to master planning skills, to learn our way around an HP12c. And we read countless prospectuses and brochures. As we mature we should learn that those tools are simply the means, *not* the ends.

## Each V6 Value "One Thing" At a Time

1. Have your head on straight. Empirically, I noticed that this was the most common trait of top advisors. Their passion was self-evident — almost obnoxious at times, frankly. Top advisors could cite chapter and verse about *why* they were an advisor — they'd describe their purpose in an almost spiritual manner. Top advisors, I noticed, were congruent. They had enough life insurance, they fully funded their retirement plans; in short, they walked their talk.

2. Systems did not appear on my list originally.[8] That was because I didn't have the volume of business necessary to expose my own weakness. However, when my career took off, I found out all too quickly that I had a mess! I had no set processes that allowed me to move effortlessly through the day. Each client was "one-of-a-kind." Each day began a new adventure in filing. Frankly, mess is a kind descriptor. I read The *E-myth* by Michael Gerber. Then, when I began The Strategic Coach™ program, I learned the value of Unique Methods™. In short, I slowly, agonizingly let go and began to delegate to others and began to create standard processes. I systematized everything I did in running my business. Systems allowed my income to grow while my time off expanded exponentially!

3. Have a marketing system that delivers a never-ending supply of the right prospects to your door. A marketing system is not the same as you marketing your services; here's how: If the typical advisor goes to the beach for two weeks, he'll have a slow schedule of new

---

[8] Yes — I called it V5 then!

prospect meetings waiting for him upon his return. However, an advisor with a marketing "system" in place shouldn't feel that drop-off when he returns from the beach. His office team should have his calendar filled with highly qualified prospects. This is true whether you're a fee-only planner or a life insurance advisor. Some of you are in the envious position of being "full" — you don't need any new clients. I still heartily encourage you to continue to market what you do to your existing clients with the same fervor you had when building your business. It's analogous to keeping the romance going even though you might be married 11 years![9]

4. Have an un-sales conversation that is all about the client. All I need to say about this is re-read Mitch Anthony's, Dan Sullivan's and George Kinder's chapters. Deena Katz, Bill Cates, Bill Bachrach and Don Phillips address this very well too! The "un-sales" conversation is about how you can be of service. I know better than most how to "close" sales. I know that nothing happens until a "sale" is made. Simply put, we've moved well beyond that. As Dave points out in his chapter, the seeming paradox is that the less you try to sell, the more you will probably make!

5. and 6. Planning and products — I'm no expert in either. What I think I can say with authority is this: Clients — people — fall asleep thinking about the ones they love. I've yet to meet a client who asked my thoughts on a CRUT or what the differences were between actively- versus passively-managed funds. Most of the world does not think about these sorts of issues. So to all of you who value planning above all else, I have bad news for you: No one really cares. Planning and cool products are *the means* to the ends people want — period, full stop, the end. So with 99 percent of people falling asleep thinking about the people they love, what do these people say they want? I'll tell you from my observations.

They want to know that they'll always have enough money to keep their standard of living; sure they'd like more, but most importantly, they don't want to have less. They want to know that they won't be a burden to the people they love because of their health. They want to know that their children and grandchildren will be equipped to flourish in the future. And they want to know, all things being equal, that when they die, all that they've worked so hard for goes to their family, *not* to the government.

---

[9] If my wife reads this I'll have to increase my dinner and movie budget!

So if that's what people want, why focus mostly on CRUTs and 529 plans? Why lead with Monte Carlo simulations? If you do, I wouldn't hire you. If you do, I suspect that the only reason people hire you, if you focus mostly on planning and products, is because their needs outweigh your inability to speak their language. Lord help you when your clients meet someone who focuses on having the kinds of conversations outlined by George Kinder, Dan Sullivan, Mitch Anthony et al — someone who's quite competent at planning but also understands where the client "lives."

### Tying It All Together

I didn't step out the door of my MBA program and become an overnight success. I struggled to master planning, products, marketing and sales. Frankly, it took me a decade before I began to put a handle on it all. Yet what kept me going was that I never forgot the pain my family endured because of the *lack* of sound advice. That pain, that unwillingness to forget, became the bedrock of my developing a rock-solid belief in my abilities to make a positive difference in the lives of the clients I helped.

As I made a few nickels I developed a taste for success. Truthfully, sometimes the success became about how "big a producer" I was. But the pain of my family's financial failures, coupled with the current realities and tough situations of my existing clients, continually brought me back down to earth.

Over time I approached the work with reverence. I saw the legacy I was helping to create for the generations of each family I touched. I began to see the effects of my work touching lives in positive ways. I got my "head on straight."

I realized that the advice I had given did not necessarily alleviate suffering. When the wife in a couple I advised began to develop Alzheimer's, no amount of money could alleviate the emotional pain the entire family suffered. Yet my advice, given many years earlier, enabled her family, so much more than my own, to focus on her health and on the draining emotional aspects of supporting her — and not on worrying about money.

As I made more money, I re-invested much of it back into the human capital of "getting my head on straight." I read book after book and listened to tape after tape[10]. I attended seminar after seminar like that of Tony Robbins. I went to boot camps and coaching programs — some good, some bad, a few quite exceptional. Many of the good and exceptional programs are produced by the people in this book.

---

[10] Okay — so that dates me a little! For you youngsters, us dinosaurs used to have devices called tape players in our cars!

Eventually I began to notice that other people at conferences were asking me questions, and that small groups of people would gather as I discussed the answers I had to give. People asked for my card and asked permission to call or visit me to find out how I did this or that. It became almost embarrassing that many advisors senior to me would ask for my guidance.

At the same time, I began to notice a phenomenon; free advice is worth what people pay for it. Often the advisors asking me "How did you do this?" would be interested in the answer, but were rarely committed to changing their ways of doing things.

I'd spent well over $100,000 on tapes, books, coaching programs, and so on to develop myself. I'd become an overnight success after a decade of failing. And the advisors asking me "how to" questions were really asking for "What is the easy, quick and painless way?" to get where I was financially. I don't think you have to starve, like I did, to get to where I am.[11] You need a compelling reason — a force that drives you when you're feeling blue and want to stay in bed; a force that reins you in a tad when you feel like you've kicked the world in the butt! In short, you need a *Compelling Reason Why*™.

A *Compelling Reason Why*™ is an emotionally charged mantra for doing what you do. For me, my *Compelling Reason Why*™ was the pain my family suffered not once, but twice, because of poor or bad advice. I never forgot the look on my grandmother's face as she struggled on $198 a month and it drove me to do the right thing every time I sat in front of a client. When you have a *Compelling Reason Why*™ that powerful, you'll never quit and you will, quite literally, overcome any and every obstacle.

## How You Implement V6

In order to implement **V6**, I believe that a quote by Dan Sullivan is apt: *All progress begins by telling the truth.*

To that end, I think that you need to look hard in the mirror and have an honest discussion with yourself about some powerful questions.

First, what have been the values you espouse in your advisory life and do they still work for you?

Second, how well do you implement what you value?

I'll give you an example of a fictitious advisor named "Jane."

*Jane is very proud of her planning skills and honestly believes she is the brightest planner in her 25,000-soul township. She spends a tremendous amount of time reading the trade journals and doing a lot of due diligence.*

---

[11] Starving, however, is a powerful motivator! Hopefully you need a less draconian stimulus to act!

*Disdaining sales and marketing, Jane struggles financially. Jane secretly feels like a fraud when she advises clients when she herself doesn't have any investments or retirement funds. Jane, however, is the Vice President of her local FPA chapter and really enjoys working with new planners.*

What does Jane value? She places planning and due diligence above having her "head on straight." Sales and marketing are four-letter words to her.

Is this good or bad? Frankly, it's neither. What it is, though, is a waste of talent. Jane's tremendous ability is being underutilized because fewer people take advantage of her skills. Most importantly, Jane is not congruent! She does not make enough money to be a good example of the work she is recommending to others!

In Tom Gau's chapter, he'd say Jane's weakest link is marketing and I would agree. Tracey Beckes would tell us that Jane has to know where Jane is at her best — and I agree here too. This seeming paradox can be explained: Jane needs better marketing to bring her amazing planning skills to those who really need her talent. For every Jane who is strong in planning and weak in marketing, there is a "flip side" advisor who is strong in marketing and sales and weak in planning. When Dave Drucker started his partnership in Bethesda, it embodied many elements of this dynamic!

Now here's the really cool part: In this book you'll find the coaches, consultants and visionaries who can help you with your One Thing — your **V6**. I urge you to re-read it, highlight it, color it up with highlighters. Start a study group on this book. Do whatever it takes to find your "One Thing" and let nothing stop you from putting it into place!

Think you need to focus on having a better "un-sales" conversation? Check out Dan Sullivan's chapter or George Kinder's or Mitch Anthony's.

Feel like you need to be more congruent about being an advisor? Read Bill Bachrach's chapter. Need to be more affirmed that what you do is valuable? Read Bill Cates' chapter.

Our interviews have affirmed what I believed; my notion of **V6** has firm grounding! Our interviews sharpened my thinking. They challenged my assumptions and gave me different perspectives. They created more questions — good questions like, "What is the most efficient way to market yourself as an advisor in this new paradigm?" I'm quite sure I'd ask Bill Cates that question because I believe his referral system is the cornerstone of this new marketing paradigm.

I have a core belief that the world is hungry for great advice that's provided in the context of a creative, open and nurturing relationship. So these interviews acted like a catalyst to my ideas on **V6** and created a framework that I hope you'll embrace.

I created the following chart as Dave and I flew around the country to do our interviews. I used it to benchmark my thoughts on **V6**.

| | Their One Thing | Core Message | V6 Value(S) I think they espouse[12] | | | |
|---|---|---|---|---|---|---|
| | | | Head on Straight | Systems | Marketing | Un-sales Conversation |
| **Mitch Anthony** | It's their story | Have a better conversation | X | | | X |
| **Bill Bachrach** | Be Congruent | Be Congruent | X | | | X |
| **Tracy Beckes** | Know where you are at your best | Work in your unique ability | X | | | |
| **Bill Cates** | Know your value | Know you are valuable | X | | X | |
| **David Drucker** | Be virtual | Have a better conversation | | X | | X |
| **Tom Gau & Ken Unger** | Always be meeting with Clients | Have a systematic approach | | X | X | |
| **David Grau** | Know you have value | Know you are valuable | X | | | |
| **Deena Katz** | It is the Connection | Have a better conversation | X | X | | X |
| **George Kinder** | It's their life not their money | Have a better conversation | X | | | X |
| **Don Phillips** | Create a Better Investing Experience | Have a better conversation | | X | | X |
| **Jerry Reiter** | Be prepared and be proactive | Have a systematic way to protect yourself | | X | | |
| **"D" Shannon** | Never Forget & V6 | V6 | X | X | | X |
| **Leslie & Paul Strebel** | Be Willing | Systematize everything | | X | | |
| **Dan Sullivan** | R-factor DOS conversation | Have a better conversation | X | X | | X |
| **Mark Tibergien** | Know your personal definition of success | Run it like a business | | X | | |
| **Bob Veres** | Know Your Value | Know you are valuable | X | | | X |

[12] My idea of which **V6** value they espouse is my interpretation of what their core message is. I am quite sure they champion the other values and have become better known for the ones I checked.

In the Introduction, we outlined the five major ideas we found in our interviews:

1.  It's relationships, *not* return on investment!

2.  We need better conversations with our clients — open-ended ones that are all about their agenda, *not* ours.

3.  You, the financial advisor, are the most valuable professional in the world.

4.  Build a business, *not* a practice, using carefully crafted systems.

5.  Be passionate, purposeful and congruent about what you do.

As I look back to that napkin on which I outlined **V6** I see an amazing resemblance to the five major ideas we found in our interviews. Until now, this information has been out in the advisory world only in bits and pieces. But now it's been pushed forward, focused and concentrated in one place.

For repetition, let me review the "old world" model — the primary focus I've witnessed at conferences and in the industry magazines:

1.  Product features and benefits

2.  Financial planning techniques

3.  Sales training

4.  And more and more compliance "driver ed" lectures

I think that the five major ideas (i.e., those in my **V6** framework) that emerged from our interviews contrast dramatically with the "old world." I'd encourage you to ponder this shift. Challenge my assertions! Walk around **V6** and the above five major ideas, kick the tires, and think this through for yourself.

In the end, it's what you think that matters. I pray this book helps you on your journey, that it sharpens your thinking, and that it helps you bring your tremendous talents to more of the world!

### Finally — Why the World Needs More Good Advisors — Our *Compelling Reason Why*™

Dave and I wrote this for many reasons: For fun, adventure, for profit and for expanding our own understanding of the advisory world we inhabit. For me, however, I kept a distant target in mind as we wrote this: "Let's move the dial forward for the advisory world!"

To that end, I believe it's important that you do this work on several levels. It's important that you do this work so that you improve your life.

It's important that you do this work so that you improve your client's lives. And it's important that you do this work so you improve our industry — because our industry is but an amalgamation of each of us as individuals.

Finally, and most importantly, it's important that we all do this work because our freedoms are based on democratic capitalism. You, as a financial advisor, are the very grassroots, the bedrock of our capitalistic society. Without you, our economic system would not function.

Dan Sullivan said, "Advisors are the nervous system of the world." I couldn't agree more.

Where you find lots of financial advisors in the world, you also find stability, relative peace, and individual freedom. Where there are few or no financial advisors, you'll find economic depression, fear, and scant freedom.

The world needs more good financial advisors to be a better, safer and freer place.

So please go prosper. We *all* need you to do so!

**In summary:**

- Never forget what your *Compelling Reason Why* is.

- "Old World" values emphasize:

  1. Products

  2. Planning

  3. Sales

  4. Compliance

- V6 values in order of priority are:

  1. Have your head on straight: be passionate, purposeful and congruent.

  2. Have a systematic approach to running every aspect of your business.

  3. Have a marketing system that delivers a never-ending supply of the right prospects to your door.

  4. Have an un-sales conversation that's all about the client and that helps them understand who you are and what you can do to help them.

  5. Be technically proficient at financial planning.

6.  Know the product universe you recommend.

* The world needs more good advisors!

 The Experienced Advisor LLC was founded by **"D" Shannon** in 2003 and is located in Bealeton, VA.

"D" has "been there, done that and got the t-shirt!" He has produced at high Million Dollar Round Table production levels as a life insurance salesman. He achieved the top production level in the nation's largest independent broker-dealer. He has been a fee-only planner and a member of the National Association of Personal Financial Planners (NAPFA).

"D" has a gift for cutting to the heart of the matter in a funny, enlightening and empowering way. "D" shows advisors how to transform their businesses and their lives so that they can live the lives they've dreamed of.

"D" can be reached at The Experienced Advisor LLC at (888) 567-4862 or at ***www.experienceDadvisor.com***.

## BONUS

We have created The One Thing Process™ that helps you take what you have learned in this book and successfully DO SOMETHING WITH IT! The three steps to implement this are:

1. Identify what your "One Thing" is that you need to work on.

2. Identify who can help you work on this and improve it.

3. Create a Compelling Reason Why™ you must do this and what your life will look like in the future when you have successfully installed this "One Thing" and what will happen to your family, your clients and yourself if you don't.

**For your 15% discount on The One Thing Process™ enter your discount code of "V6" in the shopping cart coupon**

### For more on "The One Thing"

If you enjoyed this book and want to know more about additional products and services we provide please go to:

*www.onethingforadvisors.com*

While there sign up for our FREE "One Thing" Report

If you are interested in booking "The One Thing"
as a speech at your conference please call 1-888-567-4862.

Thanks for your continued interest and patronage!

# INDEX